Architecture and Field/Work

D0218960

Positioned at a point of interchange between the disciplines of architecture and anthropology, this book is the first to identify and to critique key terms, techniques, methodologies and habits comprising our understanding of fieldwork in architecture. In the wider context of interdisciplinary spatial practice, this book explores the potential of the term 'field' and offers insight into how future research in architectural design and other practice-led disciplines might make productive links between academia and design professions.

Essays by established and emerging international scholars are arranged into three parts introduced by the editors, which move from practices to site to techniques, and are interspersed with field notes by experienced voices: Andrea Kahn (New York), Alan Dein (London) and Can Altay (Istanbul) with an afterword by Jane Rendell (London).

For students, academics and reflective practitioners in architecture, art history, theory, landscape and urbanism, this book offers a reassessment of methodologies, forms of aesthetic production and creative activity in architectural design, theory and practice.

Suzanne Ewing is an architect and academic who teaches architectural design at the University of Edinburgh. She is a partner at zone architects and contributes to public discourse on design in the UK and Europe through workshops, exhibitions and publications.

Jérémie Michael McGowan is an artist, designer and academic who has taught and exhibited in the UK, United States and Finland.

Chris Speed is Reader in Digital Spaces at Edinburgh College of Art.

Victoria Clare Bernie is an artist and academic who teaches architecture at the University of Edinburgh.

AHRA

CRITIQUES: *Critical studies in architectural humanities*

A project of the Architectural Humanities Research Association

This original series of edited books contains selected papers from the AHRA Annual International Conferences. Each year the event has its own thematic focus while sharing an interest in new and emerging critical research in the areas of architectural history, theory, culture, design and urbanism.

1   **Critical Architecture**
     Edited by Jane Rendell, Jonathan Hill, Murray Fraser and Mark Dorrian

2   **From Models to Drawings**
     Imagination and representation in architecture
     Edited by Marco Frascari, Jonathan Hale and Bradley Starkey

3   **The Politics of Making**
     Edited by Mark Swenarton, Igea Troiani and Helena Webster

4   **Curating Architecture and the City**
     Edited by Sarah Chaplin and Alexandra Stara

5   **Agency**
     Working with uncertain architectures
     Edited by Florrian Kossak, Doina Petrescu, Tatjana Schneider, Renata Tyszczuk and Stephen Walker

6   **Architecture and Field/Work**
     Edited by Suzanne Ewing, Jérémie Michael McGowan, Chris Speed and Victoria Clare Bernie

AHRA provides an inclusive and comprehensive support network for humanities researchers in architecture across the UK and beyond. It promotes, supports, develops and disseminates high-quality research in all areas of architectural humanities.

www.ahra-architecture.org.uk

Architecture and Field/Work

**Edited by Suzanne Ewing,
Jérémie Michael McGowan, Chris Speed
and Victoria Clare Bernie**

Routledge
Taylor & Francis Group

LONDON AND NEW YORK

First published 2011
by Routledge
2 Park Square, Milton Park, Abingdon, Oxon OX14 4RN

Simultaneously published in the USA and Canada
by Routledge
270 Madison Avenue, New York, NY 10016

Routledge is an imprint of the Taylor & Francis Group, an informa business

Typeset in Univers by Wearset Ltd, Boldon, Tyne and Wear
Printed and bound in Great Britain by TJ International Ltd, Padstow, Cornwall

British Library Cataloguing in Publication Data
A catalogue record for this book is available from the British Library

Library of Congress Cataloging-in-Publication Data
Architecture and field/work/edited by Suzanne Ewing ... [et al.].
p. cm. – (Critiques: critical studies in architectural humanities)
Outgrowth of Field/Work, the 6th International Conference of the Architectural Humanities Research Association, hosted by The University of Edinburgh and Edinburgh College of Art in November 2009.
Includes bibliographical references and index.
1. Architecture and anthropology. 2. Architectural practice. I. Ewing, Suzanne.
NA2543.A58A74 2011
720–dc22
                                                                        2010019470

ISBN13: 978-0-415-59539-1 (hbk)
ISBN13: 978-0-415-59540-7 (pbk)
ISBN13: 978-0-203-83944-7 (ebk)

Contents

Contents

Illustration credits

Illustration credits

Contributors

Can Altay lives and works in Ankara, Turkey. His practice is established within the realms of architecture, art, design and theory. It deals with the spatial appropriations, social encounters and forms of human improvisation within urban structures.

Martin Beattie has taught architecture at Newcastle University since 2001, gaining his PhD in 2005. His research looks at the ways cultures mix, or not, as the case may be, and how that process manifests itself in architecture.

Victoria Clare Bernie is an artist and academic. She teaches architectural design at the University of Edinburgh. Her visual art practice centres on representation in relation to the landscapes of northern and western Scotland. Her work has been exhibited both nationally and internationally and she is the recipient of awards from the Scottish Arts Council and the Leverhulme Trust.

Carolyn Butterworth runs her own practice and teaches architectural design and theory at the University of Sheffield's School of Architecture. She combines building projects with research on the performative site in architecture and its potential for user participation.

Michael Chapman lectures in architectural design and theory at the University of Newcastle (Australia) where he is completing a PhD concerned with the relationship between Surrealism and contemporary architectural discourse. His architectural designs have been exhibited and published internationally including at the 2008 Venice Biennale.

Prue Chiles is Director of Architecture at the University of Sheffield and combines design teaching, research and practice. She also directs Bureau – design + research, a research consultancy at the School of Architecture. Her work attempts to reconcile the poetics of designing for people with the practice of building.

Ella Chmielewska teaches Cultural and Visual Studies at the University of Edinburgh. Her research interest centres on place and memory materiality of text, photography and visual knowledges, urban research methodologies, and semiotic landscapes.

Alan Dein is an oral historian and broadcaster. He presents documentary features for BBC Radio, and is a freelance interviewer and oral history consultant. He is a committee member of the Oral History Society, and has been working since 2004 on the *King's Cross Voices* project.

Paul Emmons is Associate Professor at the Washington-Alexandria Architecture Center of Virginia Tech where he directs the PhD program in Architecture + Design. He holds a PhD from the University of Pennsylvania and is a registered architect.

Suzanne Ewing is an architect and academic. She teaches architectural design at the University of Edinburgh and is co-founder of zone architects. Her research explores fragilities and resiliences of the modern city and discourses of in-situ thinking and making in architecture and urbanism.

Miriam Fitzpatrick is an architect, urban designer and educator who has worked in London and Toronto. She is a member of English Heritage and Cabe's Urban Panel and is a Lecturer in Urban Design at University College Dublin and in Architecture at Waterford Institute of Technology, Ireland.

Catharina Gabrielsson is an architect, curator and researcher. She received her doctoral degree in 2007 at the School of Architecture, KTH Stockholm and was a Visiting Fellow at the Cities Programme, London School of Economics and Political Science from 2008 to 2010.

Andrea Kahn is the Principal of designCONTENT, a consulting practice focusing on design communication and presentation strategies. She is Adjunct Associate Professor of Architecture and Planning at Columbia University, and a critic at Yale School of Architecture, New York. She is contributing co-editor of *Constellations: Constructing Urban Practices* (2007) *Site Matters* (2005) and contributing editor of *Drawing/Building/Text* (1991)

Krystallia Kamvasinou is an architect and landscape architect, currently post-doctoral Research Fellow at the University of Westminster, London. Her research interests include landscapes on the urban periphery, video in research and design and 'terrain vague' landscapes as public space.

Jérémie Michael McGowan is an artist, designer and academic. His research draws on ideas of 'performativity' and 'fictive fieldwork' and the 'anthropological footnotes' of nomadism in modernist architectural projects. He has taught and exhibited in the United Kingdom, United States and Finland.

Mhairi McVicar is a Lecturer at the Welsh School of Architecture, Cardiff University. Her previous publications include 'Passion and Control: Lewerentz and a Mortar

Joint' in *Quality Out of Control* (edited by Dutoit, Odgers and Sharr, Routledge, 2010) and 'Memory and Progress: Confessions in a Flagstone Wall' in *Architectural Research Quarterly* (2007)

Igor Marjanović teaches architecture at Washington University in St Louis. His research focuses on design education, including pedagogical experiments of Alvin Boyarsky. Together with Katerina Ruedi-Ray he is a principal of *ReadyMade Studio* and co-author of *Marina City: Bertrand Goldberg's Urban Vision*.

Philipp Misselwitz is an architect and curator based in Istanbul. He co-founded the research platform Urban Catalyst in 2002. He initiated the project *Geographies of Conflict* (2002), co-curated the Israeli–Palestinian–European exhibition *Liminal Spaces* (2006–8), *Refuge* (2009, with Can Altay), and is currently working on cultural Agencies with Nikolaus Hirsch and Oda Projesi.

Michael J. Ostwald is Professor of Architecture at the University of Newcastle (Australia) and an Australian Research Council 'Future Fellow'. Michael's PhD is in architectural theory and history and his higher doctorate in design mathematics. Michael Ostwald is on the editorial boards of *Architectural Theory Review* and the *Nexus Network Journal*.

Jane Rendell is Professor and Director of Architectural Research at the Bartlett, UCL. An architectural designer and historian, art critic and writer, her work has explored various interdisciplinary intersections: feminist theory and architectural history, fine art and architectural design, autobiographical writing and criticism. She is author of *Site-Writing: The Architecture of Art Criticism* (forthcoming 2010), *Art and Architecture* (2006), *The Pursuit of Pleasure* (2002) and co-editor of *Pattern* (2007), *Critical Architecture* (2007), *Spatial Imagination* (2005), *The Unknown City* (2001), *Intersections* (2000), *Gender Space Architecture* (1999) and *Strangely Familiar* (1995).

Sebastian Schmidt-Tomczak is a PhD student in the History, Theory and Criticism of Architecture at MIT. His research is focused on representations of the city, visual urban research methodologies, and memory in cities of the East: Eastern Europe and Japan.

Emily Scott is an artist and scholar whose work explores intersections between contemporary art, geography and environmental sciences and politics. In 2010, she completed a PhD in Art History at UCLA, with her dissertation, 'Wasteland: American Landscapes in/and 1960s Art'. In 2004, she founded the Los Angeles Urban Rangers. She is currently based in Zürich, Switzerland.

Jill Seddon is Academic Programme Leader in History of Art and Design at the University of Brighton. She is currently researching the public sculpture of Sussex as part of the Public Monuments and Sculpture Association's national recording project.

Kelly Shannon is Associate Professor of Landscape Urbanism at the University of Leuven (Belgium). Her research is at the intersection of urban analysis, mapping and new cartographies, design and landscape urbanism, with a focus in particular on south and south-east Asia.

Chris Speed is Reader in Digital Spaces at Edinburgh College of Art, working on the impacts of ubiquity of digital technology and locative media on the fields of human geography and architecture.

Lindsey Stouffer teaches art and architecture at Washington University in St Louis. Her artwork represented by Bruno David Gallery explores the issues of site, place and materiality and has been exhibited around the United States, including a series of public art projects for the St Louis subway system.

Renata Tyszczuk is Senior Lecturer in Architecture at the University of Sheffield where she teaches MArch design, history and theory, and is the Director of Postgraduate Taught Masters programmes. Her research and art practice address questions of global environmental change.

Preface

Architecture and Field/Work, the sixth volume in the *AHRA Critiques* Series, acknow-ledges a late-twentieth-century 'ethnographic turn' in artistic thought and practice, which until now has remained relatively unexamined within architectural discourse. Taking this recent impulse as its focus, this volume begins to identify and to critique some of the key terms, techniques, methodologies, habits and habitual cross-disciplinary borrowings constituting our understanding of and approach to fieldwork in architectural education, research and practice.

This volume assembles a selection of critical historiographies, theoretical strategies and reflective design practices which first emerged from *Field/Work*, the 6th International Conference of the Architectural Humanities Research Association, hosted by the University of Edinburgh and Edinburgh College of Art in November 2009. The conference hosted 55 papers from practitioners and scholars from around the world, and a further selection of visual 'findings' became part of an exhibited backdrop to the proceedings. A website, www.fieldworkconference.net, was constructed and became an archive, depository, network, exhibited informal discussion space of the conference which will remain as a temporal trace for a short while. FieldSunday was a collation of associated events which took place in the field of Edinburgh.

Acknowledgements

The editors would like to thank the Architectural Humanities Research Association for the opportunity to host its sixth annual international conference in November 2009, and the members of the AHRA Steering Group for support of the event and this publication, in particular, Jonathan Hale, Igea Troiani and Stephen Walker. We are grateful to the staff and students of the School of Arts, Culture and Environment at the University of Edinburgh and Edinburgh College of Art, where the conference was held, and in particular to Sanne Dijkstra-Downie, our excellent Conference Administrator. Stephen Cairns and Ross Maclean also contributed to the conceptualisation and organisation of the conference theme. The conference was developed in collaboration with VARIE (Visual Arts Research Institute, Edinburgh) and took place in the inaugural year of the Edinburgh School of Architecture and Landscape Architecture, which is an ongoing alignment of the programmes and activities of Architecture and Landscape Architecture in the University of Edinburgh and Edinburgh College of Art. We would like to thank all academics who have attentively contributed to abstract, conference and text reviewing during the course of the project: Dr Gerry Adler, Dr Alex Bremner, John Brennan, Prof. Iain Boyd Whyte, Prof. Stephen Cairns, Prof. Richard Coyne, Prof. Gordana Fontana-Giusti, Dr Eric Laurier, Prof. Tim Ingold, Prof. Sarah Pink, Dr Peg Rawes, Dr Igea Troiani, Dr Stephen Walker and Dr Dorian Wiszniewski. We would like to thank all participants in the conference – the keynote speakers, the scholars and practitioners who contributed papers and the invaluable contribution of our postgraduate students, who all helped to shape the theme of the book. Finally, the support of Fran Ford and Georgina Johnson-Cook at Routledge has made this publication possible.

Introduction

Suzanne Ewing

Knowing and navigating the terrain

'…the more I work on it, the less I know', voices Rem Koolhaas in the early stages of the film, *Lagos Wide and Close: Interactive Journey into an Exploding City* (van der Haak 2005). This work has been criticized as reckless anthropology and as an outsider's indulgent aesthetic project, but it is part of a traceable trajectory of field *work*, which this volume argues is a practice of Architecture requiring critical attention. In the Lagos/Koolhaas project, the *work* is most visibly manifest as a film about the city and its inhabitants, a filmed documentary of the process of research and filming, and a process of architectural research-education. What is the *knowing* that Koolhaas suggests is elusive if it is overdone? Knowing how to make architecture or urbanism? Knowing a city? Knowing how to work, how to make cultural analysis? Knowing when to finish? And what are the implications for ethical architectural production when the relationship of work in the field to architectural design and responsibility is scrutinized – a contemporary condition of professional distancing from, yet personal proximity to, site: *field/work*?

Aware of the well-established paradigms, legacies and critical frameworks of other disciplines, this book probes the rich but as yet underexplored terrain of fieldwork in relation to architecture. Although this book makes no claims to be a Fieldwork Manual for Architects, or a Manual of Architectural Fieldwork, it does aspire to be used informally as a Reader, of interest to critical practitioners, researchers and scholars of Architecture. The composite bibliography offers a map of a larger scholarly terrain, the visual content is intended to extend beyond illustration to a further 'playing out' of *work* in/of/from/to the *field*, and the 'Field Notes' act as documentary anchors which acknowledge the situated origins of these discourses in a particular academic network, institutional context and two-day event, an academic conference.

How does this book relate to the wealth of tradition, contemporary critical scholarship and reflective fieldwork practice characteristic of other disciplines? As a profession founded on the coexistence of theory and practice, Architecture can study the historical model of fieldworking, acknowledge the theoretical context and under-take the practical experience. Fourteen chapters interspersed with conference 'Field Notes' are choreographed into three parts: Part I 'Field/work Practice', Part II 'Field/work and Site', Part III 'Field/work Techniques'. Each part is thoughtfully introduced by a co-editor and is sequenced as an unfolding of critical historiographies, theoretical strategies and reflective design practices. In Part I, Jérémie Michael McGowan out-lines recent relevant anthropological discourse, and suggests a potential correlation between 'fictional fieldwork' and architectural field/work. Conceptions of site as fixed and specific alongside more fluid interpretations of field and 'unfixed' networks are reflected on in Part II by Chris Speed. Acknowledgement of Architecture as a 'gleaning' discipline with its own and appropriated practised habits and repertoires, offers genera-tive potential for architectural field/work as a critical design practice operating between representation and construction, and is the subject of Part III by Victoria Clare Bernie.

This arrangement aims for a dialogic rather than a dialectical tone, weaving pertinent themes which are attentive to 'the [subject's] cultural thickness and concep-tual intricacy' (Burns and Kahn 2005: xxi) and challenge us to think seriously about our knowledge, experience and application of fieldwork in Architecture. Other threads are manifest in the texture of the volume and offer potentially innovative strategies for design-research practice. Individual and collaborative accounts of reflection-in-action and reflection-on-action (Schön 1983: 76) position author as architectural fieldworker, potentially a participant-observer of anthropology, yet also a *participant-maker* of archi-tecture. The recurring engagement with non-textual output, although familiar in Archi-tecture, agitates conventional anthropological paradigms, and within an 'ethnographic turn', encourages review of relationships between visual, aesthetic fieldwork output and construction and design, where existing discourses and techniques of the visual, the aesthetic, the critical and the spatial overlap with those of anthropology, archaeol-ogy, ecology. Possibilities of performative modes of scholarship, the 'unmethodical' and 'unfinished' as creative practices and the architect as navigator as well as con-structor are posited. Finally, there is an intriguing set of adjacencies which shed light on early 1970s United States, with revisits of the research-educational practices of Robert Venturi, Denise Scott Brown and Steve Izenour in Las Vegas (Michael Ostwald and Michael Chapman), the art practices of Robert Smithson and his collaborators in New Jersey (Emily Scott), and the influential urban analysis practices of William Holly Whyte in Manhattan (Miriam Fitzpatrick).

The co-editors of this book each come from a different disciplinary position and operate in different areas of practice – Ewing (Architecture), McGowan (Art and Design), Speed (Digital Media), Bernie (Fine Art). Having worked together over two years on the framing of the conference event, the solicitation, negotiation and management of call, content, contributors, presentations and interactions, and the subsequent evolution of this volume, our interdisciplinary overlaps have evolved into a dialogue with an increas-ing focus on questions of contemporary (and of course our own) practices, repertoires and dispositions. Initially sharing experiences of and interests in defining, exploring and understanding the current condition of architectural fields, fieldworking, sites and site knowledges, we see this project as a continuing interrogation of the dialogue between theory and practice, a promotion of thinking through doing and an uncovering of the tacit knowledges of design (Burns and Kahn 2005: ix, xiv). Understanding differences in habit pertinent to different habitual ends may nurture future dialogues and exchanges which inform reinvigorated habitual routines and innovative practices.

Critical historiographies

What are the professional habits and habitual practices of field/work in the discipline of Architecture? When and how do habits change and why? Field, like site, can be understood as a condition operating between, as well as a condition of, design intention and resolution, architectural idea and built construction. In this volume, Paul Emmons' chapter establishes an understanding of architectural work on site, and sets out a narrative of the historic disconnection between architectural representation and construction which can be understood to be at the root of the contemporary condition of Architecture. Contemporary professional habits are revealed by Mhairi McVicar, Prue Chiles and Carolyn Butterworth in their detailed accounts of experiences of site/work in architecture, opening up reflection on the architect understood as a field/worker in this situation. Habits of other disciplines are also present – fine art documentary, urban design analysis, landscape urbanism, historic taxonomy.

Histories and techniques of site/work in Architecture are related to histories of the profession, and to histories of professional architectural education. There is a traceable history of models of engagement with sites and fields of study – eighteenth-century Grand Tour, nineteenth-century English country excursion, mid-twentieth-century US field-based studios, late-twentieth-century global urban ethnography – which have influenced professional and disciplinary preoccupations and dispositions (Brianard *et al.* 2008; Ewing 2009). A shift from *sitework* to *fieldwork* as a driving concern is coupled with a consolidation of the field*work* being an end in itself rather than a habit, tool or condition which directly informs action: the constructed photographs, book and studio process of *Learning from Las Vegas* were articulated as end products, alongside urban or architectural proposals for change to this paradigmatic urban artifice. Rem Koolhaas continues this trajectory, he 'set out to learn from Lagos, rather than planning, building or changing anything' (van der Haak 2005) but paid much attention to the construction of the DVD. The evidence in this volume suggests that heightened knowledge of site/work in architecture may inform making or constructing in a particular site at a particular point in time. However, increasingly, architectural field/work 'out there' is articulated as a constructed project of research or aesthetic production in itself, whether film, text, installation, PhD or site notebook.

Clearly what is scrutinized as field/work is implicitly ascribed a value by the author(s), may be influential on 'the public eye' and potentially adopted by a wider disciplinary context, skewing or shedding light on motivations and concerns as well as outputs. In conventional architectural practice, value in field/work has tended to focus on artefact and conservation – the classical ruin or monument of the Grand Tour, the modernist project of archaeologically influenced vernacular studies, material conservation projects and, more recently, environmental rhetorics of the deep ecology movement. Is the privileging of the contemporary, the at-hand, the everyday such as the casinos of Las Vegas, the recycling networks of Lagos, ultimately just another aesthetic project or is it a catalyst for a paradigmatic shift in knowledge-based practice?

Field/work may be seen as a form of 'critical realism'. Acknowledging and working with the circumstantial, the unfinished, the decayed, the abstract conditions of site is an essential, practised skill of architects with a view to offering propositions which are ultimately definitive, finished and sustainable. Associated techniques and routines of site/work, such as the site visit, site study, site survey, site analysis condition survey, setting out, snagging, certification constitute habitual components of architectural practice – 'assemblages of knowledge' (Burns and Kahn 2005: xv). Practical knowledge engages with thinking and theorizing of thinking over time, and becomes tacit through practised habits, routines, vocabularies. Site/work, like field/work, is a circumstantial subject dependent upon the individual ethical position of a designer, couched in the prevailing collective value systems of the profession and the immediate culture, potentially complicit with tactics for project-based resolutions.

Vocabularies of *site* in architecture and urban design, including representational habits, routines and practices, have begun to be established and can become a guide to clarify a way of proceeding to understanding vocabularies of *field*. Typically, site – an area of control, an area of influence, an area of effect (Burns and Kahn 2005: xii, xx) – is understood within an architectural frame of reference as a place with potential. Students learn on fieldtrips to look for sites, to frame and limit sites, to project potential onto sites. *Field* suggests more fluid qualities, and unfixed conditions suggestive of contemporary networked conditions. In current parlance, as well as delimiting a disciplinary or subject area, 'field' describes a place to learn from, to research, to draw from. Fieldwork operates as both a noun and a verb, and this oscillation correlates with a potential oscillation of work and worker which may inflect questions about and understandings of *project*, *construction*, *design*, *work* in the field.

Theoretical context and strategies

The slash between field and work in the book's title acknowledges that the subject of field/work is, like site in art and architecture, 'A Place Between' (Rendell 2006), 'best viewed from points in between' (Burns and Kahn 2005: xxiii). Detailed attention to this recurs in a number of the book's chapters. In a prevailing context where architectural theory has pulled away from consideration of the physical and the practical, focus on field/work draws attention to the iterative relations of theory-practice design knowledges. Easy borrowings, name-dropping and cross-referencing have saturated much of recent practical and theoretical production in Architecture. How might this be resisted through engaging with the disciplinary knowledge of the other critically, navigating the written, the made and the lived as an ethical practitioner?

What are the aims, intended gains and theoretical underpinnings of field/ *work* in Architecture? What is field/work data for? Keynote speakers at the 2009 AHRA Conference exposed a range of theory-practice knowledges, discourses and hi(stories) of the architectural, visual, sensory, oral, spatial. Particular questions emerged which are registered in this book in three conference 'Field Notes':

What values guide us? To what ends? For whose gain? (Field Note 1, Andrea Kahn);

How do you acknowledge the temporal? How do you enable enfranchisement? (Field Note 2, Alan Dein);

How do you cross the threshold between research and practice? (Field Note 3, Can Altay).

Theory-practice knowledges and underpinning of the ethnographic in relation to the spatial, aesthetic, urban, are touched on by Martin Beattie, Catharina Gabrielsson, Ella Chmielewska and Sebastian Schmidt-Tomczak in chapters in this volume. A 'geographic turn' in art practice, architecture and urban studies has become characteristic of recent discourses (Rendell 2006: 18). If Architecture is to look critically at and begin to theorize the 'ethnographic turn' (Coles 2000) in thought and practice, it needs to recalibrate relevant knowledges, terminologies and thinking of field/work as design practice.

Reflective design practices

Fieldwork is a practice, not a discipline. It is practised in different ways by different disciplines towards diverging ends, and may contribute to the consolidating, deepening and extending of disciplinary knowledge. Field/work in Architecture is a tacit design knowledge, a resource for the study of site and the making of projects, enacted by learnt strategies, techniques and skills, rather than disciplinary-driven models of applied methods or articulated methodologies. Practice can be conceived of as an 'artful doing', where knowledge is inherent in practice (Schön 1983: 140, 276; 1985). 'Thinking on our feet', looking to draw from experience and from what has gone before, to connect with feelings, to attend to theories in use and to construct new understandings which inform actions in unfolding situations, may engender ways of thinking about what it might be to *practise*, within a disciplinary framework or as a professional: to reflect while acting, to reflect on acting. The 'repertoire', a collection of images, ideas, examples, metaphors, theories and actions that can be drawn on, frames of reference and routines (Dewey, 1933: 123, Schön 1983: 138; Smith 2001) are all potentially brought to bear on unfamiliar or new situations – navigating an exploding city, assessing the potential of a building site, participating in the open process of a design studio. Contributions in this volume include eloquent reflections on a range of design practices – visual/city research, on-site architecture, video-making, architectural education, landscape urbanism.

An architect making films as a field/work project, while potentially offering fresh eyes and techniques, has to develop a new repertoire of the 'artful doing' of other disciplines – film-making, cultural/urban studies – building up new skills, or relying on others to service this activity. While moving between disciplinary practices may forge new opportunities and identify new areas of concern, new fields of work and modes of field/work, there is a risk of too little critical traction. As routines are always new, they can be over-privileged and may skew understanding and reception of the output. Narratives of relationships of field and site to design work in contemporary architectural practice are rarely explicit, although study of this could provide fruitful clues for further understanding of this topic. How do we understand the relationships and connections (if any) between innovative field/work and site/work, innovative design practice, innovative speculations? We can bring understandings of repertoire, frames of reference, routines, in order to negotiate and define new terms, techniques, methodologies and habits of *Architecture and Field/Work*.

Architecture and field/work: a critical project

The theme of this book provides an opportunity for sampled disciplinary-scale readings and epistemological changes to be brought into focus alongside detailed reflective vignettes. These can be re-read through *critique*: through review and critical analysis of contemporary soundings and samplings of field/work in art, architecture, landscape architecture and urbanism. Selected critical historiographies, theoretical strategies and reflective design practices of *Architecture and Field/Work* add to understanding of this 'place between'. Examination of the 'ethnographic turn' opens up a reassessment of vocabularies and forms of aesthetic production and creative activity in architectural production and design practice. Conceptions of architectural fieldwork as 'fictional fieldwork', the architect as participant-maker and field-navigator may be posited. While Architecture has much to learn from critical discourses of field/work in other disciplines, the profession and critical practitioners need to acknowledge the histories and strengths of their own repertoires and routines. Then, they might offer other disciplines a distinctive knowledge-based practice, where long-practised translations between invention and resolution, idea and construction, precision and error, study and speculation can be brought to bear on *work* and *field*. As the contributors in this book show, a critical self-knowledge – working between personal proximity and professional or disciplinary distance – can be creatively productive. A dislocation of field *from* work may unsettle the disciplinary repertoire yet the connection between field *and* work offers a critical resource for the invention of architectures at once imaginative, beautiful and pertinent to the worlds in which we live.

Field/work practice

Introduction

Jérémie Michael McGowan

> ...fieldwork is personal, emotional and identity *work*. The construction and production of self and identity occurs both during and after fieldwork. In writing, remembering and representing our fieldwork experiences we are involved in processes of self presentation and identity construction.
>
> (Coffey 1999: 1)

> ...a crucial aspect of fieldwork lies in recognising when to be unmethodical.
>
> (Wolcott 2005: 5)

In cultural anthropology, fieldwork based on participant observation is well established as *the* defining method of data collection. Fieldwork in anthropology has rather clear traditions and a largely coherent historical lineage, dating from at least the sixteenth century. Modern anthropological fieldwork points to the key works of a handful of founding fathers (Boas, Malinowski), while the modern discipline, in turn, can be seen 'crystallising' at a precise enough moment in the 1860s and 1870s (Kuper 1988). Today, fieldwork is variously understood to be 'one of the fundamental or "paradigmatic" elements of anthropology' (Robben and Sluka 2007: 4); a 'ritual initiation experience' (Berger 1993: 174) or rite of passage (Freilich 1970: 16; Johnson 1984); and, 'the source of anthropology's strength' (Keesing and Strathern 1998: 7) as a discipline. Readers and specialist texts now address multiple aspects of fieldwork, including its varying relationships to psychology, ethics, sexuality, gender, intimacy, eroticism, globalisation, health and safety, humour, violence, identity and friendship. And this is in anthropology alone. Other disciplines increasingly emphasise the importance of fieldwork, including education (Delamont 2002), development studies (Scheyvens and Storey 2003), history, folklore, nursing, geography, social work, economics and archaeology – where concrete and practical 'how to' information, including readymade lists, checklists, equipment inventories and measurement charts may be found in pocket field manuals and user guides (e.g. Kipfer 2007). Having come through a period of 'epistemological hypochondria' (Gewertz and Errington 1991: 89), most anthropological fieldworkers today believe in the continued importance and relevance of being in the field.[1] In response to ongoing postmodern and postcolonial criticisms of their field practices, contemporary anthropologists have turned to notions of a '"good enough" ethnography' (Scheper-Hughes 1995: 418), reaffirming the long-standing disciplinary commitment to fieldwork as anthropology's primary mode and method of enquiry.

The position of fieldwork in architecture, including art and architectural history, is far less defined; a historical and contemporary ambiguity that points to a range of problems and potentialities in architectural thought and practice. As the chapters in this opening section suggest, the role of fieldwork in the present is still negotiable; despite fieldwork's growing 'cross-disciplinary "trendiness"' (Robben and Sluka 2007: 3) and an ever-expanding bibliography of titles, its meaning, use, methods and outputs remain open to change and disruption. While the anthropological paradigms of participant observation and ethnographic writing are clear references, alongside techniques and tools gleaned from archaeology and geography, such 'loosely borrowed' disciplinary models prove malleable and multi-functional points of departure.

Drawing on ethnographic traditions of inhabiting and writing about the field, anthropological approaches to fieldwork may be used in architecture as a method of observation, data acquisition and representation; a way of interacting with, documenting and responding to a specific people, time, place and circumstance. While genuine experiences of living in the field remain rare in architectural studies, Martin Beattie's first-person account of fieldwork in Barabazaar, Kolkata, India, reveals a deep personal engagement with contemporary concerns in anthropological thought and practice. Taking stock of some criticisms of anthropological methodologies, his reflexive writing draws attention to the importance and value of being 'self-conscious' (Cohen 1992b) in the field. Although imperfect, fieldwork based on participant observation remains one of the most sensitive and nuanced approaches to the difficult task of working within and representing a field, as testified by the personal fieldnotes transcribed within Beattie's chapter. Highlighting important issues of identity, narrative, collaboration, compassion, hybridity and reciprocity, Beattie poses searching questions about what it means to 'be there' in a contemporary, increasingly globalised world still saturated with lasting power hierarchies.[2]

The postmodern and postcolonial critiques of anthropology informing Beattie's approach to fieldwork may be deployed in alternative ways. When utilised critically and historiographically, politicised reflections on ethnographic methods may become theoretical frameworks through which to rethink the fieldwork activities of others. Michael Ostwald's and Michael Chapman's re-reading of Denise Scott Brown, Robert Venturi and Steven Izenour's late-1960s work in Las Vegas draws on recent anthropological writings about sex and eroticism (e.g. Kulick and Wilson 1995), provocatively exposing the repressed narrative of attraction and desire underwriting the 'dead pan' objectivity of the *Learning from Las Vegas* project. Outlining a compelling strategy for contemporary historical and theoretical scholarship, their text capitalises on the critical potential of the term fieldwork, presenting an analytical approach through which we might continue rethinking the role of fieldwork in architectural thought and practice: Ralph Erskine's 'Arctic architecture' (McGowan 2008, 2010) or Aldo van Eyck's 'field study' of the Dogon (Jaschke 2005, 2009), for example, both of which are roughly contemporaneous with the *Las Vegas* field studio. Making linkages between architecture, anthropology and popular culture in the postwar period, Ostwald and Chapman's text challenges us to reconsider all such architectural claims to scientific or 'ethnographic authority' (Clifford 1983, 1988) in the field.

The critical application of anthropological theory explored textually and 'remotely' by Ostwald and Chapman suggests the possibility for other, more hands-on and performative modes of revisionist enquiry, wherein fieldwork might become a way of critically and creatively retracing someone else's bodily and intellectual movements within a field. What happens when fieldwork experiences separated by time, place, agency and circumstance are overlaid and intertwined with each other, read and juxtaposed over and against themselves? Derek Freeman's (1983, 1996, 1999) pioneering yet controversial approach to Margaret Mead's work in Samoa, like the irreverent 'second generation' questioning of similar fieldwork sites in the anthropological canon that followed, seem to offer real potential for contemporary architectural thought and practice.

Yet there are other approaches to fieldwork that exist somewhat outside the anthropological model and its attendant body of critical theory. Using her bodily experience of Palaeolithic caves in France to creatively rethink questions of architectural origins and their implications for our understanding of spatiality, society and identity today, Catharina Gabrielsson scripts herself as a knowing 'fictor' in the field; an actor, performer and wilful inventor of archaeological evidence, architectural history and contemporary theory. Her chapter returns us, momentarily, to the 'discovery' of the Palaeolithic caves in the late nineteenth century; incidentally, a historical moment when the disciplinary boundaries of modern anthropology were still being worked out, and everyday travellers routinely produced 'amateur ethnographies' of their journeys. Must fieldworkers in the present be professionally trained and equipped with a codified set of academic and technical tools in order to detect, observe, detail and transcribe the multiple characteristics, complexities and potentialities of a field?

At the same time, Gabrielsson's chapter links, if indirectly, to lesser-known traditions of 'fictive fieldwork' in anthropology. While 'ethnographic fiction' is often dismissed as 'inappropriate for consideration as ethnography' (Robben and Sluka 2007: 493), 'a hidden lineage' of anthropologists leading double lives as novelists and fiction writers nonetheless stretches back at least as far as the late 1800s (Narayan 1999). One example, a highly influential work on later-twentieth-century popular culture, is Carlos Castaneda's *The Teachings of Don Juan: A Yaqui Way of Knowledge* (1968). When read against such fictional practices and their still-problematic place in anthropology, Gabrielsson's chapter mobilises the critical potential of fiction writing for architecture, revealing we have everything to gain by intentionally and creatively engaging with 'traumatic' disciplinary taboos. While many anthropologists continue, for the most part, to resist the age-old desire to 'go bush' or 'go native' in the field, Gabrielsson does not suppress her impulse to enter the dark and slippery (intellectual) terrain of the caves.[3]

Identifying herself as an artist rather than an art historian, Emily Scott's eloquent critical historiography of collective fieldtrips undertaken by Nancy Holt, Robert
Smithson and others in the late 1960s argues for a performative mode of scholarship
based on the creative acts she studies. Her engaging proposal to employ creative
projects as models for critical enquiry in their own right plays interestingly and sugges-
tively upon current debates in anthropology that sometimes seem to struggle with the
more artistic dimensions of classic ethnographic fieldwork (Wolcott 2005). Blurring the
boundaries between historical, critical, ethnographic and creative approaches to
working in, writing about and otherwise representing the field, Scott's chapter traces a
line of flight from established geographic and anthropological rulebooks that, while proposing to embrace creativity and non-textual modes of representation in far riskier
ways than the ethnographer, loses none of its critical capacity in translation. Arguing
for speculative and exploratory forms of art history as art practice that openly acknowledge their own performativity in the field, Scott's chapter simultaneously engages,
extends and subverts Herzfeld's seductive notion of 'an anthropology that makes an
ethnographic problem of itself' (Herzfeld 1987: x).

Notes

1   There is extensive literature, written from within the discipline, discussing anthropologi-
    cal practices from a number of postmodernist and postcolonial perspectives, revealing
    the extent to which anthropology has self-consciously taken into account external criti-
    cisms of ethnographic fieldwork and its accompanying writing strategies (Amit 2000;
    Barfield 1997; Berger 1993; Harrison 1991; Strathern 1995; Wolcott 2005). Some anthro-
    pologists now address head on previously thorny subjects such as sex and eroticism,
    for example Altork (1995).
2   For anthropological reflections on the notion, problems and necessity of 'being there',
    see Bradburd (1998), Watson (1999), D'Amico-Samuels (1991) and Cohen (1992a). Sun-
    derland (1999) has written specifically on the relationship between fieldwork and the
    phone.
3   On the taboo of going native in the field, and its current status and theorisation in anthro-
    pology, see, for example, Dalby (1983), Ewing (1994), Good (1991), Gronewald (1972),
    Tedlock (1991) and Turner (1999).

Collaborative practices

Hybrid ethnographies and fieldwork approaches in Barabazaar, Kolkata, India

Martin Beattie

Figure 1 **Old China Bazaar Street, Easter 2003.**

Introduction

James Clifford and George Marcus's edited collection of essays, *Writing Culture*, reveals anthropology's links to literary theory and practice, demonstrating how ethnographies represent a biased or partial account of social reality. Arguing that anthropological texts should be viewed as 'ethnographic fictions' rather than contributions to science, *Writing Culture* maintains that all ethnographies have literary qualities, and that the influential work of authors like Mary Douglas, Claude Lévi-Strauss and Jean Duvignaud are based on systematic and contestable exclusions, silencing incongruent voices, and omitting irrelevant personal or historical circumstances. According to Clifford, 'ethnographic truths are thus inherently *partial* – committed and incomplete' (Clifford and Marcus 1986: 7).

Addressing this problematic, Clifford and Marcus highlight the importance of Mikhail K. Bakhtin's writing for postmodern ethnographies (Clifford and Marcus 1986: 15). Bakhtin's work on language uses the term 'hybridity' to discriminate texts that are monological or with a single voice, from those that are dialogical. For Bakhtin, monologism denies the existence and validity of the other. Dialogism appears for Bakhtin where the speaker's language bears the imprint of the other; writing takes on a dialogic or polyphonic structure when it includes the voice of the other within itself (Bakhtin 1984).

Developing the notion of hybridity, Bakhtin makes a fundamental distinction between organic and intentional hybridity. Organic hybridity is a feature of the evolution of all languages that intermingle and change historically. Applying it to cultures, organic hybridity shows that they evolve historically through unreflective borrowings, appropriations and exchanges. However, Bakhtin is more concerned with an intentional hybridity that has been politicized and contested, the moment when, in a single discourse, one voice can unmask the other. Intentional hybridity sets different points of view against each other in a structure of conflict that retains a sense of openness.

In the context of India, Homi K. Bhabha's seminal book *The Location of Culture* uses Bakhtin's notion of the intentional hybrid to investigate the situation of colonialism (Bhabha 1994). Bhabha defines hybridity as an inherent part of colonial representation that can reverse the effects of colonial power. Hybridity is not just a mixing together, it is a dialogical dynamic in that certain elements of dominant cultures are appropriated by minorities and re-articulated in subversive ways. At this point, hybridity marks the jarring of a differentiated culture, whose opposing powers challenge the dominant norms.

Clifford and Marcus analyse James Walker's monograph, *The Sun Dance and Other Ceremonies of the Oglala Division of the Teton Sioux* (1917) as an example of dialogical discourse in anthropological writing (Walker 1979). They read Walker's *Lakota Belief and Ritual* (1982), the first of a four-volume edition, as a collage of notes, interviews, texts and essay fragments, written or spoken by Walker and numerous Oglala collaborators (Walker 1982a, 1982b, 1983). Describing Walker's work as 'a collaborative work of documentation … that gives equal rhetorical weight to diverse renditions of tradition', wherein the anthropologist's 'own descriptions and glosses are fragments among fragments' (Clifford and Marcus 1986: 15), Clifford and Marcus find the ethnographer no longer holding authority associated with bringing elusive, disappearing oral lore into textual form. Rather, ' "informants" begin to be considered as co-authors, and the ethnographer as scribe and archivist' (17). The result is a version of culture in process that resists any final summation.

Locating myself

Looking back, Kolkata had worried, unsettled and fascinated me all at the same time. As a newly graduated architect in 1990, I had simply wanted to build buildings, as many as possible. Just before arriving in India for the first time in 1993, this initial enthusiasm had begun to wane and I became more interested in questions of how to build. After first visiting Kolkata, and on reflection, I began to wonder if it was ever going to be possible to build again, writing in my journal of 23 July 2000: 'seeing all this poverty makes me want to do something in the long-term to ease the plight of these people and reminds me of the guilt trips I went through on my first trip here.' I realise how these thoughts linked me to the civilising mission of some earlier anthropological traditions.

I began my research for a PhD in late 1998. Barabazaar, a marketplace north of the centre of Kolkata, was chosen as an empirical focus for the thesis, because it seemed an appropriate laboratory in which to test Bhabha's ideas on cultural hybridity. Bhabha's concept of hybridity builds on Bakhtin's notion of the *intentional hybrid*, which itself is rooted in his writings on the marketplace. Bakhtin regarded the marketplace as a paradigmatic form of hybrid space. For Bakhtin, 'the marketplace was the center of all that is unofficial; it enjoyed a certain extraterritoriality in a world of unofficial order and official ideology, it always remained "with the people" ' (Bakhtin 1968: 153).

While in Kolkata, it was never enough to say to people I met that the reason I was there was to simply complete a PhD. In the context of Kolkata, with its lack of material resources, one is constantly reminded of the need to waste neither time nor sentiment. Equally, when one realises what a hard slog an undertaking like a PhD is, the long-term commitment that is required, the sacrifices that are made in one's personal life and the difficulties in communication, a project like this could not succeed without a certain amount of naive optimism. It was this tension, between the everyday reality of the city and my own curiosity to learn, that seemed so often to frame my motives.

Time and again, I felt like the first person down a particular research track. While I enjoyed the sense of making connections and finding my own path, there were times when it was very daunting. I wrote in my journal of 20 July 2000:

> I think it is going to be a longer and slower process than expected, and sometimes I feel like a bit of a lone figure in the wilderness. There is so much basic work to be done in terms of logging and recording these [courtyard] houses.

Admittedly, underlying these thoughts is a picture of the isolated fieldworker, who in Rosaldo's words is undergoing, 'his rite of passage by enduring the ordeal of "fieldwork" ' (Rosaldo 1989: 30).

While in Kolkata, some people were sceptical of my motives. What was the point of this work, and who was going to be interested in it? Was I just there to further my career and finish a PhD? Why was I so interested in Barabazaar, the most overcrowded part of a decaying developing world city, with little influence outside the region of West Bengal? Of course, while these views may be clichés of myself and the city, there was an element of truth to them, which I found difficult to deny.

Some may question my own engagement with Barabazaar as a lone white male anthropologist-architect, marked out as a member of the culture of former colonialisation. At times in my fieldwork, as Trinh T. Minh-Ha puts it, there was a sense of 'neo-colonial dependency' (Minh-Ha 1991: 68). I wrote in my journal of 12 August 2000: 'As usual Kathotia [a Marwari paper trader] was very warm and friendly, talked about his like for Europeans and their modernizing ways and the need to help academics interested in Indian culture.'

On the one hand there seemed to be little escape from the privilege of my own position and how my work was enmeshed in a world of enduring power inequalities. However, often when I met someone for the first time, I would almost consciously admit my lack of knowledge about what I was studying, which paradoxically highlighted my own vulnerability and powerlessness. Sometimes I was dismissed for not knowing what I was doing, but sometimes this made people more trusting and open towards me.

Minh-Ha's work highlights the need to avoid essentialising the other, but also to resist the urge to essentialise the self. She asserts that the question is 'that of tracking down and exposing the Voice of Power and Censorship whenever and whichever side it appears' (Minh-Ha 1991: 72, 73). In reality I was received not only as former coloniser, but as backpacker, tourist, charity worker, friend, comparatively wealthy westerner and academic. The other that I was trying to understand was no passive subject, but rather active participant.

A Kolkata architect said that if he were in my position – meaning, as he put it, 'coming from the west with money' – he would be making linkages between various developing world cities. He seemed to understand, rather pragmatically, that there were certain things that it was easier for him to do, and there were other things that it was easier for me to do. In the end I would say that I wanted to learn about the lives of people very different from my own. Often, simple curiosity became the form of motivation that raised the fewest and least difficult questions.

Reflecting on the theory I had been reading, and knowing some of the practical difficulties of working in Kolkata, I began my fieldwork. I wondered whether I could meaningfully map the social world of Barabazaar in a text. How could I produce something representative of Barabazaar, while acknowledging its partiality? Would my research methods and the theory underpinning them actually be effective in highlighting local situated knowledge?

Sites of inquiry

Four fieldwork trips were made to Kolkata as part of research for a PhD (Beattie 2005). The first one, an initial pilot study, lasted for two weeks, over Easter 1999. The second

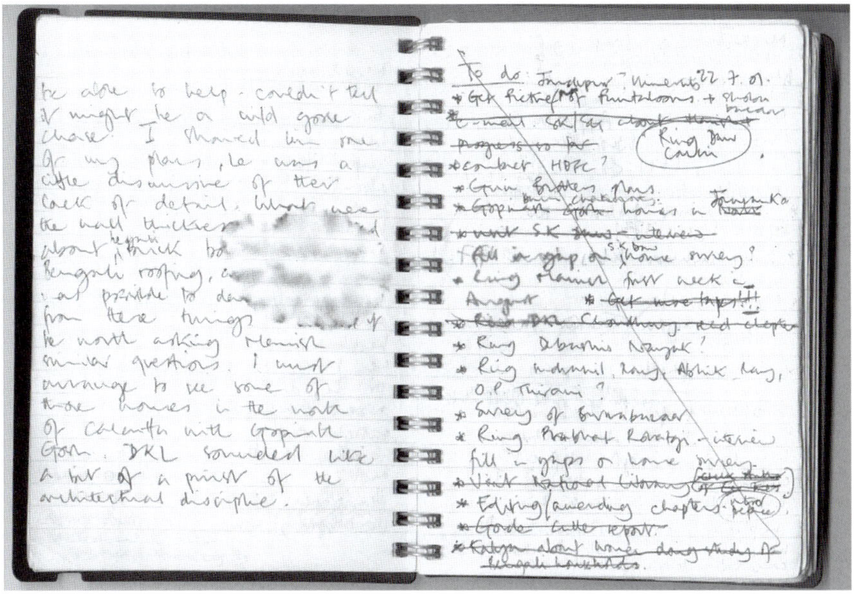

Figure 2 **Field journal.**

was for two months, over summer 2000, and the third for one month, over summer 2001. During these latter two trips, the bulk of the research was completed. The fourth and final trip was for three weeks, over Easter 2003. Dividing the research period up into smaller time periods was the only way I could manage my fieldwork between job and home commitments, and, as well as anything, reflected the part-time nature of my work.

My PhD used Bhabha's notion of hybridity as an interpretive tool, on specific architectural sites in Barabazaar. I focused on a number of research areas, or contexts for hybridisation, in Barbazaar as follows: the construction of a largely colonial urban history of Kolkata and the formation of an intertwined hybrid narrative of health and modernity; the hybrid vision that Sir Patrick Geddes adopted for proposals for Barabazaar in 1919; the hybrid sense of space found in the courtyard houses of Barabazaar; the culture of the street and the bazaar as a pradigmatic example of hybrid outside space.

Some of my analysis focused on *official* colonial discourses, specifically, city plans, conservation reports, council meeting minutes and planning inquiry transcripts. I also examined how Indians negotiated their own sense of difference, not only with the British but among themselves. In particular, I compared two distinct Indian communities within Barabazaar, the Bengalis and Marwaris. Thus, some of my study also investigated more *unofficial* debates, such as historical and contemporary Bengali texts, as well as my own interviews with individuals and groups participating in the struggles surrounding urban development and change in Barabazaar today. The thesis also drew on architectural sources, namely the urban structure of Barabazaar, and a number of courtyard houses.

Following the anthropological method of participant observation, I had originally hoped to stay as a guest, or interpreter-observer, in a household in Barabazaar.

This proved to be more difficult than I first anticipated. Of course, what this method required in the first place was getting to know a family reasonably well, and then gaining their trust and friendship in order to arrange to live with them.

Over the summer of 2000, I stayed as a paying guest with a Bengali family in their flat, which I had found through an accommodation agency in South Kolkata. This was not without some tensions, and I recorded in my journal of 2 August 2000: 'sometimes … I get a sense of envy or jealousy that comes from me being born on the other side of the tracks, in the land where all the opportunity, at least is perceived to be.' During the summer of 2001, I lived with a widow on the top floor of her family home, in Bagbazaar, North Kolkata, again as a paying guest. I met her through a mutual friend from Barabazaar. Despite its proximity to the centre of Kolkata the house felt like a retreat from the city for me, as I accounted in my journal of 1 August 2001:

> All you hear in Bagbazaar is the sound of occasional cars honking, the ring of bicycle bells, people talking on the street, and the sound of rickshaws clattering past. The balcony is a good place to watch it all go past, and I'm not the only one doing this.

Part of the fieldwork involved surveying and photographing courtyard houses in Barabazaar. These were mostly two to three storey buildings built for one extended Bengali family, often adapted as the family and/or business expanded or contracted. I surveyed six such houses, owned by five families, and interviewed all families at varying length about their own histories. Three of the houses were surveyed in the summer of 2000, one in summer 2001 and two during Easter 2003 (Beattie 2003).

For the courtyard house family histories, I spoke largely to the *male head of the family*. It was difficult for me as a European man to meet women out of familiar relationships who lived and/or worked in the bazaar (for a study which touches on Marwari women in Barabazaar, see Hardgrove 1999). According to Minh-Ha, ethnography has traditionally functioned as a method which allows the writer to 'grasp the native's point of view' and 'to realize *his* vision of *his* world' (Minh-Ha 1991: 65). Her work underlines the fact that ethnography is often a gendered subject (Minh-Ha 1989, 1991, 1992). In this sense, this study remains a limited intervention, because of the lack of opportunities offered to me in the field.

As well as getting to know the private life of the bazaar, I wanted to understand an aspect of its public everyday life, and interviewed six Marwari market traders who deal in paper and stationery in an area at the southern end of Barabazaar, called China Bazaar. They all worked on two adjacent streets, namely Old China Bazaar Street and Synagogue Street. The aims of these interviews were to gather information about the history of the business and the family, and the changes that were occurring to them. Three market traders were interviewed in 2001, and three more in 2003 (Beattie 2008).

Mostly the interviews were recorded at people's place of work during the day, among telephone calls and customers coming and going. Interviews were conducted in English and where translation services were required, these were provided informally by friends. I acknowledge that the filter of the English language excluded many from this study. I wrote in my journal of 24 July 2000:

> It was the first time I wished I could speak Hindi as not many people in these buildings seemed to speak English. How do I cross the divide to try and understand these people's lives?... Will my lack of Hindi restrict me to the English speaking courtyard houses and probably by definition the richer ones?

Networks of intermediaries

My research in Kolkata was first and foremost an exercise in building trust and friendship. Sunand Prasad acknowledges that 'in India the helping hand of the intermediary seems to be an ever present fact of life whatever it is that one wants to do' (Prasad 1998: 2.6). Anne Hardgrove describes the nature of her research in Kolkata as 'appointment anthropology', never calling 'anyone up "cold" without having first had a proper introduction from someone else, either with a letter or preferably a phone call' (Hardgrove 1999: 27, 28).

Thus I spent my time developing networks with many intermediaries. At Easter 1999, I was put in touch with Kalyan Kumar Deb because of his links to the Foundation for the Conservation of Rural and Urban Traditional Architecture. Mr Deb, a Rotarian, introduced me one Saturday evening, in July 2000, at a local meeting in north Kolkata. One of the people I met there introduced me to another Rotarian, who owned a courtyard house in Barabazaar. Another Rotarian was the chairman of the Society for the Preservation of Kolkata and put me in touch with a paper trader in China Bazaar, and member of the Kolkata Numismatics Society. He introduced me to all the paper traders I subsequently interviewed, and another numismatic in turn took me around many of the courtyard houses I visited, most of whom he knew as fellow members of the Numismatics Society. This is reflected in what I admit is a very partial view of Barabazaar.

This description of establishing networks of participants was constructed with the benefit of hindsight, and after my story had been consolidated, makes the process seem simple and rational – in fact it was anything but. Many people who seemed potentially useful at the start turned out not to be, and similarly some who seemed unpromising on first meeting turned out to be useful later on. In essence, the process was unpredictable, informal, piecemeal and involved much negotiation. Initially information was hard to come by and involved long and protracted negotiation. I wrote in my journal of 21 July 2001:

> I met a Mr. Dudhoria, who had remembered me from Mr. Beed's gathering last year. He said he would make enquiries at the College Street Coffee House to see if anybody could help with my study ... I started the day feeling disappointed that Professor D. K. L. Choudhoury could offer me few new leads but ended it thinking that a whole new network might be emerging.

There were times during my visits when I was unsure how it would all turn out. I wrote in my journal of 28 August 2000 that I thought the trip was a 'bit of a gamble', and that I felt 'exposed, insecure … I can never see further than 1–2 weeks ahead – never quite sure what's around the corner good or bad'. Equally, the reality of fieldwork in the often crowded conditions of Barabazaar seemed to frustrate any attempts at close unobserved study. I wrote in my journal of 19 July 2000:

> Most often I'm the subject of curiosity sometimes I sense ridicule. The camera draws most attention, changing film even more so – but unfortunately it's a necessary evil. The most unobtrusive way is making notes on a small piece of paper, but still people stop and look at what you are doing. Avoiding eye contact reduces much of this attention. Inevitably, trying to avoid unwanted attention you put the shutters up.

During my second visit in the summer of 2000, I reflected on how sources were scattered and how finding them was an ad hoc and uncertain process. Somebody might be able to tell you something about one particular aspect of the subject and somebody else something different. This process relied very heavily on you being able to tell somebody exactly what you wanted (which of course you might not always know), them being able to understand you correctly and remember who might be able to help.

During my third visit in the summer of 2001, I continued to develop networks of collaborators. On this trip, I took photographs of my family to show to people that I had met the previous year and felt a little closer to. Having asked a lot of personal information about people's lives, I wanted to show something of a more personal nature in return. Most of the fieldwork was located in more traditional neighbourhoods in Calcutta where families had been established for generations. Despite the seeming breakdown in extended families, people wanted to know how I fitted in and what my networks were, both familial and non-familial. This act of showing family photographs was as much about me locating myself in extended family networks as anything else.

In 2001, I began interviewing market traders and courtyard house owners. Generally, the format of the interviews with both groups of people would start with a cup of tea and introductions, which might take from five minutes up to an hour. Then there would be a formal taped interview which lasted from 30 to 45 minutes. After the interview, when the tape recorder was switched off and people began to relax, there would often be more reflective information, which I tried to remember the gist of and record in my journal afterwards.

The final trip over Easter 2003 reminded me about some of the things I had missed out, or overlooked. After seeing a Marwari courtyard house in Barabazaar, built at the beginning of the twentieth century, I realised that I made very little mention of them or of the differences to their Bengali neighbours, built mostly earlier in the nineteenth century. Another set of interviews that I conducted with market traders seemed to give a different and more optimistic picture about the state of the paper trade in Barabazaar, from the previous trip of 2001. At a Rotary Club meeting I was invited to, I was reminded of the perceived differences between north and south Kolkatans,

Bengalis and Mawaris that often coloured people's comments on my work in Baraba-zaar, and that I had forgotten too.

I did not leave the field with mountains of empirical materials, able to easily write up my findings. The little information I found from a very partial network of col-laborators was literally pieced together. Many of my own interpretations, connections and the questions I asked were often constructed with the benefit of hindsight. I wrote in my journal of 29 July 2001: 'The chapters [of my PhD] are going to be very much like those exhibits you see in museums with a few [original] chips and fragments stuck together to make a reconstructed vase, or whatever.'

Possibilities for hybrid ethnographies

Inevitably my own readings of hybridity theory sensitised my approach to the fieldwork process in Barabazaar, which was not focused on the objects of the bazaar so much, but on an open-ended analysis of cultural interaction. For Minh-Ha, it is 'vital to assume one's radical "impurity" and to recognize the necessity of speaking from a hybrid place, hence of saying at least two, three things at a time' (Minh-Ha 1992: 140). According to her, 'the ethnographer must always ask, not "*Who* am I?" but "*When, where, how* am I (so and so)?"' (157). Minh-Ha, writing as a Vietnamese woman living in America, claims to be always a hybrid, constantly negotiating 'the difference not merely between cultures, between First and Third World, but more importantly within culture' (144). She explains her 'hybrid place' as, 'not quite the Same, not quite the Other', but, 'in that undetermined threshold place where she constantly drifts in and out' (144).

The hybrid reflected my own increasing sense of shifting personal identity, as I engaged more deeply with Kolkata and Barabazaar. On the first fieldtrips I had felt out of my depth, literally a *complete foreigner*. On the final fieldtrips, when I felt more informed, I felt not quite English, but obviously never Bengali or Marwari, more some-thing in between. I learnt that being a foreigner sometimes made it easier for me to act as intermediary between sometimes conflicting communities in Barabazaar, and helped me get access to people and places that would have been difficult for locals.

Of the five families I met who owned courtyard houses in Barabazaar, the closest relationship I forged was with Prahbat and Shashi Rohatgi. The relationship revolved around regular Sunday morning discussions over a breakfast of vegetable curry, parathas, mangoes and sweets. I reflected in my journal of 30 July 2000,

> Prahbat Rohatgi was someone highly educated with a clear sense of himself and his Indianess, as seen from the outside ... he could slip in and out of it quite easily. There's always a sense ... that not only are you beginning to understand another person's way of life but also reassessing yours. Maybe this two way process is the mind state of the hybrid.

With hindsight I realised that this, as Rabinow relates, and quoting from Paul Ricoeur, is 'the comprehension of the self by the detour of the comprehension of the other' (Rabinow 1977: ix).

Conclusions: collaborative practices

Bakhtin's notion of dialogism and of the hybrid points towards more collaborative field-work practices. Collaboration in such a hybrid context becomes fluid, fluent and dynamic – truly *dialogic* in the Bakhtinian sense. This notion of collaboration derives in part from Bakhtin's notion of the intentional hybrid, which is created through incommensurable, not simply multiple positions, remaining contested, challenged and divided.

Above all, modest ambitions are necessary for these collaborations, with tolerance for the others' motives required on all sides. This approach to collaboration is exploratory and experimental, rather then definitive. Sometimes this process works, other times it is less successful, often it is seemingly wasteful. It is based on knowing and acknowledging your own weaknesses. Despite the ambiguity and uncertainty of one's position, it requires commitment and patience to cope with the inevitable frustrations. It is tempting in collaborations to opt for a safe zone of generalities, but it is important to recognise the significance of parallels and differences. This form of collaboration keeps us alert to what Marilyn Strathern calls 'compatibility without comparability', that is, the constant work of making connections within the recognition of difference (Strathern 2004: 38).

To a certain extent, such collaboration was beyond what I was able to manage in my PhD, which, with hindsight, was constructed more out of acts of cooperation than collaboration in the Bakhtinian sense. In a place like Barabazaar, such a way of working points towards multi-voiced, cross-cultural collaborations across Bengali and Marwari communities, ethnographer and informant, academic and local, material and textual, and the powerful and the oppressed.

Luke Lassiter defines such an approach 'that deliberately and explicitly emphasizes collaboration at every point in the ethnographic process, without veiling it – from project conceptualization, to fieldwork, and, especially, through the writing process' (2005: 16). But more than this, collaborative ethnographers must also be willing, as Glenn Hinson writes, to 'surrender the interpretive authority they have historically assumed, seeking instead a collaboration that draws [informants] into the analysis as equal partners and then creates textual space for the ensuing conversation' (Hinson 2000: 324).

For some, such a view of collaboration may seem utopian. Bhabha disagrees, arguing that ' "conflicting interests forming temporary strategic alliances" – is a good popular front tactic that has been part of many movements for revolutionary social transformation' (Bennett and Bhabha 1998: 40). According to Bhabha, 'the difficult *non-utopian* thought that one has to think: what structures and strategies of praxis, organisation, interpellation, coalition can be held, painfully and paradoxically, "in common" between antagonistic political philosophies in the performative and practice-bound realm' (40). Admittedly, I have written elsewhwere about the difficulties of accommodating such a model within the current politics, oppression and corruption that are part of present-day Barabazaar (Beattie 2008: 53).

While my PhD would not have been possible without some form of collaboration, I was the sole author of both my PhD and a number of articles published from it. In no way could my work be seen to be the textual collage of collaboration that James Walker suggests. I remain decidedly uncertain about whether I managed to blur the dividing line between the observer and the observed, acting as cultural critic and writer-as-scribe for the other. Gillian Rose has argued that 'the proliferation of disruptions, subversions, instabilities, undecidabilities' in hybridity theory, insisting on the failure of the powerful from within, is worryingly optimistic (Rose 1995: 371). For Rose, discourses of the powerful 'have not so far subverted themselves away' (371). This vision of hybrid ethnographies and collaborative fieldwork practices can only flourish in a more evenly democratic terrain of power than is characteristic at present.

The erotics of fieldwork in *Learning from Las Vegas*

Michael J. Ostwald and Michael Chapman

Preface

This chapter is focused on uncovering the relationship between scientific fieldwork and repressed sexuality in *Learning from Las Vegas*. Fieldwork is especially significant in *Learning from Las Vegas* because that work set out to use scientific methods and techniques to provoke a revolution in architecture. Fieldwork is also central to two similarly important types of revolution that shaped *Learning from Las Vegas*. The first is Thomas Kuhn's theory of scientific revolutions, proposed in the 1960s for understanding how change is promoted in a discipline. The second is the sexual revolution, which became widespread in the 1960s and which drew some of its inspiration from the fieldwork of anthropologist Margaret Mead. The chapter revisits the fieldwork undertaken for *Learning from Las Vegas* in 1968 and questions both its objectivity and its ambivalent and inconsistent attitude towards gender and sexuality. As a key component of this investigation, the chapter adopts the anthropological notion of the 'erotics of fieldwork' to illuminate these previously ignored dimensions in Venturi, Scott Brown and Izenour's work.

Introduction

First published in 1972, Venturi, Scott Brown and Izenour's *Learning from Las Vegas*[1] is an iconic example of twentieth-century architectural research. This work, which famously adopted the methods and rhetoric of anthropology, set out to provoke a revolution in architectural thinking. Since its publication, *Learning from Las Vegas* has been described as 'a seminal statement in the history and theory of architecture [and] one of the defining texts of postmodernism' (Vinegar 2008: 1). It has equally been condemned as condoning 'ruthless kitsch' and providing a 'mask for the concealment of the brutality of our own environment' (Frampton 1992: 291). In *Learning from Las Vegas* Robert Venturi, Denise Scott Brown and Steven Izenour provocatively argue that the 'ordinary and ugly' architecture of the commercial mainstreet is a valid urban condition and that parallels can be drawn between the Las Vegas strip and the Roman piazza. In contrast, they condemn the 'heroic and original' propositions of Modernity, decrying its reliance on contrived formal compositions to achieve an often-unwarranted monumentality. By developing a rhetoric of 'ducks' and 'decorated sheds', and a heraldic reading of advertising, *Learning from Las Vegas* was instrumental in the rise of postmodernism; one of the great revolutions in twentieth-century architectural thinking.

While the central message of *Learning from Las Vegas* has been repeatedly revisited, the present chapter offers an alternative, discursive exploration of two, seemingly disconnected themes in the work: its scientific framing and its apparent neglect of issues associated with gender and sexuality. In the first instance, when *Learning from Las Vegas* is reviewed today, its scientific aspirations and its revolutionary agenda are rarely questioned. The contemporary reader accepts these features, much as they accept the curious structure of the work.[2] However, when seen in the context of the intellectual culture of the 1960s (when the work was initially formulated), the language and structure of *Learning from Las Vegas* strongly mirrors Kuhn's blueprint for supporting a paradigm shift in a discipline. At the heart of Kuhn's argument is a call for objective evidence to be gathered as part of the process. Venturi and Scott Brown adopted the methods and nomenclature of science in general, and the fieldwork practices of anthropologists in particular, when they constructed their work to ensure that it was capable of provoking a paradigm shift in the discipline. However, just as a reading of the work from the point of view of 1960s intellectual culture is revealing, so too is a review of its apparent neglect of a major component of Las Vegas popular culture in the 1960s: its alleged 'sexual freedom'. While various critics have attacked Venturi and Scott Brown's lack of commentary on sexuality in Las Vegas (Frampton 1992; Leach 1999), none have been able to provide a reasonable explanation for their inconsistency when it comes to handling issues of gender and sexuality.

This chapter is focused on fieldwork; the practice which is simultaneously central to Venturi and Scott Brown's appeal to scientific objectivity and their failure to confront the gendered, the libidinous and the sexual in Las Vegas. The chapter commences by drawing on Kuhn's theory of scientific revolutions and Latour's sociology of science to explain the significance of fieldwork in *Learning from Las Vegas*. Connections are then made to popular cultural representations of fieldwork in the 1960s including the work of Margaret Mead and Claude Lévi-Strauss. Then, through an account of the fieldwork undertaken by Venturi and Scott Brown in Las Vegas in 1968, a series of questions are raised about the apparent objectivity of the work and its lack of recognition of the commodification of sexuality in that city.

In order to reconcile the problems of the scientific and the sexual in the fieldwork of *Learning from Las Vegas*, the chapter refers to recent research from the discipline of anthropology which has identified the problem of the 'erotics of fieldwork': the moment when the boundaries separating the observer and the field disintegrate and a range of complicit and provocative relations develop (Newton 1993; Kulick 1995).

Regardless of whether this breakdown is as a result of being seduced by a person or an environment, the end result, the loss of objectivity, has the same affect on the project; it undermines its capacity to support revolution. Because evidence of the breakdown in objectivity as a result of seduction is frequently hidden in a text, anthropologists have identified three types of behaviour that may collectively signal that an erotic fault is present in the work. This chapter identifies instances of each of these three forms of behaviour in *Learning from Las Vegas*.

Through a close analysis of *Learning from Las Vegas* and identifying parallels with the fieldwork of Margaret Mead in Samoa, the chapter proposes that Venturi and Scott Brown's failure to consistently confront the sexual and the gendered is a direct result of their desire to deny its influence on their fieldwork and thereby retain their aura of scientific objectivity.

The attraction of science

Venturi, Scott Brown and Izenour present *Learning from Las Vegas*, in 'respectable scientific' (1977: 6) terms, as an unbiased study combining both laboratory scholarship and fieldwork (Chapman and Ostwald 2009). According to Golec (2009), their fieldwork set out 'to maintain an aura of objectivity and a tone of scholarly dispassion' (32). The word that was repeatedly used by Scott Brown to reinforce the impartial nature of the fieldwork was 'deadpan'; a concept which implies that 'the facts are [recorded] while "creative" interventions are largely repressed' (Stierli 2009: 25).

If, as Scott Brown claims, their work set out to provoke a 'revolution' (quoted in Rattenbury 2008: 18) in architecture then, from the perspective of Kuhn (1962) who defined the notion of scientific revolution, this means that their research must be able to support a shift in thinking from a 'pre-science' state to a 'normal science' state. By bridging this gap a 'crisis' occurs in a discipline and a new paradigm is in turn promoted and promulgated. Kuhn (1962) describes this process as 'revolutionary science'; a phrase which resonates with the 'revolutionary' agenda of Venturi and Scott Brown. That this parallel exists is not surprising; Kuhn's famous *Structure of Scientific Revolutions* was published in America five years before Venturi and Scott Brown visited Las Vegas. Kuhn's work was widely debated at Yale, where Venturi and Scott Brown were based, during the intervening period, where it was later responsible for the rise of one of the first History and Philosophy of Science courses (Fuller 2000: 15). What is most significant in Kuhn's work is his identification of 'a blueprint for how a community of inquirers can constitute themselves as a science, *regardless* of their subject matter' (Fuller 2000: 234). This is the same 'blueprint' that Venturi and Scott Brown embraced to support a paradigm shift in architecture, and at its core is a parallel appeal to authority and demonstration of objectivity.

Bruno Latour (1987) identifies that there are several critical elements in any scientific proposition and the first of these is the 'argument from authority' (31); a balanced appeal to history demonstrating an awareness of the normative principles of a discipline. *Learning from Las Vegas* contains multiple appeals to historic precedents and methodological approaches fulfilling this requirement. Latour (1987) then proposes that further support is garnered by offering evidence that a proposition is unbiased, methodical and repeatable. One way to ensure this status is to locate the research in a laboratory environment. However, it is equally possible to conduct research in the field, provided sufficient protocols are in place to ensure the separation of the observer and the subject. This second approach, fieldwork, is the one embraced in *Learning from Las Vegas*.

In the 1960s, when Venturi and Scott Brown were formulating their research proposal, fieldwork had entered both the academic mindset and the popular consciousness for two major reasons. First, Lévi-Strauss's fieldwork in the Amazon basin was widely celebrated following the publication of *Tristes Tropiques* (1955), though the publication of *Structural Anthropology* (1963) had a more significant impact on the American academy. More importantly, the renowned anthropologist Mead's fieldwork studies were instrumental in supporting the sexual revolution that swept through American society in the 1960s. Mead's landmark work, *Coming of Age in Samoa* (1928), noted that young Polynesian women were more sexually promiscuous than their American counterparts but that their actions were guilt-free and presented no barrier to them living successful lives. The works of both Mead and Lévi-Strauss, which were much romanticized in the media in the early 1960s, raised the status of fieldwork as an important scientific method for investigating primitive societies. These cases were not only widely debated at Yale, but Scott Brown also had the opportunity to be aware of this work through her involvement in the Independent Group in London. Indeed, according to Hans Ulrich Obrist (Fischli *et al.* 2009), the 'field research approach' adopted by *Learning from Las Vegas* 'was very much driven by' Scott Brown, who grew up in Africa and had a well-known 'anthropological interest' (167). As a result of Scott Brown's background, Rem Koolhaas argues 'it was logical [for] the trip to Las Vegas [to be framed as] a kind of anthropological exercise' (Fischli *et al.* 2009: 167).

In hindsight, the combination of Kuhn's explanation of the structure of disciplinary revolutions and the heightened awareness of anthropology and fieldwork as agents for change was ideal for Venturi and Scott Brown's purposes. Moreover, this merging of popular culture (Mead, fieldwork and sexual revolution) and intellectual culture (Kuhn, fieldwork and scientific revolution) perfectly mirrored Venturi and Scott Brown's own predilection for merging high and low culture. For example, in *Learning from Las Vegas* they famously compare the merits of grocery store parking lots and the gardens of Versailles.

Early signs of an affair

In October 1968, following three weeks' preparation, the fieldwork for *Learning from Las Vegas* commenced. Thirteen students from Yale University had enrolled in a 'technical studio' entitled 'a significance for A&P Parking lots, or learning from Las Vegas: a studio research problem' (Venturi et al. 1977: xi). The trip lasted for a total of 14 days, with the students spending the first four in Los Angeles and the last ten in Las Vegas.[3] While in Las Vegas the group set out to methodically map the city, paying particular attention to the relationship between cars, signs and buildings. Over 5,000 colour images were taken, along with several films, and around 40 analytical figures were produced. The focus on documentary images was deliberate; the strategy of 'replacing the human eye's selective perception with the camera's mechanical gaze' was central to their desire to work with 'an absence of emotion' (Stierli 2009: 27). While these aspirations of the fieldwork are well known, the group's desire to remain objective and independent is the focus of the present inquiry.

On arrival in Las Vegas the group were transported to the Stardust Hotel, where they stayed, free of change, for the duration of the fieldwork. This is the first of many examples of a blurring of the boundaries that would normally isolate the observer and the system. The team was also supported by free car hire and special access was provided to millionaire playboy Howard Hughes' personal helicopter. Denise Scott Brown was invited to the 'gala opening of the Circus Circus Casino' and arranged for the rest of the studio group to 'semilegally' attend as well (Venturi et al. 1977: xii–xiii). The newspaper headlines that heralded their arrival also suggested that their services, and the results of their research, had been secured in advance by the city for the sum of $8,925. Where precisely this money came from is never adequately explained but the commercial nature of the transaction, a fee for service, already suggests a prostitution of values.[4] While all of this information is recorded about the group's time in Las Vegas, significant details are missing. For example, Venturi and Scott Brown describe the Stardust Hotel where they were staying as 'one of the finest on the strip' (1977: xi); but they neglect to mention that its fame was largely as a result of its glamorous, if risqué, Lido revue. According to the Las Vegas Journal of 1965, in the foyer of the Lido ballroom, a series of platforms were automatically lowered from the ceiling and then raised again, each one supporting a 'bare-bosomed beauty' (quoted in Rinella 2006: 83) draped in gold cloth (see Figure 1). When the Learning from Las Vegas group arrived in 1968 the publicity posters for the Lido described the show as featuring 'pretty girls' with 'naked chests' along with a swimming pool with 'naked mermaids' (2006: 84).

While it is not recorded if Venturi and Scott Brown attended the Lido revue, as residents of the hotel they were given tickets to it (Rinella 2006) and it is unlikely that they or their team of, predominantly, young men were able to avoid its ballroom and foyer, with the famous topless platform show, for the entire ten days. Yet, the Lido is never described in their work, in much the same way that the rampant commodification of sexuality that is present across Las Vegas is largely ignored. There are some exceptions to this, but they are typically isolated. For example, the presence of 'strip shows' is recorded in several analytical diagrams and images and in true 'deadpan' tradition these are presented without commentary. However, only a small selection of the strip show signs that lined Fremont street in their photographs are recorded in the diagrams, as if some decision was made to include a few and remove the rest. But other examples of sexuality are presented in a more ironic way. For instance, a sign

Figure 1 Lido platform show at the Stardust Casino.

advertising 'Burlesque, Girls, Girls' is positioned above a strangely phallic sign for a hot dog and one for the leaning tower of Pisa (Venturi *et al.* 1977: 61). The team also note that outside Caesars Palace guests are greeted by replicas of the '*Rape of the Sabine Women* and statues of Venus and David' (1977: 51) while inside an advertisement depicts a toga-clad woman who 'eagerly await[s] your every summons' (1977: 55). In total, the instances of sexual commodification recorded in the fieldwork are, for the most part, frustratingly oblique, as if somehow clumsily repressing the role of the carnal and the licentious both in Las Vegas and in their fieldwork.

In this context it is especially significant that during the time the group were in Las Vegas a 'Polynesian Revue' was playing in their hotel. The team methodically charted the existence of this show in their map of the 'written word' (Venturi *et al.* 1977: 30–31), just as they carefully recorded that these 'living dolls' (1977: 30) of the Pacific were performing nightly in their documentary photographs. However, their famous physiognomic diagram of the sign contains a curiously Freudian slippage when the 'living dolls' of the Pacific are mis-transcribed as simply 'naked' (1977: 67) (see Figure 2). Was this a mistake or an ironic attempt at 'truth in advertising'? Those who

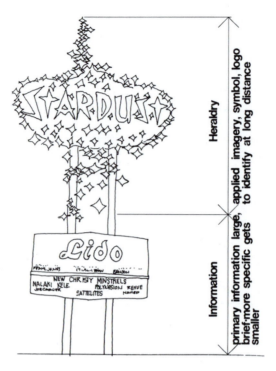

Figure 2
Physiognomy of a typical casino sign.

attended the show would have seen an interpretation of a traditional island dance before the 'Polynesian' girls discarded their fake grass skirts and shell-encrusted brassieres to swim unfettered in the base of a huge waterfall on stage. For the audience, the ersatz island sojourn was completed with a complimentary pineapple liqueur cocktail in the nearby Tiki Lounge. Once again, it is not known if the team saw this show, entered the Stardust's Aku Aku restaurant or drank at its Pacific-themed bar, but it would have been impossible to ignore its presence; from the check-in counter to the room-service menus, the casino was decorated with a Polynesian theme (Rinella 2006: 84). It would have been equally impossible for the Polynesian Revue to occur at all if it weren't for the fieldwork of Margaret Mead. Without Mead's (1928) descriptions of wanton and joyous sexuality in Samoa it is unlikely that the young women of the South Pacific would have found their way into the erotic imagination of the Las Vegas entrepreneur. But what would Mead have made of her beloved island girls, now depicted on stage by American women with their skin and hair artificially darkened, their individual identities suppressed beneath a false cultural mask?

The first tragedy of Mead's Samoan fieldwork was that it was directly responsible for presenting the Polynesian islands as 'a paradise of adolescent free love' (Freeman 1983: 226). First published in 1928 as a record of a 'detailed intensive investigation' (1983: 207) among the Ta'û islander people, Mead's fieldwork was widely influential and credited with 'revolutionising the field of anthropology' (Freeman 1999: i). However, by the time Venturi and Scott Brown were invited to attend the 'Polynesian Revue' during their own fieldwork, Mead's research had come under increasingly critical review. By 1968 anthropologist Derek Freeman had methodically retraced Mead's steps, re-interviewing the same people and studying transcripts and notes of the original research. By 1971, he had collected extensive evidence that Mead's conclusions were based on mischievous lies told to her by young Samoan girls (Freeman 1983). The motive for the lies may never be known, but feelings of sexual jealousy may have been the cause, as it was known that Mead was attracted to a young man in the local community (Freeman 1999: 137). In his findings Freeman argues that Mead's judgement in the field was clouded by pressure from her academic supervisor and, at barely 24 years of age, her own growing sexuality. Jones (1993: 37) is less forgiving when he argues that 'Mead's anthropological conclusions were drawn primarily from her own personal unresolved sexual conflicts'. This is the second tragedy of Mead's fieldwork: she had failed to maintain the required degree of objectivity.

Latour, reviewing the case of Mead and Freeman, is carefully balanced when he notes that the issue is not whether one is right and the other wrong, but rather that a breakdown has occurred in the 'etiquette' of the field (1987: 84–85). At the heart of this failure is the paradox that to develop a detailed understanding of a place or culture requires immersion in it, but to remain a credible witness, a veil of objectivity, however diaphanous, must clothe the observer. It is the frisson that results when an observer and the environment come in contact that has since become recognized as the 'erotics of fieldwork' (Kulick and Wilson 1995).

In Flagrante Delicto

The anthropologist Don Kulick notes that the underlying problem with sexuality in the field is not that it is immoral, nor even that it might be unethical, but rather that it compromises the 'objective recording and analysis' (1995: 3) of the field. From the work of anthropologists Newton (1993), Kulick (1995), Altork (1995) and Morton (1995) it is possible to identify three typical stages in the process wherein objectivity in the field is sexually compromised. Because a common characteristic of sexual relations in the field is their immediate denial or concealment, these three stages are also useful for confirming that the independence of the fieldworker has come into question. However, it must be remembered that while the theory of the erotics of fieldwork was developed to explain actual sexual relations between observers and subjects, it also covers the broader seductive influence of a culture or place on the researcher.[5] In addition, the theory explains the allure of certain topics to the observer, many of which are sexual, and which may be outside the frame of reference of the research, but which continue to intrude on its reporting. It is these latter two dimensions that are most relevant for the present work.

The first sign of the breakdown of the objective relationship between a researcher and their field often occurs in advance of the fieldwork. People tend to be drawn to fieldwork for emotional as well as scientific reasons. The longing for adventure, the desire for self-discovery and the fear of the unknown all have an impact on the observer's imagination before they set foot in the field. For example, Morton (1995) talks about a personal desire, inspired by the work of Mead, to conduct research in the Pacific Islands and be 'seduced by the naïve vision of an idyllic paradise' (169). Altork (1995) observes that the 'seductive nature of the field has been alluded to frequently by ethnographers who, at times, seem to radiate intensity as they speak of – or write about – their field locations and experiences' (109). The intense romanticization of the fieldwork, in advance of the project commencing, is often seen as prefiguring a loss of independence.

In *Learning from Las Vegas* this pattern of behaviour can be traced throughout the preliminary work. For example, 1968 was not the first time Venturi and Scott Brown had visited Las Vegas. In 1966, shortly before they were married in Santa Monica, they arrived in Las Vegas, where Scott Brown described their reactions as follows; '[d]azed by the desert sun and dazzled by the signs, both loving and hating what we saw, we were jolted clear out of our aesthetic skins' (quoted in Gilbert and Moore 1981: 310). Golec argues that in a city dominated by 'gambling and sex', Venturi and Scott Brown unexpectedly 'found beauty' (2009: 38). However, it wasn't until the following year that they would propose that Las Vegas contained a potent antidote to the sterile and puritanical architecture of modernity. Specifically, they protest that 'Modern architecture has been anything but permissive' (Venturi *et al.* 1977: 3), and that even the 'most necessary messages, like LADIES' (1977: 7) are only begrudgingly accepted. Both their prior experience in Las Vegas, and their desire to destabilize Modernity – a desire already expressed in gendered and sexual terms – would have preconditioned Venturi and Scott Brown for the seduction of Las Vegas.

The second dimension of the erotics of fieldwork is associated with scopophilia and the 'loss of self'. By its very nature, fieldwork is voyeuristic. It privileges one individual's observations of others; authorizing behaviour that would not otherwise be socially acceptable. Moreover, the more intently the observer focuses on the subject, the more likely they are to become entranced or fixated on it. This is an example of the 'erotic subjectivity of the fieldworker' (Kulick 1995: 23); it is a source of natural tension and attraction both between individuals and between a researcher and the society they are observing (Cupples 2002). In practice, it can be seen in the unexplained veneration of an overtly sexual image, subject or event. In affect, the image is fetishized as representing the myriad amatory and erotic dimensions of the fieldwork that have otherwise been hidden or repressed.

The covers of the first two editions of *Learning from Las Vegas* share a single common feature: the 'Tanya' image (see Figure 3). This incongruous photograph, which is explicitly referred to only once in the book,[6] must have held some significance for Venturi and Scott Brown for it to be so prominent. To the right of the image, a black road vanishes into the desert horizon and dusty neon signs advertise hotels, gas stations and casinos. A billboard dominates the left side of the image. Raised on timber posts above the desert landscape, the billboard depicts a reclining female form clad only in a floral bikini. The expanse of naked flesh is advertising an artificial tanning agent made from 'coconut oil and cocoa butter'. The focus of the billboard is unashamedly the odalisque form, her long brown legs and sensuous contours dominating the lower part of the sign. Moreover, her body is stripped of individual identity with the edge of the sign literally slicing part of her face away, rendering it a body without a specific identity. But the body does have a cultural identity, the eroticized Polynesian girl, her skin tanned by the Hawaiian sun, her face transformed into a willing, if anonymous, smile, and her hair adorned with a single frangipani. However, this billboard, with its innocent depiction of youthful sensuality, is ultimately, like the Polynesian Revue in the Stardust lounge, hollow and contrived. Not only is it advertising a product that seeks to falsely replicate the Pacific lifestyle, but its very framing, on aged scaffolding, suggests a degree of artifice in its message. When viewed in its totality, scanning from left (billboard) to right (street), the image initially evokes the romance of island life, a message which is soon diminished with visions of commercial transactions in tawdry hotel rooms.

The meaning of the Tanya image has been debated in many works, being in turn eulogized as an abstract, pop-art gesture and condemned as sexist and demeaning. For example, Aron Vinegar argues that Venturi and Scott Brown selected the image as a provocation; a symbol that during their fieldwork they had braved the 'sexual temptation' (2008: 46) of Las Vegas and were not afraid. Yet, for the remainder of their work, sexuality seems to be deeply suppressed as if through guilt or denial. Conversely, Neil Leach identifies Tanya, the 'woman-as-commodified-image', as 'blatantly exploit[ing] female sexuality' (1999: 64). This latter position is reliant on bringing a late-twentieth-century political sensitivity to bear on a 1960s image. Neither of these interpretations is particularly compelling when taken in the context of the larger work or the era in which the image was taken.

Viewed in the context of the late 1960s, the Tanya image evokes the great romance of sexual liberation and the appeal of exotic places; both of which can be traced to the fieldwork of Mead. Its secondary significance lies in its evocation of the experience of staying in the Stardust hotel during their fieldwork in 1968 and being surrounded by Pacific Island images, names and performances. The Tanya image, the single most overtly gendered sign in the entire work, ultimately functions as a type of

Figure 3 **Tanya billboard, Las Vegas.**

memento mori for Venturi and Scott Brown's romance with Las Vegas; a static reminder not of death, but of an otherwise repressed and innocent sexual desire. The documentary photographs of the fieldwork support this reading; they contain images which Koolhaas describes as depicting a team lead by 'two lovers', a 'romantic couple' on a 'honeymoon with students' (Fischli *et al.* 2009: 162).

The third and final characteristic of what Newton (1993: 14) calls the 'erotic equation of fieldwork' is that it is frequently hidden or repressed and may only be subliminally present in the researcher's notes.[7] Newton argues that there is a 'black hole enveloping this non-subject' (1993: 5) and that the sexual and romantic allure of fieldwork is consistently erased after it is complete. Killick (1995: 76) similarly notes that while 'the ethnographic literature becomes ever more [sexually] explicit' in its accounts of the field being examined, 'the anthropologist's sexuality remains a subtext that is systematically erased'. This neutering of the anthropologist's notes and actions, which has been described as one of the last taboo subjects of anthropology (Whitehead and Conaway 1986), has an unusually clear presence in *Learning from Las Vegas*.

In the preface to the revised edition, Scott Brown records that one of the changes that she made to the work was to ' "de-sex" the text' (Venturi *et al.* 1977: xv). While she implies that this procedure is warranted by a growing political awareness of the equality of women, the process of de-sexing the work draws even more attention to the act of repression. In a book about a city where women are systematically commodified and objectified, the minute alterations to the prose to ensure that it is more objective, neutral and scientific is precisely the practice that anthropologists warn is used to deny the influence of sexuality in the field.

The end of the affair

Looking back on the fieldwork in 1976, Scott Brown was drawn to admit that her relationship with Las Vegas was of a 'hate–love' kind: '[w]e recommended learning [from] not loving … Las Vegas' (1976: 103). With distance, the seductive lure of Las Vegas had been diminished, reinforcing her view that the second edition of the book should be less artfully designed, less tactile and without the translucent, fetishized, cover. Where the first edition was an object to be admired and coveted in its own right, Scott Brown called for the second issue to be abridged and presented as a simple scholarly work. This repression of the sexual, the de-sexing of the text and the denial of the commodification of women, has been noted in various critiques of *Learning from Las Vegas* but rarely explained.

This chapter proposes that when *Learning from Las Vegas* is seen, in its totality, as an attempt to provoke a paradigm shift in architectural thinking through appeals to science, then the centrality of the fieldwork becomes apparent. Yet this same fieldwork, which seeks to suggest a degree of objectivity and independence, can trigger an erotic shift in the relationship between the observer and system, resulting in hasty denials and belated censorship in the face of evidence to the contrary. This is the reason why the interpretation of *Learning from Las Vegas* through the erotics of fieldwork is so useful even though it remains unproven; it provides a single explanation for so many of the controversial dimensions of the original work, and especially its indecisive and hesitant attitude towards issues of sexuality and gender.

Epilogue

In the late 1970s Denise Scott Brown was invited to feature alongside Margaret Mead in a book about prominent women and their impact on society. By the time the book by Gilbert and Moore (1981) was released, Margaret Mead had died and the legacy of her work was slowly unravelling. At that same time Scott Brown was drawn to make the first of many careful denials of any deep feelings towards Las Vegas, confronting, in part, the questions of sexuality and fieldwork that Mead had never been called to account for. But while Mead and Scott Brown at least had the opportunity to reflect on their experiences in the field, what of the field itself?

In 1983, after the publication of Freeman's work, the Polynesian people could finally celebrate the wresting of their culture from the hands and fevered imaginings of foreign anthropologists. Their consistent rejection of Mead's findings was finally justified and the first great example of twentieth-century fieldwork was exposed to ridicule. In 2007 the Stardust Casino, where the majority of Scott Brown and Venturi's fieldwork was based, was subjected to demolition by controlled implosion. In the intervening years the Polynesian Revue had been closed to make way for a large sports betting facility and the Lido had been diminished in size until it had become an anomaly. It would be nice to think that Las Vegas, in some way, learnt from Venturi and Scott Brown's fieldwork, but in the end, the Stardust was simply demolished to make way for an even larger palace of hedonism and consumption.

Notes

1   While the authorship of *Learning from Las Vegas* is conventionally attributed to three people – Venturi, Scott Brown and Izenour – many of the sections of the book had been previously published or circulated as the work of just the first two named authors. Moreover, it is also apparent that some sections, like the preface to the revised edition, were written entirely by Scott Brown. In this chapter, where the work is clearly that of one or two authors, it is generally credited to them in the text, even if the citation leads to the complete work.

2   The structure of *Learning from Las Vegas* shifts from polemic, to graphic display of evidence, then back to polemic and finally to examples of the work of Venturi and Scott Brown, not all of which are well connected to the themes of the book.

3   The unpublished field notes record that the first four days in California commenced with an appointment to see the artist Ed Ruscha and a visit to Disneyland. The time in Ruscha's studio is readily explained by the team's desire to borrow his graphic techniques and 'deadpan' method. No explanation for the visit to Disneyland has ever been offered and there is a conspicuous lack of reporting of it in any of the texts.

4   The headline was 'Yale Professor Will Praise Strip for $8,925' (Venturi *et al.* 1977: xii). While neither disagreeing with the implications of the headline nor rejecting it, Venturi, Scott Brown and Izenour then record that they requested additional money from the city, with the result that the next day's headline was 'Yale Professor Ups Price to Praise Strip' (Venturi *et al.* 1977: xii).

5   The chapter uses the latter definition of the 'erotics of fieldwork'; that is, it occurs when the observers have lost their independence and been seduced by the values, preferences or practices of the field. There is no suggestion that any members of Venturi and Scott Brown's team actually had sexual relations with other people in Las Vegas during their fieldwork.

6   The image may appear twice in the body of the text, and once on the cover, but the only explicit reference to it simply draws attention to the Roman practice of celebrating events with bas-relief representations.

7   Newton (2000) also describes the work of Mead as a major influence on her own personal revelations about the flirtatious nature of fieldwork.

Inside the cave, outside the discipline

Catharina Gabrielsson

> The historian is, in every sense of the word, only the *fictor*, which is to say the modeller, the artisan, the author, the inventor of whatever past he offers us. And when it is in the element of art that he thus develops his search for lost time, the historian no longer even finds himself facing a circumscribed object, but rather something like a liquid or gas expansion – a cloud that changes shape constantly as it passes overhead. What can we know about a cloud, save by *guessing*, and without ever grasping completely?
>
> (Didi-Huberman 2005: 2)

Introduction

In *The Eternal Present: The Beginnings of Art*, published in 1962, Sigfried Giedion writes on parietal art or cave art. Although we 'are free to interpret the fantastic forms occurring in these caverns as cathedrals, galleries, chapels', he writes, 'these sequences of forms, sometimes sharply defined, sometimes utterly amorphous, are not architecture' (Giedion 1962: 526). He insists: these spaces are not architecture, because architecture is man-made, architecture – as a spatial art – depends on light, and the darkness of the caves eliminates space. Giedion admits that spatial perception is not entirely visual, that it also involves touch and hearing (which, incidentally, is considered crucially important in many current accounts of these caves)[1] – he even, habitually, quotes Le Corbusier to underline the acoustic significance of space – nevertheless, Giedion maintains that these spaces are *not* architecture.

Most people would agree. Deep caves are strange environments, where the prehistoric markings made by humans sometimes require climbing and crawling several hundred metres, even kilometres, into the entrails of the Earth.[2] By popular account, these are the sites for the Beginning of Art, even the Birth of Man as some have imagined it; a 'transition from animal to man, from twilight to conscious life' (Bataille 1980: 31), a discovery of man's 'strangeness to his own humanity' (Nancy

1996: 69) – and if not a birth, at least an early record of the exteriorization of information characteristic for modern man (Leroi-Gourhan 1993; see also Derrida 1976). In common with these readings is an understanding of the emergence of 'man' through a process of distancing from nature, either made manifest or produced through acts of creation. This creation, multifarious as it may be, is not seen to include architecture. The traces left by prehistoric dwellings may be few and scanty, yet the caves themselves bear proof of some of the most ancient forms of spatial practices and spatial productions known to Western civilization. Relatively little has been written on the spatial aspects of parietal art that goes beyond a mere acknowledgement of the caves as a given (albeit extraordinary, possibly sacred) context.

But if the natural quality of these caves is such a self-evident fact, why is it so important for Giedion to repeatedly claim that we must not think of them as architecture? What is at stake here, and what would happen if we indeed *did* think of them as architecture? In this chapter, I will investigate the caves as a site for architectural thinking based on the following assumptions. First, it seems to me that the 'art' of these caves – if we agree on calling it that – cannot be approached without considering the spatial situation in its entirety. Second, their lasting significance as practised spaces means that these caves were integrated in a social, religious and possibly also political context, which makes them cultural rather than natural. And finally, that by forging an alternative beginning for architecture than the one maintained by generations of architects and scholars – who, much like Giedion, have shied away from ambiguity – architecture might begin to recognize the uncertainties inherent to its own, highly speculative nature.

Figure 1 **Inside the cave. Lithography from the nineteenth century showing one of the halls in the Galerie Infèrieure in the cave of Gargas (Aventignan).**

Architectural origins

Fieldwork can be understood as a form of reality check, a means of adjusting one's thinking and practice to the exterior world. In its traditional anthropological setting, fieldwork draws on an epistemology that sees reality as a reservoir of 'facts' to be used as 'the material base for an argument', thus aligning with a positivistic scientific model that ignores one's complicity with the work (Rogoff in Doherty 2004: 86). The so-called discovery of the painted caves of Europe in the late nineteenth century and their gradual acceptance into the academic world is in fact a case in point for how perception is formed by 'habits of mind' and disciplinary framing (Lewis-Williams 2004: 18–68; Rosengren, forthcoming; Burns and Kahn 2005).

My own interest was ignited by a random first encounter with the cave of Rouffignac in 2003. Situated in the Dordogne district of France, this vast and unusually brutal cave contains more than 250 animal representations with almost portrait-like qualities, located some 4 km underground. Although it has been visited repeatedly during the last 500 years (as shown by the writing on the walls), the prehistoric art was only officially recognized in 1956 and has since been dated to the Magdalenian era, some 13,000 years ago. If my initial visit sparked a childlike sense of excitement, my return to the caves in 2009 – more precisely, to the south-western part of France where many of them are concentrated – was also driven by scholarly concerns, linked to my research on how notions of beginnings become operative in architecture. In comparison to the mythological, literary or tendentious archaeological sources that have been used to feed speculations on architecture's origins, the Palaeolithic caves are *real* and part of the physical world. But doing research on these caves – as physical places, imaginary sites and theoretical outsets – is also to venture outside the realms of architecture into an interdisciplinary field. If largely disregarded in terms of space and ignored in terms of architecture, there is an enormous amount of literature on what the caves presumably reveal concerning early hunter-gatherer societies. And the bodily experience I have of these caves, of treading and slipping in the darkness, feeling the cold, the silence, the wonder, is inseparable from my mental activities – searching for differences, making associations, comparing one guide's account to another's. The interplay between sensory and psychic factors in sense-making processes thus furthers an understanding of the complexities inherent to fieldwork. For the field is never merely physical ground, an unmediated reality we can presume to have direct access to via our senses. It is always a juxtaposition of different fields, including that of our own predisposition.

Granted there was no official knowledge of the prehistoric caves until the late nineteenth century, and that scholars of architecture had no way of including them in their theories – but would they ever have done so? The mythologies of architecture's origins, from Vitruvius onwards, have always involved progression – stories of how primitive man abandons his animal-like existence, raising structures of wood or stone into precise functional forms. In identifying architecture as form, and of building as conditioned by necessity, reason, climate, God or some other external factor (and thereby founding architecture in principles beyond the realm of the social), these spaces whose art reveals a level of sophistication that defies any notion of progression simply do not fit in. It is only with Giedion we arrive at a point in history where the prehistoric caves *could* be written into a treatise, and although he knowingly traces a linear path of gradual progression true to the genre, the caves are not so much omitted as rejected from architecture. There is clearly some prohibition here, some kind of taboo, some risk we are running as architects.

The notion of origins in architecture has always served an operational purpose. As Anthony Vidler has noted, modern architecture resides on the 'more or less coherent narratives of origins and progress' fabricated by historians and theoreticians in order to authorize a certain style (Vidler 2008: 1–12). But if the origin has a privileged position in Western thinking – if not a source for truth and authenticity, then at least as morally or aesthetically superior – its use in writings on architecture reveal an almost obsessive need, not merely to argue for a certain style, but to justify the discipline as such (Forty 2006: 4). Le Corbusier famously linked nomad temples to fishermen's shacks to argue for 'the principle of the straight line' – thereby promoting an architecture which, in its basic adherence to reason, would be of eternal value. And this kind of thinking re-emerges whenever attempts are made to ground architecture in so-called essential principles. It finds its most explicit form in uncritical phenomenological writings but is equally embedded in the 'humanist' tradition whereby form is supposed to harmonize with the idealized human body (Hight 2008: 17–31).

So origins are not innocent – they are charged with ideology and intent. They have less to do with the past than with the future, in setting out the path for architecture ahead – thus 'speculations intensify when the need is felt for a renewal of architecture' (Rykwert 1981: 183). What is rarely brought to the fore, however, is the wilful creativity of these acts, even their inherent critique: how origins are invented and made operative in discourse for a certain end. There is thus a tactic and rhetorical side to architecture's engagement with origins that enters into almost complete contradiction, with the formal and cognitive closure that origins in themselves represent. For Edward Said, origins are teleological in nature and therefore 'divine', whereas beginnings are historical, dynamic and constitutive for an altogether more productive category of ideas (Said 1997: xxiii). By proposing the Palaeolithic caves as an alternative beginning for architecture, then, I am stepping in line with an architectural tradition but also consciously breaking with it. The purpose here is to undo the determinacy of architecture as form and physical construction, opposing the 'tone of certainty' dominating in art history (Didi-Huberman 2005: 2) which hems the architectural imagination, too.

Alternative beginnings

Suggesting the painted caves as a beginning for architecture – a milieu from which architecture comes into being, on which an alternative architecture may be forged – evidently calls for careful considerations.[3] Needless to say, I am not proposing that we should all go back and live in caves. The widespread view that we were once cavemen is in fact without substance: the decorated caves in Europe and elsewhere in the world were never used for human habitation (Leroi-Gourhan 1993: 102, 318). People may have lived in the openings, and under rock shelters, or in dugout hollows along the rivers, but never in the depth of the caves themselves. It is not difficult to imagine that for these hunter-gatherer societies, following the seasonal movements of game across the lands, the most common form of shelter must have been something like a tent. Nevertheless, and perhaps because of that, many of the caves show signs of sustained practices over thousands of years, pointing to a high level of integration in the structures of these societies.

Considering the close-knit relationship between art and architecture, made particularly vivid here, the neglect of the spatial aspects of this art is indicative for the rigidity of disciplinary thought. The standard accounts on parietal art have an almost exclusive focus on objects and imagery, thereby delimiting the issue of space to *represented* space – that is, as the outcome of the composition and perspective possibly revealed by the motifs. Although current archaeological research has done much to contextualize the caves in climatic, biological and anthropological frameworks of interpretation (Bahn and Vertut 2001: 170–211), questions concerning the nature of these presumably 'sacred' spaces necessarily remain open. Therefore, it is primarily through their association with shamanistic practices that the spatial and material aspects of the caves are brought to the fore. Here, a particular focus is made on the great variety in size and location of spaces used as settings for the art. The differences in techniques and material engagement – ranging from 'tags' and hasty sketches to elaborate murals and carvings – are seen as suggestive for a distribution of public and private spaces, of communal and individual activities (Lewis-Williams 2004: 228–267). Drawing on the pioneering work of the Marxist art historian Max Raphaël (1946), Lewis-Williams interprets the imagery as productive for the formation of hierarchies, power relationships and identities – as well as reflecting a cosmologic belief that included transgression to the 'beyond'; a theory that is sufficiently controversial to be bypassed in silence in more general accounts (Bahn 2007).

Figure 2 **Cave documentations. Plan and figurative content of the caves of Pech Merle (Cabrerets) and Les Combarelles (Les Eyzies) after André Leroi-Gourhan. Numbers and letters refer to a system of categorisation devised to analyse the structural principles for what he discerned as 'mythograms'.**

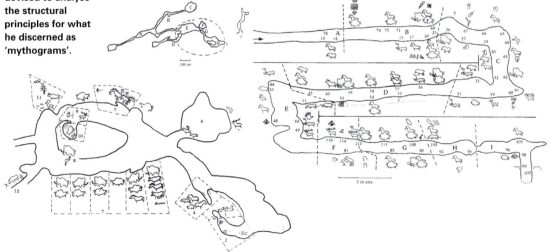

Giedion is thus quite alone in addressing the Palaeolithic spatial perception – and certainly in writing from an architectural outset. Although 'spatially speaking, the caverns are empty', the sense of space displayed by the imagery clearly fascinates him. Giedion discerns a bewildering order of freedom and independence, resembling the order of the stars 'which move about in endless space, unconfined and universal in their relations' (Giedion 1962: 519). Something is clearly going on here that projects into the future, *his* future: the spirit of modern architecture. So why the taboo – even enforced by his assurance (flaunting a remarkable insight) that 'prehistoric man did not regard the caverns in any way as architectural space' (1962: 529)? Hovering between the sacred and the unclean, the meaning of 'taboo' is ambiguous. Its functionality at a social level has a connection to the repression of early traumas and forbidden sexual impulses into the unconscious of the individual, deemed by Freud as necessary for the formation of the socialized subject (Freud 1950). And so we may indeed speak of a taboo, for in order for Giedion to maintain his episteme he must deny the disturbing architectural implications put forward by the caves.

For the caves may be dark, but they were lit up by people – hundreds of oil lamps were found in Lascaux whose paintings must have required extensive preparations, including the building and raising of scaffolding. They may be interior spaces, but then again, hadn't architecture only recently been defined as precisely that? According to the late-nineteenth-century aesthetics developed by Riegl, Wölfflin and Schmarsow – forerunners to the conception Giedion is advancing – architecture is understood in terms of the hollowed-out space, the art of forming the interior (Giedion 1964: 499–504). But the argument that Giedion is making and spends his life defending is 'architecture being the masterly, correct and magnificent play of masses brought together in light', that is, architecture as the building of intentional form, as the creation of an authored space that encompasses the entire environment (1964: 507). So the problem here is not so much that the caves are formless, natural or dark – what is at stake is a major shift in architectural theory, one concerning the identity and legitimacy of the architect. The caves limit the scope of the architect, and perhaps not merely in terms of their interiority, but as evidence for a collective and ongoing production of meaning that stretches into the present – with each experience and each contested interpretation (see also Ballantyne 2004). The caves have the capacity to undermine everything Giedion holds holy, and that continues to be holy for an architectural culture centred on the stability of narrative and meaning, on autonomous form and programmatic determination.

In his book *Walkscapes*, Francesco Careri suggests that the humanization of space began with wanderings, with the appropriation of territory across the Palaeolithic landscape. He discerns another beginning for architecture, not one based on settlements and physical walls, but of spaces made by routes, paths and relationships (Careri 2002; see also Petrescu 2007). Striving to undo the primordial duality separating nomads from settlers, Careri nevertheless champions an 'original' spatial conception, similar to what Leroi-Gourhan identifies as 'itinerant' space (and then drops in favour of lengthy ruminations on 'radial', settled space) (Leroi-Gourhan 1993: 325–335). The presence of the painted caves complicates this scheme, for their status as practised

Figure 3 Fieldnotes. The author's notes from an expedition with artist Eva Löfdahl to the *grottes décorées* located in Dordogne, Lot and the Hautes-Pyrénées districts of south-western France (31 May–6 June 2009).

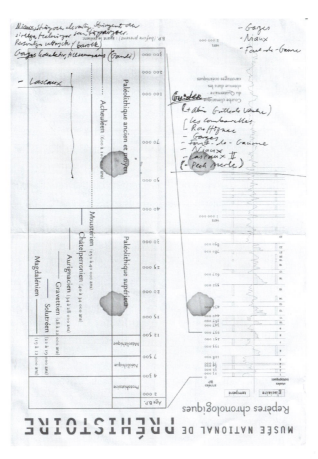

spaces are neither itinerant nor radial in character. They must have served as nodes in the nomadic landscape, permanent places for temporal use, which points to the need to negotiate between different spatial modes in a non-dialectic fashion. While some of these ideas are developed in philosophy and are investigated in environmental archaeology, the full implications of the caves in terms of space, in terms of architecture, remain to be explored.

Preliminary conclusion

What is commonly referred to as 'the beginning of art' tends to be envisaged as a homogeneous body of imagery. In fact, parietal art is as differentiated as the visual culture of today. Although there is a consistency in motives – mostly animals, handprints and signs (and very few human figures) – the great varieties in terms of techniques and locations suggest disparate meanings or functions (Bahn and Vertut 2001: 213). And if the naming of the spaces – the Great Hall of Lascaux, the Salon Noir at Niaux – reveal their architectural affinities, the caves themselves are so dissimilar that one may even think of them as *stylish* (the gothic of Gargas, the baroque of Niaux, the modernist Rouffignac, the art nouveau of Pech-Merle). These differences are scarcely conveyed by photographs. The topographical settings for these caves, their gigantic halls, narrow passages, ante-chambers and salons are *species of spaces*, to paraphrase Georges Perec (2008). And if his precise account of the multiplicitous, complex and fragmented nature of space is precedent to what is presently cast as heterogeneous space, suggesting a knowledge of space that has been repressed in architectural thinking (Hensel *et al.* 2009), it is already present in the caves, with the same crucial imports for our thinking on space, self and society. Thus the trauma repressed in the caves, why we as architects must not go there, is their capacity to convey a different idea about architecture. Not architecture as building, but one created by the multifarious uses and experiences of space, an architecture in continuous emergence – ambiguous, ephemeral and contextual.

Notes

1   The theory that acoustic properties had a decisive influence on placement of markings within the caves was put forward by Iegor Reznikoff and Michel Dauvois in 1988 (Reznikoff and Dauvois 1988). It sparked a broad range of responses, from scholarly studies on 'archaeoacoustics' to more free-flying speculations on the connection between sound and sacred places. Within the shamanistic framework of interpretation, touch and sound are especially important: signifying a desire to physically merge with the 'underworld', the markings left by humans are seen to derive from various consciousness-altering rituals in which drumming and chanting played an essential part (Lewis-Williams 2004: 223–226). Even the sober archaeologist Paul G. Bahn acknowledges that it is 'extremely likely that they [the prehistoric artists] would have used any acoustic peculiarities to the full' (Bahn and Vertut 2001: 199).

2   André Leroi-Gourhan describes the passage into the underground sanctuary of Etcheberriko-Karbia as one requiring 'full speleological equipment . . . crossing little lakes, moving along narrow ledges, and climbing over slippery stalagmites several yards long, before reaching an entrance that opens on a very narrow tunnel; the tunnel ends at a sheer cliff more than six feet high with no handholds'. The figure made at the very bottom of the cave is placed in such a way that 'we can only suppose that a colleague was holding the artist by the back of his garments over the void' (Leroi-Gourhan 1968: 164).

3   In order to situate the caves more precisely in architectural theory, it is necessary to engage more fully in a conversation with epistemology, archaeology and aesthetics than it is possible to do here. The project outlined in this chapter will be extended to form a chapter in a forthcoming book, tentatively entitled *Beginnings: Rethinking Architecture from the Inside*.

Group pioneering

Robert Smithson and circle's early forays to the field

Emily Scott

Beginning in 1966, American artist Robert Smithson and a circle of his friends set out on a series of field excursions to the outskirts of New York City, motivated in part by their growing desire to create large-scale artworks on the actual land. Most of these group trips were to what Smithson termed 'backwater' or 'fringe' sites in New Jersey, including defunct rock quarries, suburban wastelands and the desolate Pine Barrens in the southern part of the state. Smithson would publish two New Jersey 'travelogues', though the more famous of the two, 'A Tour of the Monuments of Passaic, New Jersey' (Smithson 1967c), is based upon a solo journey undertaken to his former hometown.[1] Smithson's 'preoccupation with place' (AAA, Smithson 1972) was deeply embroiled with art world debates of the day and is only decipherable relative to a knot of interrelated critiques he began waging in the mid-1960s: against nineteenth-century Romantic views of nature, pictorialism and Abstract Expressionism, to name a few targets. His early site-based activity also responded to emerging land-use patterns and politics (e.g. the rampant suburbanization of postwar America, the shift of industrial production from inner cities to exurban reaches, increasing public concern about ecological degradation). In contrast to practitioners coming from empirically oriented disciplines such as architecture and geography, Smithson invented field destinations as a creative-critical act. The field, in other words, functioned as a space in and through which to stage a particular set of critiques. More specifically, New Jersey's 'backwaters' operated as an *other space* to the New York art world he associated with studio-based art making *and* to wilderness, at least as defined by a rapidly expanding back-to-nature movement toward which he held fundamental objections.

Scholars have devoted tremendous attention to Smithson's ambitious, if convoluted, theoretical project, especially his idea of 'site' and 'non-site' dialectics. Art historian Jennifer Roberts, for instance, notes the degree to which his Passaic essay has assumed cult status within the fields of architecture, landscape architecture and urban planning, 'where it serves as a benchmark for its exploration of what would later come to be called *terrain vague*: the liminal or interstitial landscape' (Roberts 2004: 60–61). My own chapter, by contrast, foregrounds the social nature of early art-making expeditions conducted by Smithson and his peers.[2] (I am as eager to counter-monumentalize Smithson, the lone artist, as to consider the import of these activities for contemporaneous and subsequent collaborative art making.) More broadly, it seeks to shift attention from the products to the processes of these trips, thereby returning to them some of the temporality and spatiality that were crucial to their project. Within the limits of this text, I can at best evoke a sketchy impression of these now-historical events and the circumstances out of which they arose. I offer them up nonetheless as a provocative instance of fieldwork as creative experiment, of the permeation of practice with theory, of an updated (if decades old) formulation of the site visit.

My own attraction to these long-ago trips also stems from the fertile methodological dilemmas they pose to contemporary art historical scholarship. What would it mean, I wonder, to employ Smithson's artistic project as a model for critical enquiry, particularly in a discipline without any identifiable fieldwork tradition? This chapter embarks upon art historical research as experimental terrain, intending to put forward, rather than conceal, the messy entanglement between the art that is its subject and its own speculative practice of art history. To be upfront, my relation to the trips examined here is fundamentally parasitic: using them as a window and vehicle to engage in field-based research, to 'inhabit' historical landscapes. Paralleling the artists I write about, my own predilection is for the worldly spaces of the field as opposed to the interior spaces of the library and archive. I am exhilarated by, and curious about, the continued creative and critical possibility in what Smithson refers to as 'primary process', the artist's experience of coming in direct contact with the physical world and its raw materials in actual time, of 'discovering data … that hasn't been unearthed … and making something out of this' (AAA, Robbin n.d.). I similarly want to probe the potential of the site visit, *not* as a means to authenticate research or achieve some sort of unmediated access to the world 'out there', but rather to mobilize the kinds of theoretical and methodological questions haunting my own historical-spatial research.

January 1966: Greenwich Village, New York

Smithson walks up the worn stairs of an old factory on Greenwich Street, in a district of Manhattan quickly transforming from one of the city's central manufacturing corridors into a residential neighborhood for artist-pioneers such as himself. He plops down on the sofa in the renovated loft he has shared with Nancy Holt (then Smithson, his wife) since 1962. Sifting through the day's mail, he spots a letter (dated 22 January 1966) from Dale McConathy, the audacious new literary editor at the fashion magazine *Harper's Bazaar*.[3] In it, McConathy makes a startling proposition to the young artist and hopeful author: 'I have been trying to think of a subject which you might write for us … I was particularly thinking about the disappearance of the artist as an individual identity. See what you think' (AAA, McConathy 1966). Smithson decides to construct an essay around a fieldtrip to some New Jersey quarries he'd prowled as a youth, and immediately begins arranging plans. He invites along Minimalist sculptor-critic Donald Judd, one of the most influential voices in New York's avant-garde at the time, as well as both men's wives. The actual journey takes place sometime before 12 February, when a postcard arrives from Dan Flavin, who mentions that Judd has just shown him a draft of Smithson's essay and enquires if he might have his own copy as well (AAA, Flavin 1966). A month later, a third correspondence appears, this time from Dan Graham, which makes reference to the Judds' reaction to the text:

> Julie said about the geology piece that it is definitely to be published because 'This is Dale's baby.' She complained that it was unreadable ... Don likes the way your ideas that you attribute to others eventually fall apart at the end ... But he says he's taking up oceanography. He's sick of geology ...
>
> (AAA, Graham 1966)[4]

The couple's dismissive tone aside, it is noteworthy that Smithson's writing-in-the-making was circulated among and commented upon by his colleagues. Sol LeWitt, who, along with Graham, would also publish in *Harper's Bazaar* at McConathy's request, retrospectively described the ambiance of exchange among artists in this period in terms variously interpretable as symbiotic or cannibalistic: 'We were all feeding on one another, and it was a crucial time. Dale caught it right on the wing' (Meyer 2001: 138).

'The Crystal Land' (Smithson 1966a), Smithson's first published travel piece, materializes in the May 1966 issue of *Harper's Bazaar*, though we can only conjecture as to whether or not he conceived it as a direct response to McConathy's provocation, as a representation of the artist's ego dissolving into group identification. He sets up the two couples' 'rock hunting' excursion to the Upper Montclair and Great Notch quarries as the outcome of his and Judd's 'mutual interest in geology and mineralogy' (Smithson 1966a: 72). With no apparent self-consciousness about his chauvinistic tenor, he writes of their time at the first quarry: 'For about an hour Don and I chopped incessantly ... with hammer and chisel, while Nancy and Julie wandered aimlessly around the quarry picking up sticks, leaves, and odd stones' (1966a: 72). Of the second quarry, mirroring his taste for 'de-naturalized' landscapes (Bear 1970: 53–54), he describes: 'The quarry resembled the moon. A gray factory in the midst of it all looked like architecture by Robert Morris.... It was an arid region, bleached and dry.... A chaos of cracks surrounded us' (1966a: 73). This text, like his subsequent travelogues, substitutes documentary-style observation with its antithesis: a cacophony of chaotic impressions, esoteric references and confounding metaphorical slippages. In spite of its difficultness, a certain pop sensibility suffuses the piece, consistent with its stylish print-based destination. In addition to criss-crossing highways that 'become man-made geological networks of concrete', Smithson chronicles 'shiny chrome' diners, glass-windowed shopping centers, the car's cigarette-packed ashtray, pages of the Sunday newspaper, and row upon row of suburban houses painted in 'petal pink, frosted mint, buttercup, ... antique green, Cape Cod brown, and so on' (1966a: 72).

A main fault line running through the article is the contrast between the increasingly systematized and streamlined landscape and the gritty space of the quarries,

Figure 1 **Great Notch Quarry, Passaic County, New Jersey, December 1966. This photograph was taken on a fieldtrip by Robert Smithson, Nancy Holt and Robert Morris.**

from which its base materials are excavated. In a 1969 interview, Smithson would speak to such a relation:

> I first got interested in places by taking trips and just confronting the raw materials of the particular sectors before they were refined into steel or paint or anything else. My interest in the site was really a return to the origins of material, sort of a dematerialization of refined matter. Like if you took a tube of paint and followed that back to its original sources. My interest was in juxtaposing the refinement of, let's say, painted steel, against the particles and rawness of matter itself.
>
> (Norvell 1969: 87)

My own text, written some 40 years later, likewise revisits these trips with an interest in their exploration of particular sectors before being refined into artworks (and, moreover, artworks attributed to individual artists) – sort of a dematerialization of art historical matter. Like if you took an essay and followed that back to its original processes, juxtaposing the refinement of, let's say, reprinted words, against the particles and rawness of collaborative, field-based enquiry itself.

April 1967: Pine Barrens, New Jersey

The Rent-a-Car station wagon lurches to a halt as it turns off the New Jersey pavement and onto an unmarked, sandy road. Five travelers – Smithson, Holt, Robert Morris, Carl Andre and gallerist Virginia Dwan – spill out, into the silent springtime air. (The rock-and-roll radio station faded out miles ago, somewhere past the nearest human settlement.) Having left Manhattan early this morning, the group has already made several diversionary stops along the Garden State Parkway en route to this remote location, an obscure airfield that will, in time, become the 'site' of Smithson's *A Nonsite (an indoor earthwork)*, the first in a series of 'non-site' pieces he'd complete between 1968 and 1969.[5] The urbanites begin ambling down a series of intersecting roads aimed in the direction of the de-vegetated airfield visible in the distance. Upon climbing a small rise, they are stunned by the landscape's unbroken expanse of space, not unlike that experienced in deserts of the American West. Below spreads a sea of scraggly pines, only six or seven feet tall and forming thickets that make cross-country travel daunting, if not impossible. Their lively discussion about 'landscaping, earthworks, sites, and monuments' eventually dissipates as each individual becomes absorbed in the details of this foreign terrain (Smithson 1967b: 357). One of them bends over to inspect the ground underfoot and calls to the others, 'Come look at this!' The sense of exhilaration among them is palpable, as they re-imagine themselves as modern-day artist-pioneers.

Smithson's 'restoration of nothing but a trace' of this preliminary 'cartographic expedition' to the Pine Barrens, on 16–17 April 1967, makes reference to one of their stopovers along the way: 'Under a vast concrete bridge near [Perth Amboy] are brick and tile furnaces, a carborundum plant and a lead factory. Nancy and Virginia took some photos in that area' (Smithson 1967a: 332).[6] Among Holt's documentary photographs of the group exploring this site, one pictures Smithson and Andre below the sublime-scaled infrastructure of the highway, flanked by its colossal pillars as they make their way along this weedy inversion of the pulsing transportation corridor overhead. Holt also experimented with her young photographic art practice while at one of the industrial materials yards nearby. Her series of four snapshots, *Concrete Visions* (1967), captures neat, linear stacks of just-manufactured cinder blocks – not dissimilar from those materials and forms utilized by contemporary sculptors of a Minimalist persuasion – zooming in closer and closer until one of the infinite squares is transformed into an aperture.

Holt recounts that she and Smithson were often drawn to 'their own sites' during fieldtrips together (Holt and Scott 2009b). One of her favorite finds – an overgrown architectural ruin comprising a crumbling mansion and 'mysterious garden in the woods', just up the road from Great Notch Quarry – became the basis for the first in a series of 'site-specific' tours she developed in the coming years (Holt and Scott 2009b).[7] After taking Smithson and artist Joan Jonas there during the summer of 1967, she would again lead *Stone Ruin Tour* in January 1968, during an action-packed day in which she and Smithson brought Claes and Pat Oldenburg and Allan Kaprow and his family to Passaic County for companion tours of Holt's ruin and Smithson's by-then famous 'monuments', along with snow angels and other amusements between.

Figure 2 Robert
Smithson and Carl
Andre under a bridge
near Perth Amboy,
New Jersey, April
1967, photographic
print: b&w,
25 × 20 cm.

*Figure 3 Stone Ruin
Tour II* led by Nancy
Holt, Cedar Grove/
Little Falls, New
Jersey, 6 January
1968. Participants
included Robert
Smithson, Allan
Kaprow and his
family and Claes and
Pat Oldenburg.

Dwan has vivid memories of early scouting trips to the Pine Barrens, of which she remembers there to have been five or six. As owner of the infamous Dwan Gallery in New York City, an epicenter of Minimalist and what would become known as 'earth art' activity, she was not only an active participant in such endeavors, but also a key facilitator – i.e. she was the financier of both the trips and their prospective land purchases. Of one such venture, undertaken during the winter of 1967–1968 with Smithson, Holt, LeWitt and Mary Peacock (McConathy's then editorial assistant at *Harper's Bazaar*) in order to 'dig up the dirt for this *Site/Non-site* that Bob had in mind', she details:

> We didn't really know for sure what he was doing, but we loved doing the fieldtrip part of it.... I have photographs that I took of all of us standing around in fur coats in this really frigid landscape, with nothing in sight, and Bob digging very important shovelsful of dirt ... I just adored going off on these fieldtrips; they were just marvelous. And the conversations were so rich, all these people coming from their various disciplines and so forth, mingling at these moments in a very casual way, a very easy way. Sitting in diners, you know.
>
> (AAA, Dwan 1984)

One might deduce from Dwan's account that socializing among these same people *otherwise*, for instance, at gallery openings and parties once back in the city, was somehow *less* rich. She seems to suggest, in other words, that the form and context of the group expedition – e.g. out in the world, away from the everyday, with a mutually experienced sense of discovery – disarmed its participants, lending vibrancy to their social interactions. This is precisely why such 'inter-disciplinary' exchanges – inevitably lost to history because of their spontaneous and informal nature – are so captivating to imagine.

Four days after returning from the first Pine Barrens excursion, Dwan signed and sent six identical letters (dated 21 April 1967) to local county clerks inquiring about available land:

> Dear Sir: Would you please inform me immediately of prospective tax sales land. I am interested in a small parcel (a few acres) in the Pine Barrens plains area. Enclosed is a self-addressed self-stamped for your convenience in answering. I await your prompt reply. Thank you, Virginia Dwan.
>
> (AAA, Dwan 1967)

Holt had composed the template and carried out the administrative legwork leading up to it, for example, by tracking down various Chambers of Commerce in the Pine Barrens area. Throughout the next year and a half, leading up to the seminal 'Earth Works' exhibition that Smithson and Dwan organized at the Dwan Gallery in October 1968, Holt played the lead role in investigating real estate opportunities for the group: looking into potential land purchases, leases, donations and short-term loans. When later asked if she considered such administrative tasks to be part of the art making, she responds without hesitation, 'Yes, it was all part of it' (Holt and Scott 2009a). Despite the fact that these efforts to secure land for outdoor works ultimately failed (i.e. the exhibition was held indoors), Dwan acknowledges Holt's behind-the-scenes labor as laying 'groundwork that was important later on to her and to Smithson particularly' (AAA, Dwan 1984), for example, in facilitating future artworks that relied upon the acquisition of land (e.g. Smithson's *Spiral Jetty* of 1970, Holt's *Sun Tunnels* of 1973–1976, both in the north-western corner of Utah).

In 1967, the Pine Barrens covered roughly an eighth of New Jersey. As author John McPhee described in a two-part essay that appeared in *The New Yorker* at the end of that year (the second part of which remains in Smithson's archive), the place was, above all, anomalous, the geographical center of an ever-developing and highly industrialized megalopolis stretching between Boston, Massachusetts and Richmond, Virginia (AAA, McPhee 1967).[8] He opens his portrait of this 'bewildering green country' by contrasting it to New Jersey's central transportation corridor to its north and east, where the 'traffic of freight and people is more concentrated than … anywhere else in the world … one great compression of industrial shapes, industrial sounds, industrial air, and thousands and thousands of houses webbing over the spaces between the factories' (McPhee 1968: 4–6).

The Pine Barrens' incongruousness – geographically, historically and perceptually – is what attracted Smithson. It was Holt, however, who introduced him to this part of the home state they shared in common, which she'd avidly explored since childhood. She recalls that the lure of the Pine Barrens lay not only in its wilderness character, which possessed a consistent 'shock effect' for those arriving from Manhattan via the Garden State Parkway, but also in the remnants of forgotten industrial histories that remained embedded in the landscape (Holt and Scott 2009a). Smithson was particularly taken with sites that represented incongruous temporalities, places where, for instance, 'remote futures meet remote pasts' (Smithson 1968: 50). The agriculturally unproductive and economically evacuated Pine Barrens, inhabited by a people self-named 'the Pineys' who still gathered pinecones and berries and sphagnum moss in the woods like their pioneer forebears, was such a place: a scene of perpetually unrealized land speculation, 'perhaps the country's only permanent non-existent land boom', a cycle in which Smithson and cadre attempted to participate (McPhee 1968: 145).

For Smithson, 'backwaters' such as the Pine Barrens, strip mines, slag heaps, polluted rivers, remote islands, swamps and other sites cast aside by society and/or on the margins of consciousness, symbolized a critical frontier. Dwan recalls that he possessed a 'kind of magical facility … for taking very strange sorts of things that we would normally bypass … and turning them into something mysterious and fascinating' (AAA, Dwan 1984). For him, places and materials as yet unused by artists 'broke down the usual confining aspect of academic art', posing new frontiers for the vanguard artist (AAA, Smithson 1972). Art historian Julian Myers has argued that earthwork artists including Smithson, in reaction to the intense abstraction and bureaucratization of space that characterized postwar urbanism, sought to engage and produce 'no-places': 'empty, unfinished, or obsolete spaces on the peripheries of the urbanist "plans" that increasingly subsumed the American landscape in the 20th century', places at the 'edges and interstices of the grid, ... where the limits of its imagined totality are visible' (Myers 2006: 7, 9). In the late 1960s, the Pine Barrens was not only the blankest spot on the map within striking distance of New York City, but also it *embodied* dead-ends (e.g. roads to nowhere, streams without outlets, soil incapable of productivity), inherently resistant to the 'front country' that encroached upon it from all sides. For Smithson and his circle, this peculiar region represented not only a rupture in New Jersey's vacuous development, but also an opening for path-breaking artists – the prospect of a place still under the radar, where one might even be able to stumble upon cheap, available land.

Dwan's over-exposed photograph of a landscape collapsing into splintered disarray – from an excursion with Smithson and others to a slate quarry in the summer of 1968 – served as the frontispiece for Smithson's essay, 'A Sedimentation of the Mind: Earth Projects' (Smithson 1968), which itself served as a manifesto for the art-works displayed in 'Earth Works'.[9] Another, unpublished, image, taken moments before or after, reveals Smithson and Dwan together in the field, providing a provoca-tive juxtaposition to its printed counterpart. Side by side, the two lanky figures explore this brittle terrain, wrapped up in their own meandering thoughts. Smithson leans over with a canvas sack to gather specimens for one of his sculptural 'non-site' bins.[10] In the background, Dwan wanders off with camera in hand toward a fractured gulley, some fleeting detail (out of the picture's frame) having piqued her curiosity.

Figure 4 **Virginia Dwan and Robert Smithson at slate quarry near Bangor, Pennsylvania, 1968, photographic print: b&w, 21×25 cm. Smithson here gathers specimens for his 1968** *Nonsite (Slate from Bangor, Pa.),* **while Dwan prepares to snap a photograph later highlighted in Smithson's essay, 'A Sedimentation of the Mind: Earth Projects' (Smithson 1968).**

August 2008: Passaic, New Jersey

The art historian wakes up in the 'vapid and dull' space of a chain motel room on the outskirts of Passaic, New Jersey, or, more accurately, amid the bleed of suburban-small-town–corporate development that oozes across every seeming inch of the region.[11] She has brought along a collection of Smithson's writings, a digital camera, an audio recorder and a text on geographical field methods. As she makes her way down to the motel lobby for a coffee, she is compelled to snap a series of photographs – some riffing on Smithson's *Hotel Palenque* slideshow from 1969, others depicting monuments, or art historical 'non-sites', scattered across the motel's grounds: a dumpster housing that resembles Tony Smith's imposing sculptural cubes, a pool cover not unlike Carl Andre's horizontal floor pieces.

She and her field companions – her six-month-old baby and her mother, along to help with childcare – load into the car and use a New Jersey road map to locate the official starting point of their expedition, the bridge where Smithson hopped off a bus from Penn Station in September 1967 and began his own legendary tour of Passaic. She first notices the bridge's fixed architecture, which has changed since Smithson's time (the opening photograph of his Passaic essay is of a rotating 'bridge monument'), wondering what clues this might offer into the industrial history along the river. After crossing it, she and her fellow travelers attempt to skirt the river's edge, as Smithson had. The scene is more treacherous now, however. Whereas he had leisurely rambled through the then-construction site of a new highway, now cars zoomed past, barring pedestrian access. 'This is no place for a stroller', the grandmother warns. The art historian glimpses a homeless encampment in the overgrown brush between the highway off-ramp and riverbank, reminding her of similar settlements she'd encountered while developing an art project on freeway landscapes in Los Angeles a few years prior. Later, she discovers a small cement operation, where she is able to speak with several aged workers about their memories of Passaic in the 1960s. (Regretfully, she is too shy to ask permission to record them.) She learns that the Passaic River was once the most polluted in the United States, that industry had declined dramatically in recent decades, that the new bridge went in ten (or was it twenty?) years ago, because barges no longer needed to travel up and down this stretch of the river. Eventually, the trio makes their way to Main Avenue, a simultaneously dilapidated and commercialized jumble, which appears readily interchangeable with any other number of places in the United States that are economically impoverished, predominantly inhabited by first- and second-generation immigrants and dotted with familiar fast-food franchises. The art historian feels increasingly self-conscious about the remoteness of her art historical task – shouldn't she rather be focusing on the conditions before her? Producing her own work rather than stalking another's? (She prefers to think of herself as an artist rather than an art historian.) Giving in to her own nostalgic impulses, she searches for the folksy-sounding Golden Coach diner where Smithson had grabbed his lunch, hopelessly (and in spite of her 'critical' self) looking to satisfy her craving for an 'authentic' historical vestige, a respite from the alienating environment around her. Instead, she finds that a Dunkin' Donuts® now occupies its site.

She is overcome by a distinct sense of non-arrival, or absence, and confronts an abyss of methodological questions: What exactly *is* she in search of here? Is her intent to re-perform Smithson's act or to borrow his methodology and use it to explore the contemporary? What is to be witnessed *in situ*, when this and other artworks she studies are ephemeral and/or exist now only in documentation? More

Figure 5 **Above: Emily Scott,** *Dunkin' Donuts® Monument* **(2008), Passaic, New Jersey, USA. Below: The author's (mother and son) field companions, Passaic, New Jersey, August 2008.**

importantly, how is one to co-navigate meaningfully the historical and spatial? Does her research resemble that of an art historian, an artist, an urban geographer, or all of the above? She recognizes that part of the confusion originates from her own knotted relationship with her supposed subject's project. Still, she will attempt to take the data she unearths and to make something out of it.

I will conclude with the provocation that the most compelling site-based art from this period not only paved the way for but also demands new forms of art history and criticism. Just as Smithson and his cohort, among other artists in the 1960s, developed practices that pressured the boundaries of art – aiming to exceed the confines of its inherited spaces, borrowing from diverse fields of knowledge, blurring the edges between art and its presumed others, attempting to intervene into the spatial politics of their day – so, too, must the art historian forge methodologies to meet the task of interpretation, cobbling and crafting tools along the way. (I deploy these historical projects, then, as a critique of contemporary art history that fails to question and/or push against established edges of the discipline. For me, too, the field is a space in and through which to stage a particular set of critiques, but also to seek new creative ground.) My own aspiration is to produce art history that merges with critical landscape practice, site-specific art and what artist-geographer Trevor Paglen calls 'experimental geography' (Paglen 2008), extending dialogues across and beyond academic disciplines. More generally, I advocate for art histories that are self-reflexive about the politics of their subjects and their own making (e.g. where they operate, which communities they address), that acknowledge the performative dimension of their research and production (e.g. in my case, the degree of re-enactment involved in visiting artists' former field sites) and that test the potential of various formats (e.g. collaborative fieldtrips as research, guided site tours as pedagogy and scholarly product) in order to effectively investigate and communicate their insights.

Notes

1   The other is 'The Crystal Land' (Smithson 1966a), which chronicles a fieldtrip Smithson made with Nancy Holt and Donald and Julie Judd in early 1966.
2   In early December 2004, Holt gave a lecture about group fieldtrips in the mid–late 1960s, sharing related documentary photographs for the first time publicly, at the Museum of Contemporary Art, Los Angeles. During this talk, she claimed that the artists involved perceived the *social aspect* of what they were doing to be nothing short of 'revolutionary' (Holt 2004). I wish to acknowledge the influence of her comments upon my own thinking and also her generous assistance with my subsequent research along these lines (Holt 2009, 2010; Holt and Scott 2009a, 2009b).
3   McConathy was the literary editor at *Harper's Bazaar* from 1966 to 1969. For a detailed account of his flamboyant career, see James Meyer (2001). According to an email to the author (Holt 2010), Holt worked with McConathy as a part-time assistant literary editor in 1966–1967, during which time she introduced him to Smithson and many of their artist friends. She adds that she and McConathy were together eager to extend the reach of cutting-edge poetry and prose to a wide audience of readers, 'in beauty parlors, doctors' offices, and homes around the country' (Holt 2010).

4　The couples' unflattering reaction to the article as well as Graham's decision to pass this on together forecast remarks Graham made years later about people distrusting Smithson because they perceived him to be a social climber (Tsai 1991).

5　*A Nonsite (an indoor earthwork)* was exhibited in Smithson's second solo show at the Dwan Gallery in March 1968. Smithson created roughly a dozen subsequent 'non-site' pieces in 1968 and 1969, most of which comprised a sculptural container filled with geological specimens from a specific site, together with cartographic and photographic representations of the same location (Hobbs 1981: 104–131).

6　Smithson's date book entry for 16–17 April 1967: 'New Jersey Pine-Barrens/MORRIS – ANDRE' refers to the same trip described in this passage (AAA, Smithson 1967). Smithson's text 'Atlantic City (H-13)' is listed in Flam's anthology as being from 1966, likely based on a mislabeling by Smithson himself. My own research as well that of art historian Suzaan Boettger, however, point to it being from no earlier than Spring 1967 (Boettger 2004: 63); I have taken the liberty to list it here under this revised date (Smithson 1967a).

7　Holt's subsequent tours and 'visual sound zones' include: *Studio Tour* (October 1971, revised in January and March 1972), a tape-recorded tour of Smithson's and Holt's studio; *Visual Sound Zone* (July 1972), which was looped and repeatedly played through speakers at 10 Bleecker, Alanna Heiss's earliest Art and Urban Resources exhibition space; and *John Weber Gallery Tour* (February 1972). None of these tours have been published (Holt 2009).

8　McPhee's Pine Barren piece appeared in *The New Yorker* in 1967 (McPhee 1967a, 1967b). My own citations correlate with his 1968 book version (McPhee 1968).

9　Likewise, Dwan's black-and-white photograph of tire tracks through dirt served as the announcement for 'Earth Works' at the Dwan Gallery via two striking, if cryptic, advertisements that appeared in *Artforum*: in the first, the picture takes up a half-page, with only the caption: 'Photo: Virginia Dwan'; in the second, it fills a whole page, with the text: 'EARTH WORKS OCTOBER DWAN NEW YORK' (*Artforum* 1968a, 1968b).

10　The slate he gathers here is for *Nonsite (Slate from Bangor, Pa.)* (1968).

11　I borrow the phrase 'vapid and dull' from Smithson's essay, 'Entropy and the New Monuments': 'The slurbs, urban sprawl, and the infinite number of housing developments of the postwar boom have contributed to the architecture of entropy.… But this very vapidity and dullness is what inspires many of the more gifted artists' (Smithson 1966b: 27).

Field note 1

On inhabiting 'thickness'

Andrea Kahn

Site is a thick concept with a historically thin discourse attached, and *Site Matters* was born of a desire to address this fact. As Carol Burns and I were getting close to submitting our manuscript for publication we had to decide on an order for the collected essays. To sort out the variables, we invented a tool we dubbed our 'didactic table of contents'. It took a while to figure out the best working format (columns? matrices? bubble diagrams?) and to settle on parameters. We drafted it many times. In the end we used the concepts, terminologies and disciplinary positions that emerged as powerful shapers of

DIDACTIC TABLE OF CONTENTS				
Constructs Author	**Concepts/Topics**	**Localized Adjacencies**	**Structure of the Volume Discourse**	
site as a relational construct				
Burns, Kahn	introduction		Design Theory	
Lippard	photo essay		Art Theory	
site as socially constructed			Terminology *(Grouping I)*	
Jacobs	ownership and property controls		Property	Planning
Beauregard	place precedes site (sequential)	Jacobs + Beauregard: site as area of control	Place	History *(Grouping II)*
site as experimental/material construct		Beauregard + Dripps: "site are full"		
Dripps	ground precedes site	Dripps + Meyer: site as area of influence	Ground	Landscape
	retrieving 18th c. concept *tirer-parti*			
Meyer	site as "armature" "figure" "fragment" "experience"		Landscape	
	19th c. site readings as design tactics	Meyer + Isenstadt: writing new history		
site as historiographical construct				
Isenstadt	context and temporal dimension of site	Isenstadt + Redfield: modernist history as departure point/	Context	Architectural history
	late 20th c. context debate	modernist history reassessed		
			Practices *(Grouping III)*	
Redfield	"site suppression"		Site Design	
	corrective to received knowledge of Le Corbusier	Dripps_Redfield: site design strategies		
site as construct of analysis techniques / modes of representation				
Hess	site analysis as way of seeing/not seeing	Redfield + Hess: conditions *in situ* / recasting history	Site Analysis	Urban Design/Planning
	corrective to received ideas of suburban sites	Hess + Marcuse: resetting site boundaries		
Marcuse	"site as area of concern"		Site Definition	
	boundary definition as problem framing	Marcuse + Kahn: parameters of site definition		
Kahn	"site reach"		Site Representation	
	the multi-scaled urban site	Hess_Kahn: site study practices as conceptually formative		
Burns				Architecture

Figure 1 'Didactic table of contents', *Site Matters: Design Concepts, Histories and Strategies.*

perception, representation and methods of engagement with the construct of site. *Our Didactic Table of Contents* grapples, graphically, with a 'thick concept' capturing a few, but hardly all, of the many meanings that accumulate around the construct of site.

To make sense of the 'thickness' of site requires continual crossing and re-crossing of knowledge categories. No matter the methodology adopted, in the site study process discoveries occur in the spaces between: imagination and precision; creative enterprise and rigorous analysis; field and field work; the real and the represented; one disciplinary lens and another. By asking us to 'acknowledge the significance of disciplinary borrowing as a critical resource for design practice' the Field/Work conference prompted us to explore in-between spaces, to venture beyond our habitual disciplinary lenses.

As American philosopher John Dewey notes, habit wields decisive influence because:

> all distinctly human action has to be learned, and the very heart, blood and sinew of learning is creation of habitudes. Habits bind us to orderly and established ways of action because they generate ease, skill and interest in things to which we have grown used and because they instigate fear to walk in different ways, and because they leave us incapacitated for the trial of them. Habit does not preclude the use of thought, but it determines the channels within which it operates.
>
> (Dewey 1954: 160)

The remarkably thick tangle of questions around field and fieldwork in the call-for-papers that accompanied my invitation to attend the conference speaks volumes. It talks about a 'habit of mind' familiar to many of us, myself included, educated in the design fields – in that designers delight in speculative practices and expansive thought. It also tells us a lot about the predilections of academics (I include myself here as well) who take great pleasure in posing difficult questions and unpacking rich concepts. Dense questions and thick concepts attract our attention because they invite theorization, because they prompt us to explore and inhabit intellectually rich territories 'in between' received ideas and understandings. But when our concepts and questions become over-saturated, when they come to stand for (or, even, 'stand in for') an excess of ideas, or actions, or conditions, they have a way of getting *in our way* – of occluding the very world we expect them to illuminate.

Given that risk, we should be mindful of just how much we lard into, or onto, the concept of 'fieldwork'. We need to be careful not to overlook the basic questions (as yet unspoken) stashed in between the many already provided, questions such as: What values should guide us as we strive to expand the arena of our knowledge? And to what ends (and to whose benefit) should these expansive efforts be put?

As we search for answers, we also should remain alert to the force of our habits.

Dewey's comments in *The Public and Its Problems* (1954) bear directly on the core ambitions of the conference, as I understand them: to 'walk in different ways', to arm us for the trial of our disciplinary predilections and practices. Immediately following his observation that habit determines channels through which thought operates, he writes: 'thinking is *secreted* in the interstices of habit.' When I first came across that line, it stopped me short (a sign, perhaps, of my intellectual upbringing – schooled in poststructuralist philosophy and comparative literature, I take pleasure in language play).

On one hand, Dewey's words sound a cautionary reminder: read as 'thinking is secreted (concealed, stashed or squirreled away) in the interstices of habit' they refer to the inhibitive powers of habits of mind – of their potential to lay serious obstacles along our path for new knowledge. But if we read the passage as 'thinking is *secreted* (released, emanated, generated) in the interstices', it beckons us to inhabit those charged spaces between orderly and established ways of working where opportunities for innovation reside. With this line, Dewey gifts us, his readers, that exhilarating experience of escaping the confines of habit – of thinking in the in-between. He also makes a compelling point: each of us holds within ourselves the capacity to stash away or share knowledge, and how we act will always be a matter of choice.

Even absent its in-between slash, 'fieldwork' belongs to a category of concept that seems inevitably to entice architects: heavily freighted terms that encompass acres of discursive wiggle room, where connotative and denotative references shift precipitously, depending on who's speaking, what they're speaking about and why.

At once verb and noun, *field* can signify an action (to field a question, handle a situation, tackle a problem) or, equally, an area subject to action. That area acted upon could be material (an agricultural field, meadow or pasture, a green field, a brownfield); intangible (a body of knowledge, or disciplinary field); or professional (as in, 'What field are you in?'). Associate these many connotations with those of *work* (another saturated term) and the interpretive possibilities enlarge even further.

In pedagogical circles, fieldwork can refer to a period of study or empirical research undertaken outside the academy in the world at large (an internship). Or, it could suggest more reflexively focused academic endeavors such as analyzing the means and methods of a particular disciplinary field, work aiming to critically assess the practices and habits of mind associated with a specific knowledge area. For architects and others in the design disciplines examining fieldwork, the dual (or should I write dueling?) reference – to working *in* the field and working *on* a field – evokes the locus of our professional activities (the actual places, or physical fields where we operate) as well as presumptions about our very modes of operating (what we understand to be constitutive of that arena of theory and praxis known broadly as 'the field of architectural design').

In design discourse, 'fieldwork' collects assorted understandings of the real. The term embraces material objects and epistemological subjects, pointing to constructs at once intangible, empirical, discursive and experiential. It too may be best described as a thick concept. Similar to the concept site, fieldwork begs for our attention precisely because it straddles so many domains. Setting up an oscillation between reflection and action, this saturated term highlights the essential inseparability of design theory and praxis in the daily routines of design professionals as well as design scholars. So doing, it provokes us to ever more critical consideration as to the exact modalities of their interaction, wherever and whenever they are played out.

Note

1   Drawn from Field/WORK, a lecture delivered 20 November 2009, Edinburgh.

Field/work and site

Introduction

Chris Speed

> Once the whole social world is relocated inside its metrological chains, an immense new landscape jumps into view. If knowledge of the social is limited to the termite galleries in which we have been travelling, what do we know about what is outside? Not much.
>
> (Latour 2005: 242)

In the last ten years contemporary communication mediums have fostered a rich awareness of many dimensions of local and global environments that were previously abstract. Social, political and economic factors that affect how designers interpret the concept of context and audience are being fed back through digital networks in real-time. This constant feed from people, devices and environments is contributing to a new interpretation of 'field', one that may be better understood as a 'cloud' with indeterminate temporal and spatial dimensions.

In seeking new methodologies for interfacing with these *magnetic* fields, a series of practical and theoretical design processes are beginning to emerge from a wide variety of industrial, academic and creative contexts. These new methodologies are collapsing previous distinctions between science and art, and are constructing new inter-disciplinary vocabularies for not only understanding what, when and where the contemporary site is, but also how we understand our place inside and outside them. As sites open themselves up to being interpreted and examined from many new perspectives, we are able to extend our opportunities for reading them. As demonstrated through this section we see how we are able to trace historical connections across landscapes and through social connections, understand how conversations about a place offer themselves as 'semantic webs' for interpretation, and use 'top-down' maps alongside 'bottom-up' experiences to better understand the movement of urban material. In this context, visions for architectural initiatives and strategies for research projects cannot remain fully controlled by a designer or researcher, but adopt a reciprocal quality within an entire web of social and environmental relations.

The chapters in this section, all to some extent case studies of architecture and field/work, offer a breadth of understanding of site and, through a recurring theme of the social, encourage the architect to relinquish any singular representation of space and accept that site is subject to a constant process of transformation, negotiation and reinterpretation. In this way 'Field/Work and Site' embraces an interpretation of site as something indeterminate in form and closer perhaps to a network, a field of oscillating priorities in which difference between time and space, outsider and insider, top-down and bottom-up views all become artificial distinctions.

Jill Seddon's chapter investigates the work of the Public Monuments and Sculpture Association (PMSA), in and around the town of Brighton in Sussex. Providing a critical analysis of the limitations of recording and documenting the many forms of public sculptures, Seddon identifies the deeper temporal significance of monuments in the site. Here, the sculpture and the monument operate as 'ghosts', their material and formal absolutes dissolved, only to configure as pertinent markers in an indistinct historical narrative looked on by 'the public eye'. Seddon offers stone statues a form of agency within the definition of a site. Familiar markers in the urban landscape, monuments, loaded with historical significance, become over time part of an integral, mnemonic vocabulary of a place, activating and reactivating the temporal and spatial consciousness of its inhabitants.

Architecture's acknowledgement of the network qualities of site allows the naturally contingent dimension of the social to place further value on the role of field/work and the need to get out of the studio. Miriam Fitzpatrick's analysis of William 'Holly' Whyte's Street Life Project reminds us of origins of models of Field/Work that places people at the centre of interpretations of how spaces are produced. Whyte's preoccupation with people led him and his team to adopt time-based media as a method of recording the transactions that define the quality of an environment. Fitzpatrick uses this focus (among others) to demonstrate the sensitivity of the 'leg work' that ran counter to the planning of the high-Modern sites under investigation. Concentrating on people, actions and dimensions in and around Mies Van der Rohe's Seagram Tower and the Seagram Plaza on Park Avenue, New York, the Street Life project laid the ground for practices of urban design analysis and a contemporary concept of Social Navigation, a precursor to and subsequently defining characteristic of contemporary experiences of the digital networks.

Kelly Shannon sees field/work as a kind of critical realism and 'ground truthing'. Her chapter uses water and water mapping as a mechanism to demonstrate the need to study site coincidences, reflections and actualities from both the ground and the air. While reconciling the split between top down and bottom up is a common theme in spatial discourse, Shannon identifies how water as a medium binds disparate representational frames with an environmental, cultural and economic complexity. For Shannon, understanding water from above and below leads to a synthesis of 'vision and strategy', of imagined potential and pragmatic solution. She interrogates water as a catalyst for formal change in the pressured hydro-infrastructure of Hanoi, deploying chronology, political analysis and participatory practices.

Where the first three chapters elucidate aspects of fieldwork data collection in historic landscape, urban and exploding global situations, the final two open up more experimental approaches to working in and with the field. Exploring the theoretical and practical characteristics of 'Open Form' developed by the architect Oskar Hansen during the late 1960s and early 1970s, Renata Tyszczuk identifies the integration of theory and practice that Hansen asserted for architectural design practice and the inter-pretation of a site. In this relational mode, non-hierarchical methods 'play out' in an emergent and unstable manner to inform a unique and 'open' production of space. Revisiting Hansen's use of film in a contemporary architectural studio context, Tyszc-zuk provides evidence of the ways in which Open Form techniques can encourage understandings which offer possibilities of 'the unfinished' as an experimental practice, and refute the closure of any architectural reading of site.

Ella Chmielewska and Sebastian Schmidt-Tomczak's carefully composed chapter is a dialogic reflection on the positionality of research and researcher 'in the field'. Where is the work situated? How is the work affected by transposing to other situations? How might conscious collaborative exchange enhance and clarify know-ledge? Reciprocal characteristics of the fluidity of field yet particularity of urban are acknowledged. Here, the two researchers exchange through text and image, reflect on their shifting positions in relation to each other and their subjects, and negotiate re-readings where the site as object slips between the geographical frameworks of space and language, between Warsaw, Berlin, between artist and her studio. Sensitive to (the relational qualities of) vocabulary and translation, Chmielewska and Schmidt-Tomczak identify a field/work that is temporal, discursive and definitely in-between.

'Field/Work and Site' reconfigures 'site' from the perspective of architec-tural design as socially, environmentally and economically contingent. Contingent because the very term field/work is presented as a process of reflection and action. Subjects sustain perspective while developing engagement. Such a position, or perhaps disposition, engenders a fluid interpretation of context. An acknowledgement that no coordinates for site are fixed, that conditions are subject to change according to a multitude of metrological conditions.

Landscape with statues

Recording the public sculpture of Sussex

Jill Seddon

Within anthropology, ethnography, archaeology and cultural geography, the concept of fieldwork has become problematised. As social anthropologist Ulf Hannerz wrote, 'we do not seem to know what the field is or where it should be, if it is real or perhaps virtual and even if there has to be one at all' (Hannerz 2006: 23). Despite this, there appears to be a consensus that fieldwork is fundamental to these disciplines; a recent report on university archaeology courses concluded that 'graduates felt they should have been exposed to more fieldwork opportunities during their degree, and that this element of the course should be compulsory and its importance emphasised' (Jackson and Sinclair 2007: 28). The importance of being 'out there' in the field continues to be stressed, but the meanings of that experience and the deployment of the data gathered through it have come under scrutiny. Recent cross-disciplinary debate has encouraged a move away from what once appeared an uncomplicated performance of set procedures of recording and compiling data, towards a much more reflexive consideration not only of the significance of the role of the fieldworker, but also of her/his acts of interpretation.

Drawing upon some of these debates, this chapter takes as a case study the National Recording Project conducted by the Public Monuments and Sculpture Association (PMSA). It is acknowledged that the fieldwork necessitated by this project, the measuring, examining and photographing of cultural artefacts, is not the same experience as the 'intensive participant observation' (Amit 2000: 1) that remains a defining criterion of anthropology, nevertheless new levels of self-reflexion in that discipline and others propose a new range of ways of thinking about the role of the fieldworker, the gathering of data and subsequent acts of interpretation.

The PMSA is a registered charity founded in 1991, 'which campaigns for increased care and appreciation of public art' (NRPD n.d.). With Heritage Lottery funding, it initiated, in 1997, a national recording project to make an electronic survey of public monuments and sculpture in Britain. The work is undertaken by regional archive centres, mostly hosted by academic institutions, throughout the country. The research is published by Liverpool University Press in its *Public Sculpture of Britain* series, similar in format to Pevsner's *Buildings of England*, with volumes devoted either to counties or large metropolitan centres. As described by the PMSA, 'the undertaking is part conservation, part archival' (NRPD n.d.), with the characteristics both of an audit and, through the recording of 'types' of sculpture, the establishing of a taxonomy in the tradition of nineteenth-century engagement with the natural world. A small research team based at the University of Brighton is currently engaged in the compilation of a comprehensive and permanent record of the rich and diverse range of public sculptures and monuments of Sussex. Each piece is photographed and recorded on a standard PMSA template, which provides precise details of location, sculptor, patron(s), construction and installation, together with a detailed visual description, including current structural condition. It is then uploaded onto a publicly accessible database, hosted by the university.

Although they are presumed to be straightforward and intended to be objective, these procedures in themselves raise questions concerning the collection of data in the field and questions of judgement and interpretation of collection criteria, thus, applying PMSA parameters presents it own challenges. Fieldworkers are asked to record:

- commemorative or other freestanding statues;
- 'art' sculptures;
- any commemorative or sculptural outdoor feature (carrying a commemorative inscription or with sculptural content);
- commemorative columns;
- clock towers, ornamental/drinking fountains, pumps, mile posts etc. containing inscriptions or sculpture (or both);
- street furniture which has sculptural content or shows fine stone or ironwork;
- commemorative plaques or tablets where these carry elaborate or long inscriptions and/or sculptural content or fine stonework;
- architectural sculpture where this stands out from the basic texture of the building or where this relates particularly to local history;
- any of the above on private premises but in the public eye;
- statues or sculptures on estates where the grounds are open to the public.

The criteria for inclusion gather around definitions of 'sculptural' and 'public', which are taken as given, but not overtly stated. These concepts are open to subjective interpretation, which is often inflected by histories of fashion and taste. For example, the Long Man of Wilmington, once thought to be Neolithic but now regarded as an eighteenth-century folly, has a particular meaning as sculpture in relation to the emergence of Land Art from the late 1960s.

Once the judgement has been made to include a particular piece of sculpture or monument, further opportunities for subjective interpretation on the part of the fieldworker ensue. The essence of the recording process is the act of standing in front of, or walking around, a sculpture and carefully recording what can actually be seen. The procedure is a convincing example of cultural geographer Gillian Rose's claim that 'fieldwork is all about looking … Just as fieldwork is central not only to cultural geography, but also to the discipline as a whole, … so too the visual is central to claims to geographical knowledge' (Oakes and Price 2008: 171). There is, however, no PMSA guidance or standard procedure for looking or for photographing the pieces. It is not stipulated how many photographs should be taken, nor whether they should be taken from certain viewpoints or should include particular features; such decisions are left to the discretion of the photographer. Thus the consideration of the relationship of a sculpture or monument to its surroundings, whether architectural or landscape features, becomes almost incidental, a tacit personal decision.

The Sussex research team takes up to 20 photographs of each object, from which four are selected, often on aesthetic grounds, to appear on the database. More purely informative shots, such as close-ups of signatures and inscriptions, are kept within the archive. This experience reinforces the widely acknowledged view that the taking of a photograph is not a neutral act, but one that involves judgement and selection as well as physical and technical restraints despite the best efforts of a body such as English Heritage to standardise and neutralise its recording of archaeological and architectural sites (Schofield *et al.* 2006: 39–42). In addition to visual recording, PMSA project researchers are required to provide a written record of the pieces. This ranges from factual details such as measurements, through the choosing of object and subject types from prescribed lists, to observations of current condition and physical and iconographical descriptions, representing a further process of selection and interpretation.

While remaining conscious of the subjective role of the data recorder, the research team must also consider the ways in which that data might be used; how it might begin to be interrogated as a way of understanding the complex webs of historical and present-day relationships between landscape, society and culture. One approach involves an examination of the vulnerable and transitory nature of sculptures and monuments, often regarded as permanent landmark features of our towns and villages. Many instances of their removal and disappearance, for a variety of reasons ranging from new building development and road widening to processes of decay and changes of fashion, have been revealed, although in some cases they retain a residual presence. In his article 'Ghosts of Place', rural sociologist Michael Mayerfeld Bell explains that he uses the word ghosts in the

> sense of a felt *presence* – an anima, *geist* or genius – that possesses and gives a sense of social aliveness to a place … Ghosts help constitute the specificity of historical sites, of the place where we feel we belong and do not belong, of the boundaries of possession by which we assign ownership and nativeness.
>
> (Mayerfeld Bell 1997: 813–814)

The potency of this lingering 'ghost of place' is acutely felt in the many temporary memorials frequently encountered on routes through our towns and cities, but it also applies to those which were intended to be permanent but have subsequently disappeared, such as the Prince Albert memorial clock tower in Hastings. This memorial to Queen Victoria's husband, who died of typhoid, was designed by Edward Heffer of Liverpool and installed on 10 June 1864. The clock was illuminated by gas and arranged to light automatically at 9p.m. every evening. Re-siting of the memorial was proposed several times in the period following the Second World War, usually for reasons of traffic congestion as the town continued to develop; redevelopment plans in 1952 even suggested demolition. Following arson attacks in 1973, the clock was damaged and the surrounding stonework cracked, and there was little opposition to getting rid of the memorial. Albert's statue was bought by a local resident and stands in Alexandra Park in Hastings; two lamps and columns from the clock tower stand outside the local Museum and Art Gallery. Despite its rather ignominious end, the clock tower occupied a central place in the identity of the town; there was a regular news column named after it in the local newspaper in the 1930s and residents of the town continued to refer to it when giving directions or arranging meetings long after its physical disappearance.

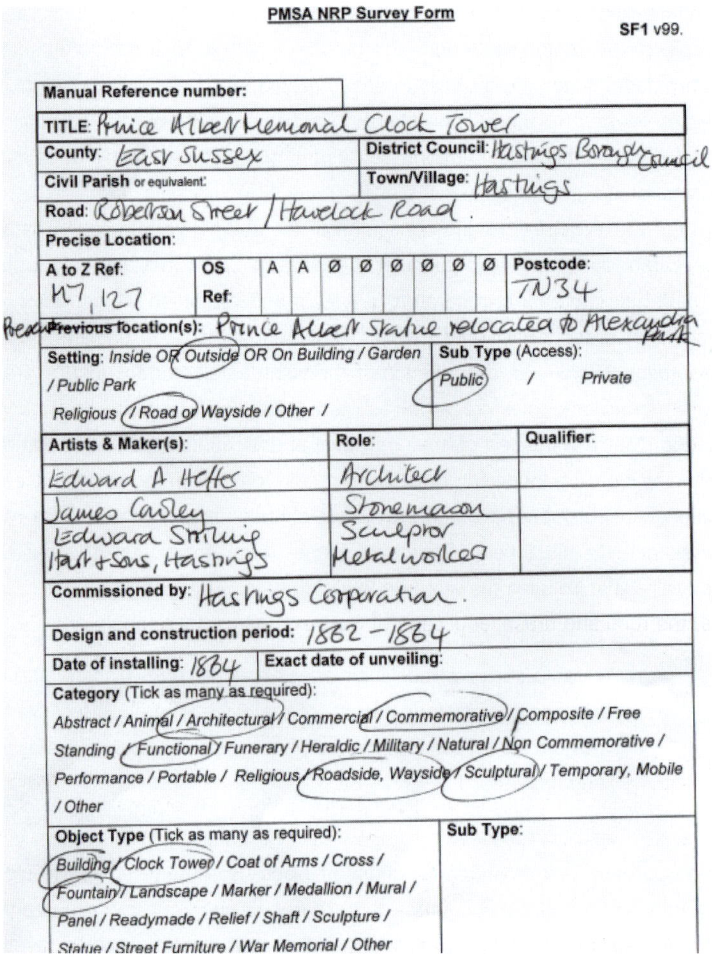

PMSA NRP Survey Form SF1 v99.

Manual Reference number:

TITLE: Prince Albert Memorial Clock Tower

County: East Sussex | District Council: Hastings Borough Council

Civil Parish or equivalent: | Town/Village: Hastings

Road: Robertson Street / Havelock Road.

Precise Location:

A to Z Ref: K7, 127 | OS Ref: A A Ø Ø Ø Ø Ø Ø | Postcode: TN34

Previous location(s): Prince Albert Statue relocated to Alexandra Park

Setting: Inside OR Outside OR On Building / Garden / Public Park Religious / Road or Wayside / Other / | Sub Type (Access): Public / Private

Artists & Maker(s):	Role:	Qualifier:
Edward A Heffer	Architect	
James Casley	Stonemason	
Edward Stirling	Sculptor	
Hart + Sons, Hastings	Metalworker	

Commissioned by: Hastings Corporation.

Design and construction period: 1862 – 1864

Date of installing: 1864 | Exact date of unveiling:

Category (Tick as many as required): Abstract / Animal / Architectural / Commercial / Commemorative / Composite / Free Standing / Functional / Funerary / Heraldic / Military / Natural / Non Commemorative / Performance / Portable / Religious / Roadside, Wayside / Sculptural / Temporary, Mobile / Other

Object Type (Tick as many as required): Building / Clock Tower / Coat of Arms / Cross / Fountain / Landscape / Marker / Medallion / Mural / Panel / Readymade / Relief / Shaft / Sculpture / Statue / Street Furniture / War Memorial / Other | Sub Type:

Figure 1 **Record entry for the Prince Albert Memorial Clock Tower, Brighton.**

There are many such examples of the social and geographical significance of a particular sculpture or monument. Since the database has been constructed so that it is possible to search not only by individual object or maker, but also by town and by date, the researcher can now move beyond authorship and location to discern geographical clusterings of pieces. Perhaps unsurprisingly these are at their most dense along the coastal littoral and in the towns along the A23, the Brighton to London axis. Currently Brighton has the highest PMSA recorded number of sculptures at 57, followed by Chichester at 46. Along the coast from east to west, Rye has 8, Hastings 16, Newhaven 8, Shoreham 8, Worthing 21, Littlehampton 5 and Bognor 3. Inland, Horsham has the highest number at 12, followed by Crawley at 10 and Haywards Heath, quite a large town, has only one so far recorded. In addition there are numerous small towns and villages with a single piece of sculpture, usually a war memorial or a millennium project.

From this initial reflection of the significance of location, fundamental questions arise as to when and why sculptures and monuments were erected. Searching the database by historical period reveals that the decades that saw the greatest activity in the erection of public statues and memorials were at the turn of the century, between 1898 and 1908, when Victorian 'statuemania' was at its height; the years immediately following the First World War; and the period from the 1990s onwards, when some local councils, notably in Brighton and Hove, which established an independent Arts Commission in 2004, were developing sustained public art policies and encouraging implementation of the Percent for Art scheme.

In considering ways in which the landscape has shaped, and been shaped by, its monuments, it is important to take into account not only their siting and their dates, but also their subject matter. Due to the history of Sussex as a predominantly rural county devoted to agriculture, fishing and, later, to the pursuit of leisure and pleasure, there is a distinct lack of 'men on plinths', those wealthy philanthropical self-made men frequently immortalised in stone or bronze in Victorian industrial cities. Instead there is embodiment of royal and aristocratic connections, subjects reflecting the proximity of the sea, memorialisation both of local 'characters' and of the county's dead in two world wars, the embellishment of architecture and the marking of the new millennium.

In beginning to analyse what this fieldwork may tell us about the field, that is, the rural and urban landscape of Sussex, it is useful to adopt John Schofield's position that 'a building or monument is an object of communication because different people, institutions and interest groups connect different goals and interests with it' (Schofield *et al.* 2006: 7). He refers specifically to sites of conflict, the places where these issues are most starkly illustrated, but it is a point that has a more general application. The Victoria Fountain in Brighton is one such example of the changing meanings of a site and its sculpture. It is the centrepiece of the gardens in the Steine, a place that until the late eighteenth century was an ill-drained, swampy area used by fishermen to dry nets and store boats in bad weather. As the small, decaying fishing village of Brighthelmstone began its transformation into the fashionable seaside resort of Brighton, however, its potential as a level, sheltered promenade brought about a conflict of interests. The draining and enclosure of the space during the eighteenth century effectively excluded the fishing community, despite their vociferous claims of 'inalienable rights' to its use. Thus there was a radical shift from the site of specific occupational activity to one devoted to leisured recreation. The Steine rapidly became woven into the civic fabric with the building of fashionable hotels, lodgings and private houses overlooking it. Its embellishment with gardens and a fountain, designed by local architect Amon Wilds, to honour the new queen, reinforced its role as a focal point in Brighton's new incarnation as an elegant seaside resort.

The inauguration of the fountain, on 25 May 1846 to celebrate the queen's twenty-seventh birthday, was marked with great ceremony. The proceedings were launched by a royal salute fired from the pier head at noon, the same time as the fountain was turned on. Specially commissioned music, including *Fountain Quadrilles* by Charles Coote, was played. Local shops and businesses closed at 3 p.m. for a celebratory Fête Champêtre, admission one shilling, in the Royal Gardens, which concluded with fireworks. The Steine Gardens and their fountain continued to provide a focal point for the southernmost point of the town. Despite being encircled by a one-way road system, this open space functions both as a place to sit and eat (in a café converted from the old public conveniences) and as a rallying point for meetings and demonstrations. At a further inauguration ceremony, when Prince Charles visited the Steine to unveil a plaque to commemorate the restoration of the fountain in 1995, there was a security alert when it became the focus of a protest about live animal exports from nearby Shoreham harbour. In an inversion of the original ceremony, the local newspaper noted that the protestors were waving flags, while also yelling abuse.

Inauguration ceremonies and subsequent events surrounding public sculptures introduce a performative element into the study of the field. In the nineteenth century in particular, unveiling ceremonies were public spectacles and a form of urban mass entertainment, but it should also be noted that levels of participation were dictated by issues of class and wealth. These were hierarchically structured events that often represented the culmination of local power struggles over contested sites and representations. The celebrations, and the lasting memorials that they left behind, both marked the significance of specific public spaces and reinforced Victorian values of loyalty to queen and country and of public philanthropy, in quite transparent ways. Nevertheless, their subsequent history can illustrate the temporal and shifting nature of civic values and beliefs and the ways in which later generations could subvert or undermine them.

The changing nature of a sculpture's relationship to its environment may also be observed in present-day commissions from the private sector, a Sussex example being 'Twins', designed by Charlie Hooker as part of the redevelopment of Churchill Square in Brighton by the Standard Life Insurance Company in 1998. The demolition of the 1960s shopping centre to make way for the new mall entailed the destruction of a public sculpture, William Mitchell's 'Spirit of Brighton' (1968), which subsequently became hardcore in the new building site. Hooker's marble constructions that incorporate soundscape and lighting, based on the rhythms of local life and weather, are sited in front of the entrance to Churchill Square, on what was originally a wide curved plaza with shallow steps. Since the inauguration of the piece, this space has been gradually given over to fast-food outlets that significantly diminish the visual impact of the sculptures in ways that were clearly not envisaged either by the original planners or by the sculptor.

The PMSA recording project aims to promote public awareness of, and concern for, public sculptures and monuments, highlighting their significance within our urban and rural landscapes. Now that most of the data has been collected, the process of its interpretation and reflection on the interpretative processes of this fieldwork is only just beginning. This raw material may be inflected in many different ways both by the fieldworker and other researchers with differing perspectives, but it is crucial to remain alert to the lessons that may be learnt from current debates within archaeology and anthropology concerning the role of the fieldworker and the processes in which they are engaged. The relation of a sculpture or memorial to its landscape and its social context raises complex issues concerning class, gender, ethnicity and regional identity. As Mayerfeld Bell has pointed out, 'Place is a notoriously difficult concept to define, and therefore pick up and inspect with the mental tweezers of an objective social science' (1997: 814). Layers of meaning and subjectivities of perspective militate against such objectivity and constitute the interest and richness of this project. The research team shares geographer Dennis Cosgrove's belief, that 'the evidence of cultural products ... can provide as firm a handle on the meanings that places and landscapes possess, express and evoke, as do more conventional "factual" sources' (Oakes and Price 2008: 181). The data collected in the field provides a continuing resource for an extensive range of approaches to reading the text of a landscape through specific examples of its material culture.

Fieldwork in public space assessment

William Holly Whyte and the *Street Life Project*
1970–1975

Miriam Fitzpatrick

This chapter outlines the twin roles of analysis and intuition in the assessment of public space through an example of urban fieldwork. The territory for this 'creative legwork' is the public spaces of Modernist Midtown Manhattan, much of which was built as a result of 1961 zoning regulations. This fieldwork creatively adopted methods usually used by other fields, and, through 'legwork', changed legislation and encouraged better designs: 'When architects and planners designed by intuition, Holly gave them facts' (LaFarge 2000: vii; Goldberger 1999: 55)'.[1]

The purpose of the fieldwork was to understand why some spaces 'work for people, and some do not, and what the practical lessons might be'. This is from the opening lines of *The Social Life of Small Urban Spaces*, written by William Hollingsworth Whyte Jr (1917–1999), or Holly Whyte as he was known. This pre-book and film (Whyte 1980) recorded the findings of a special fieldwork group which Whyte established, called the *Street Life Project*. He regarded both book and film as stop-gaps to change planning legislation. With the publication of *City: Rediscovering the Centre* in 1988, he completed a trilogy of urban design guides which remain core texts in many Urban Design courses today.

Whyte's own field was journalism, a role he shares with many noted reformers in urban design, Lewis Mumford, Jane Jacobs and Ian Nairn. What distinguishes him and makes his work critical to a discourse on fieldwork is not only his connections to and from other fields, but his life-long dedication to seeking the universal from the particularities of place.

Whyte was an ex US Marine Corps Captain and Intelligence Officer who joined *Fortune* magazine in 1946. As its assistant managing editor from 1952 to 1958, he turned a few magazine series into successful books. His most popular was on corporate America, which grew from observations in Forest Park, Illinois and was based on some 'good old-fashioned shoe leather' (Whyte 2009: xiv), and led to his best-selling book *The Organization Man*, first published in 1956. Another work turned attention from the suburbs to the design of the city, and resulted in *The Exploding Metropolis* (1958). The latter text brought Whyte to the attention of the conservation philanthropist, Laurance Spelman Rockefeller, whose patronage, together with consultancy work for a number of state bodies, freed Whyte from *Fortune*'s publishing house, Time Inc. A period of work influencing legislation relating to the effects of sprawl, a term coined by Whyte, was followed by a move to urban fieldwork from 1969.

What predisposed Whyte, a successful editor and best-selling author, to spend the rest of his career walking the streets of Manhattan recording how vendors, buskers and undesirables use its steps and street corners? The shift from piecework to fieldwork, 1969 to 1979, from *Organization Man* to *Observation Man* (Birch 1986) was marked by the establishment of his *Street Life Project*. This chapter is organised around three phases: before the field, to set the context; in the field, for methodology; and after the field, for post-production analysis.

Despite the vast quantities of fieldnotes assembled by the *Street Life Project*, an archive does not exist for it or for William Holly Whyte. This is due partly to his peripatetic and episodic professional life, and in part to a couple of fires at his home. The *Street Life Project* and its influence are relatively undocumented as a result. In researching this project, uncatalogued archives of the American Conservation Association Archives and the Rockefeller Brothers' Fund held by the Rockefeller Archive Center and files in storage by Project for Public Spaces, 1970 to 1975, were used. The details are pieced together using his vast writings, interviews with colleagues, his alma maters (St Andrew's School, Delaware and Princeton University) and Whyte's family and by walking the spaces he documented.[2]

Before the field: context

Andreas Feininger's 1948 image of Fifth Avenue, 'all tense and unsmiling' (Whyte 1988: 4) sums up a congested and miserable *Anti-City* image that was gaining sway in the 1950s and 1960s. Funnelled between street face and queuing traffic, the telephoto lens foreshortens the pedestrians, suggesting overcapacity and congestion, while the hazy light recalls images of contagion; either way it played to a popular worry about the 'spectre of overcrowding' (Whyte 1988: 4) and a default dystopia driving decentralist planning policy. Whyte's intuition was that density and concentration made cities prosper. His fieldwork deliberately set out to capture an antidote to a gritty and pejorative image of the city.

Impetus came in the late 1960s, with an opportunity to challenge recent policy that was prompting the proliferation of new urban spaces. With its set-back from Park Avenue as well as its popularity, the Seagram Plaza of 1958 had given the city the idea for a plaza bonus or a new planning tool, namely Incentive Zoning, which was implemented by the New York Planning Commission in 1961 to extract planning gains: for every square foot of new plaza space provided, the developer could add ten square feet of office space. The bonus, or Open-Space zoning provision, proved almost embarrassingly successful. Floor space grew by 20 per cent, but did benefits accrue to the city to balance the net gain of developers? Hundreds of new spaces were created but many of these were poorly considered and were empty. Whyte's intuition led him to ask how they were working in reality. Nobody knew and it seemed that nobody wished to know. This affront to civic justice incensed Whyte. Were people attracted to quiet spaces or did they prefer more congested places? Whyte set out to record where people chose to be and whether their behaviour suggested a preference for either. Informed by the adage of cultural anthropologist, Margaret Mead, that 'What people say, what people do, and what they say they do are entirely different things',[3] Whyte was curious to separate perception from fact.

Whyte was able to pursue his enquiry as an outsider within the planning department. Under the pro-city bias of John Lindsay, New York Mayor 1966–1973, he had been invited to edit the draft City Plan. He agitated for an evaluative unit and contested that the City should evaluate the effectiveness of these expensive public spaces. The Plan itself was criticised for its lack of substantive analysis which held resonance with Whyte, so he offered to substantiate his long-held anti-city scepticism with an immediate challenge. If he could prove what makes the good spaces good and the bad ones bad, he could amend the code. He was driven to convert his suspicion to facts and arm himself with evidence aimed at officials, planners and legislators.

It is unclear how the 18 spaces[4] finally documented in the *Street Life Project* were selected but they included a range of sizes and a spectrum of popularity, mostly concentrated in Manhattan's midtown, a short walk from Whyte's own office. They were nearly all associated with office developments due to the incentive zoning bonus. Whyte credits a serendipitous street encounter for becoming the first-ever recipient of a grant-aided National Geographic Domestic Expedition. The grant formally established the *Street Life Project* as an expedition unit and it received funding for two consecutive years. Marilyn Russell was the first member to join Whyte in 1970 and, early in 1971, she was joined by Nancy Linday. Their initial findings fortified Whyte's belief in the viability of a small evaluative group. Their observations were supplemented by social commentaries undertaken by sociology students during Whyte's year-long Professorship at Hunter College. Later members rotated between Fred Kent, Ellen Asher, Marge Bemiss, Ann Herendeen and Elizabeth Dietel representing a range of disciplines, plus interns.

In-the-field methods of the *Street Life Project*

> A word about methodology. Direct observation was the core of our work.
>
> (Whyte 1988: 4)

The group's method focused on behavioural mapping, social commentaries and time-lapse photography. Their expedition began when Whyte mounted time-lapse cameras on the McKim, Mead & White's Racquet Club building directly opposite one of the archetypal icons of high-Modernism, Mies Van der Rohe's Seagram Tower and the Seagram Plaza on Park Avenue, Manhattan, to record 'dawn to dusk patterns' (Whyte

1988: 105). This was by far the most popular of recently completed public plazas. 'Many thought it should not be but it was and we were curious to know why' (Whyte 1979).

Reflecting on the team's work, Jan Gehl confirmed that they established the primary tool for understanding how people use public space: 'eye-ball observation', which is to observe at eye-level and jot down on paper what you observe on the ground.[5] They backed up fieldnotes with a record of physical characteristics in order to explore correlation of levels of activity with actual location. They noted what people did, where they met, how and where they shook hands or took leave. They recorded the time of day, logged the weather and tallied the total on each chart. They jotted down a head count at regular intervals. They circled the social groupings; the proportion of people in groups, the size and gender composition of each. Countless charts are testimony to their diligence. When viewed today, their method seems accessible and possible to be repeated by relatively untrained fieldworkers. Each chart fitted on a clipboard and was notated by hand on gridded maps or on characteristic blue-graph paper. 'There is primitive power in the tools Holly used to craft his thesis: simple observation, time-lapse Super 8 movie cameras, hand-drawn maps and charts made with press type' (Whyte 2002: xii).

To test where people stopped to talk, whether people moved to the side or out of the way of the main pedestrian stream, they tracked movements. Well-edited video footage captures the silhouettes of bodies, and their long shadows, moving across the pale gridded granite of the Seagram Plaza, which is timeless footage amid the otherwise colourful 1970s setting, while the honking sounds of the city are temporarily muffled by its water fountains.

Dimensions mattered and records of the physical characteristics of public spaces studied indicate the hours of measurements that the team invested. The overall square footage was noted. So was the length and breadth of spaces as they wished to monitor the prevalence of long-narrow plazas. Steps and level changes were of interest due to the predominance of partially sunken or raised plazas. The rise and going (tread) of every step was measured with Eadward Muybridge precision, picking up on rhythm and mood. Notwithstanding the time invested assessing the level change of steps and plazas, it should be noted that because Whyte was not a designer, there are some spatial shortfalls regarding plan analysis. For instance, the Seagram Plaza has a fall of nearly five feet from end to end which changes the granite edge on one side from bench level to a seven-foot-high fairly blank wall at the opposite end. Also, all the field maps of the plazas end at the kerb-edge of the plaza and do not include the surrounding buildings, so the connection to street activity is less apparent from the visual charts, giving the time-lapse a distinctive edge. They followed up with interviews to find out why people were there, where they had come from, how frequently they used the space and what they thought of it. This is where activities and a cast of characters were recorded. A fieldnote on Washington Square from Monday, 12 April 1971 (noon, weather sunny, temp. 65 to 70) noted, 'Chess was underway at the corner of Washington Place and McDougal; there were half a dozen games underway'.[6]

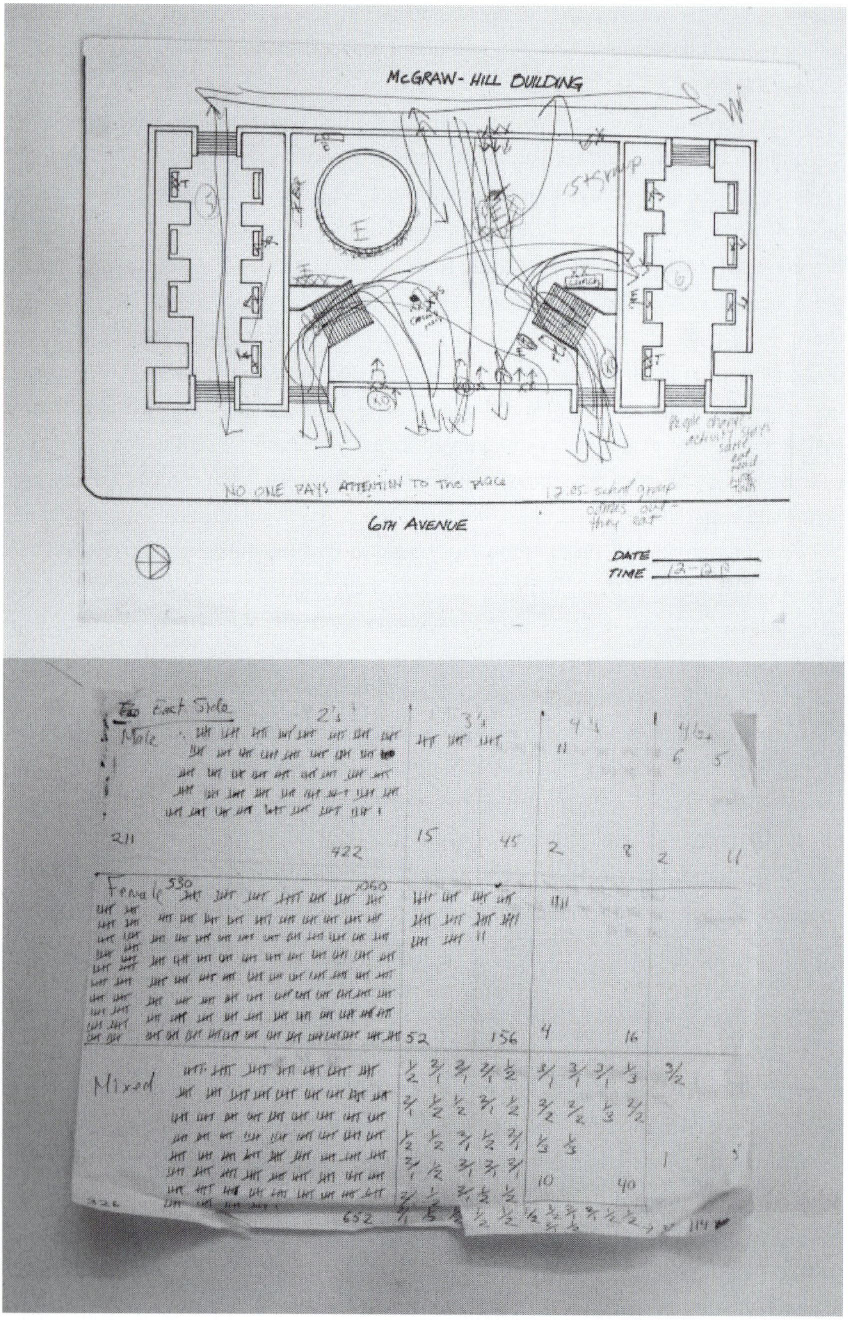

Figure 1 Above: Movement of people, McGraw-Hill Building. Below: Fieldnote: group, size and gender composition of public space use.

While working on the New York City Plan, Whyte had significantly influenced the inclusion and use of images in relation to text, so it was a small step for him to narrate and co-create a film commissioned by the City to promote the plan 'What Is the City But the People' (Whyte 1969). As a journalist, Whyte embraced this media as a means of public communication, accurately capturing the dynamic field they were interrogating. Whyte's interest in the visual documentary of time-lapse photography offered the advantage of gathering a large amount of information relatively quickly *in the field* and of speeding up analysis of patterns *after the field*. 'Time-lapse does not save time, it stores it. What you have to do is … hypothesize: ask questions of the film' (Whyte 1980: 109). The analysis of thousands of feet of film footage was time consuming and required skilled editing for visual frames to be appealing to a wider audience.

Encouraged by evidence that overall numbers using the open space of the city were increasing by 25 per cent year on year (1972–1973 and 1973–1974),[7] the *Street Life Project* concentrated on specific characteristics that differentiated popular spaces from empty ones. Whyte focused on choice. Why were people choosing to be in some spaces and what hindered the inhabitation of others? In their after-the-field analysis, findings were distilled into legible charts tabulated by popularity. A pattern began to appear. What was found was that the busiest, densest places are where people are most likely to congregate. Despite protestations to the contrary, the team observed that most people cannot resist a tendency towards self-congestion, that they are propelled into the thick of things, to what he termed the '100% location'. Far from moving out of the way, most people, not just the gregarious, have an innate urge to move further into the flow. The longer the conversation, the more likely they were to stand 'smack in the middle'. Spaces that attracted groups, generally in twos or threes, signalled the most popular spaces and registered the highest use overall, confirming that people, when alone, also gravitated towards these spaces.

Figure 2 **Bryant Park, 2009.**

After 16 years walking the streets and plazas of Manhattan, Whyte was apologetic about the deceptively simple findings. 'No matter how many other variables we checked, one basic point kept coming through; people sit where there are places for them to sit' (1988: 110). In the film, he explains the merits of movable seats by showing a choreography of chairs at Paley Park, a space that had registered the highest occupancy numbers but which was also perceived as the least crowded of spaces. He attributed this overlap of a sense of control and comfort within density, to 'that fine old invention, the movable chair' as people enjoy 'being around strangers more when there is a little something they can control; like a chair they can move' (1980: 35). An antithesis was unfolding between perception and facts, between what people said and what people did. Whyte wound down the *Street Life Project* in 1975 once he had sufficient data to amend the 1961 plaza bonus but supported his researcher, Fred Kent, to set up Project for Public Spaces to continue their methodology

After-the-field analysis

Communicating the findings was to take more time than arriving at them.

(Whyte 1980: 15)

The fieldwork on the plazas took five years and the analysis continued for another 13 years until the publication of *City* in 1988. Complex charts on pedestrian flows, seating patterns and other data were converted to simple graphics showing comparative analysis. The film represents this analysis of bar charts like the relief score of a wind-up music box with a clear narration as to patterns of use. Margot Wellington, ex-Director of the Municipal Art Society of New York, which sponsored Whyte's film and provided a space to show early screenings as a silent film, recalls how Holly would perform live and hone his narration through reaction from live audiences.[8] At one screening, at the Urban Land Institute, a number of significant developers of the Midtown area were in attendance. Whyte led them into his research, in a matter-of-fact manner, only to disarm them by revealing which spaces did not work and which used artistic effects to hide blank walls or empty plaza behind.

Whyte's aim was to work within the system to cause change, to establish an influence on the planning process, a link between good design and the evaluation of good places. The most immediate practical application of the findings was that Whyte wrote detailed amendments to the Open-Space zoning provisions which were adopted by New York City in May 1975. The new zoning revisions imposed higher design standards, mandated amenities and open space standards, restricted height above natural grade and differentiated between sidewalk widening and useable plazas. In all, it impacted two-thirds of the total 503 spaces created by the code (Kayden 2000). The ubiquitous presence of street vendors and movable chairs in New York today is evidence of the influence of their findings. Dan Biederman of Bryant Park Corporation credits Whyte for reforming Bryant Park in the 1980s to securing its status as one the most popular spaces in Midtown Manhattan today.

Conclusion

William Holly Whyte's work with the *Street Life Project* is seminal for what it did, for when it did it, for the immediacy of its effect and for the enduring lessons of its method. This chapter has outlined the contribution of this 'outsider's' urban fieldwork. Perhaps the prime legacy of this particular fieldwork is its drawing from both particularities of the place and observations of social use. Whyte's intuition that people are attracted to other people and to the city centre was proved using methods that range from dimensional measurement to empirical, post-occupancy observations.

Their methods and findings appear to benefit from a non-designer's viewpoint. Their study began with the Seagram Plaza because it was popular; much of its deliberate clean lines and grand dimensions made it attractive for the public to use to sit. And although the fact that people congregated there came as a shock to its architect, Mies van der Rohe, and his assistant, Philip Johnson, it demonstrated that good urbanism is based on principles that could coexist with high Modernist architecture. Because the *Street Life Project* was based on fieldwork and hard evidence of what worked well, it remained relatively independent of aesthetic judgement about the Modernist spaces it examined. This work represents an intimate study of the public spaces of high-Modernism which ran counter to received assumptions of the time. Its lack of bias regarding aesthetics is of special value to any urbanist researching Modernist space today. Holly Whyte's tenacity in pursuing empirical facts of the inhabited urban realm characterised his fieldwork. Many colleagues commented on his intuition for the spaces he studied because he could predict people's behavioural patterns in any part of these spaces. 'He taught all of us, more than anything, to look hard, with a clean, clear mind, and then to look again – and to believe in what you see' (LaFarge, 2000: ix). By his legwork, designers could become more creative.

Notes

1   In 1961 New York City Planning Department established a developer incentive to create more open space in Manhattan by set-backs and plazas in exchange for increased floor areas. This is known variously as incentive zoning, plaza bonus and Open-Space zoning provisions. The code created over 500 spaces, at least two-thirds of which were improved by Whyte's zoning prescriptive amendments in 1975.
2   Ex-colleagues of Whyte were generous in their recollections and include Kathy Madden, Fred Kent, Don Elliott, Margot Wellington, Jan Gehl, Albert La Farge, Alexandra Whyte, Madge Bemiss, Nancy Linday. Clayton West Frye, Peter Laurence, Ricky Burdette, Rutherford Platt and Prof. Hugh Campbell also assisted in understanding the context.

3   This adage is a simplification of extensive writing by Mead on the fieldwork of anthropol-
    ogists. See, for instance M. Mead, and R. Metreaux, (1953: 53) *The Study of Culture at a
    Distance*:

> The essence of the study of a living community is that it provides multi-faceted
> material, so that report, observation, retrospective comment, the difference
> between oratio oblique and oratio recta, explicit social behaviour and inarticulate
> social behaviour, can all be integrated.

4   The spaces included in the final documentation were: 77 Water Street, Greenacre Park,
    Time-Life, Exxon, Paley Park, GM Headquarters, Seagram Plaza, JC Penney, 345 Park
    Ave, Exxon Minipark, Burlington, 277 Park Avenue, 630 Fifth Avenue, CBS, Pan Am, ITT,
    Lever House and 280 Park Avenue. The *Street Life Project* did a number of other studies
    on parking, street width and concourse exits but these did not form core to their zoning
    amendment work.

5   Jan Gehl, telephone conversation with author, 15 July 2009.

6   From files of the *Street Life Project* held by Project for Public Space, 700 Broadway,
    New York 10003.

7   Data from Rockefeller Archive Center, Sleepy Hollow, New York, Files of the American
    Conservation Association, Box 33, Letter Holly Whyte to LS Rockefeller (March 12,
    1975: 4).

8   Margot Wellington interview with author, 8 July 2009.

Vietnamese field/work

The case of Hanoi's water urbanism

Kelly Shannon

This chapter discusses fieldwork through the development of interpretative mapping and projective cartographies in order to (re)read and (re)write potentials in the existing water and urbanization logics of the millennium-old capital city of Hanoi, Vietnam. Fieldwork is understood as a sort of critical realism (critical in the process of selection of what to map), as well as the initiation of 'design research'. A diachronic perspective frames Hanoi's urbanization from the feudal, through to its colonial, Soviet and present-day *doi moi* development impositions and tendencies. Although Vietnam's *doi moi* is popularly likened to the Soviet Union's Perestroika (meaning 'restructuring'), it is actually a reform programme of renovation. According to William Duiker, in the years following the end of the Second Indochina War, Hanoi became one of the most orthodox practitioners of the Stalinist approach to nation-building, with its emphasis on socialist industrialization. Even after the Party leaders decided to embark on the road to reform at the Sixth National Congress in December 1986, the new programme was not nearly as much a departure from past practice as was the case in China or even in the Soviet Union. It is equally clear that, for some members of the senior leadership, the ultimate goal of building a fully socialist society has by no means been abandoned (Duiker 1995: 159).

A synchronic perspective elaborates the research-motivated gaze of foreign urbanists in order to reveal the often contested, layered realities of the city and its metropolitan territory in relationship to its complex network of rivers and natural and man-made lakes and canals. The second perspective is developed from the author's fieldwork with postgraduate students in Hanoi in the winter of 2009.[1] Fieldwork was employed towards a 'ground-truthing' of the tensions in Hanoi's process of rapid urban development. Ground-truth is a term used in cartography and refers to information that is collected on specific location. It is often used to calibrate findings of remote sensing, and aids in the interpretation and analysis of what is being sensed. The terms are used here to denote the process of data collection during fieldwork and its interpretation to map-making (Pickles 1995).

Fieldwork specifically focused upon the city's relationship to water as a precursor to proposing an alternative to present-day urbanism, which offers possible scenarios for developing the city in tandem with (as opposed to) the dynamics of its rich liquid landscape.

The biography of Hanoi remains dependent upon the agents and purposes of mapping. As J.B. Harley has posited, cartography is itself a form of knowledge and a form of power – and maps have historically been an 'invention in the control of space and facilitated the geographical expansion of social systems' (Harley 2001: 55). The wonderfully rich historical maps of Hanoi reveal a series of progressive ideologies and layered narratives, which articulate particular positions with regards to the landscape and water, many of which remain visible in the urban tissue. At the same time, the present-day structure of the rapidly expanding city is readable from 'above' (particularly with the aid of Google Earth) and understood from 'below', where a method of descriptive – landscape – urbanism reveals the everyday appropriation of space. This chapter argues that the two views – from above/from below (Cosgrove 1984, 2008) – are both necessary to unromantically comprehend and intervene in the multiple contested territories and *genius loci* of Hanoi.

Mapping as designing

It must be stressed that the requalification of space from contested territory to a supportive frame requires new design tools in order to maximize its potential. What is required is a series of operative methods which develop understandings of existing spatial realities and structuring potentials. Suggesting strategic interventions and outlining project scenarios can then be developed. These new methods are built on the vast knowledge base of descriptive urbanism, employing methods such as reading the city as a complex text, with multiple, layered narratives; graphically analysing cities to discover the syntax and vocabulary of the urban text; creating morphological syntheses of cities; establishing taxonomies of urban fabrics; naming new urban patterns and understanding the logics and ecologies of landscapes. Intensive fieldwork forms the base of interpretative mapping and critical questioning which, in turn, frames the projective cartographies in the form of visions for the (regional) territory and strategic urban projects which follow.

The entire process was seen as research by design and the interpretative mapping built upon James Corner's notion of the 'agency of mapping'. According to Corner,

> Mapping is a fantastic cultural project, creating and building the world as much as measuring and describing it. . . . Analytical research through mapping enables the designer to construct an argument, to embed it within the dominant practices of a rational culture, and ultimately to turn those practices towards more productive and collective ends. In this sense, mapping is not the indiscriminate, blinkered accumulation and endless array of data, but rather an extremely shrewd and tactical enterprise, a practice of relational reasoning that intelligently unfolds new realities out of existing constraints, quantities, facts and conditions.
>
> (1999: 213, 251)

The 'tactical enterprise' of mapping has been tangentially linked to what could be seen as an emerging school[2] in the creation of new cartographic methods. Mapping is always subjective – never neutral – and both what is drawn and the manner in which qualitative, quantitative and geographical information and documentation is framed, scaled, gathered, reworked and assembled is a highly creative act. Far beyond mere description acting as a mirror to reality, interpretative mapping – often comprising dense collages with diagrams, maps, photographs, quantitative data, etc. – reduces to an essence, reveals hidden potentials, discloses conditions for the emergence of new realities. Mapping, as projects in the making, may unfold and uncover potentials through inevitable abstraction, selection and omission of facts. Speculative techniques of mapping are operative in the sense that they reformulate readings of existing territories and set the stage for the inauguration of new worlds in complex territories. Combining multiple views and scales through innovative representational techniques results in new associations between the disparate facts of urbanization over time.

Interpretative mapping and projective cartographies are particularly instrumental in the design of large-scale regions and territories. Ultimately, the aim of such mappings and cartographies is to distil intrinsic logics and create synergies between interdependent systems (natural and man-made) that (re)balance ecology, economy, growth (including urbanization and infrastructure development) and sociocultural values. Mapping holds the capacity to critically and synthetically document the multifaceted characteristics of urban development. It is a method of discovery, a means of comprehension and, at the same time, a spatial instrument which may guide future development. Mapping techniques can depict simultaneity and coexistence and can therefore juxtapose systems and elements that are physically separate into a spatial system of relationships and unseen interdependencies. The analytical and interpretative aspects of map-making create previously unseen landscapes and inevitably lead to projected cartographies of a possible future. Fieldwork is a key for new insights of diachronic and synchronic perspectives. The views from 'above' and 'below' together constitute an intelligence of place. They encompass geographical, topographical and climatic realities, tangible and intangible heritages and the messiness of everyday urbanity. The critical assessment and construction of mappings, overlays, narratives and urban biographies convey social realities on the ground, a haptic view. And since the descriptive and paradigmatic can never be fully disassociated from one another, a back and forth method oscillating between the two, between critical observer and scientific researcher is necessary.

Hanoi: shifting urban and water ecologies

The mapping and design research focused on Hanoi, the capital of Vietnam, and its evolving relationship to water. Historically, the relation of urbanization to water holds a privileged position in this millennium-old city. Hanoi is spatially structured by water – in the form of the mighty Red River (Hong Song or Song Ca (Mother River)) – and an extensive, yet disappearing, network of natural and man-made lakes. Historically, the Hong Song was a lucrative trade route to China. The river is 1,149 km long, of which 510 km flows in Vietnamese territory and includes a basin area of 60,000 sq. km. The river empties into the Gulf of Tonkin, just over 100 km downstream. In Hanoi, ancient traditions of *phong thuy* (the science of wind and water) placed special reverence on water bodies and the relation of settlement to them.[3] Hanoi once had a strong relationship to the river and an interconnected network of natural and man-made canals and lakes. Ancient ingenuity in agricultural irrigation methods are disappearing traces of the city's urban periphery, yet remnants of its regulating water structures remain. Urbanization took hold within the south-west curve of the Red River and was expanded extensively during the French colonial sojourn in Indochina and the Soviet era of 'socialist man' city-building. More recently, the socialist project has given way to footloose capitalism and frenzied real estate speculation. Old urban fabrics are mutating beyond recognition, new 'generic city' imprints are blanketing the territory and productive landscapes of the urban periphery are progressively being eroded by development that is largely uncontrollable. Hanoi, along with the rest of Vietnam, is undergoing a rapid and massive investment cycle. Ports, highway systems, industrial parks, electricity plants and networks, universities, tourist resorts and other infrastructures are planned and built at astonishing speeds.

Historically, Vietnam's water paradigm integrated a range of actors, forces, aspects of life, adaptation and a certain degree of accommodation of the forces of nature. Today, in a period of economic liberalization and the transition from tradition to modernity, water is often regarded from a singular and dominating perspective whether political, technical or commercial. As both urbanization and climate change challenges increase, water issues are on the rise while plural and adaptive responses are sidelined in favour of single actors or single sector dominance. There is a host of complex and intertwined issues regarding water science. Water impacts on ecosystems and societies, water law, policy and politics, water economics and water ethics and equity (Swyngedouw 2004; Yoshinori and Shinde 2004). Business as usual will only spell disaster for the city's future. Today, Hanoi is facing incredible challenges. The existing urban core is stretched far beyond its carrying capacity and infrastructure provision simply cannot keep pace with urban transformations. At the same time, the consequences of increased flooding are severely felt – as revealed in a two-day period from 31 October to 1 November 2008 when 600 mm rain per day rain fell and the city was paralysed. The city's pipes are designed for a maximum rainfall of 300 mm a day.

Yet people keep pouring into the city. As the capital, Hanoi continues to receive a large number of migrant workers from the rural countryside. The population is swelling and real estate speculation, from Vietnamese and other Asian tiger economies including South Korea and Japan, is rampant. The 2020 master plan placed the Red River at the heart of the city's expansion to the north and east. However, a more ambitious plan triples the city's area and opens up the west as the primary direction of growth. Politics and speculation are the primary drivers of the new plan that was approved by the highest level of government in August 2008.[4] The centre of gravity of the city will shift, as will the entire ecological balance in the surrounding urban periphery.

The main issues of the design research and mapping of the 2009 fieldwork included, first, the relationship of new development and water accessibility in relation to the river which has seasonal variation in water levels (varying from 1.5 m in the dry season to 14.13 m in the wet season). Second, the new development in the periphery and landfill processes that support urbanization. Third, the disappearance of water bodies, canals, rivers and lakes which result in the city and region's decreased capacity for water retention, a loss of public space and an increased vulnerability to flooding. At the same time, the city's protective dykes are being raised and extended. The main research question asked: What is a possible future for a renewed water network in Hanoi – ecologically, spatially, culturally – which goes beyond a reliance on defensive dykes and requalifies the river, lakes and canals?

(Re)reading and (re)writing the Red River Delta and Hanoi's territories

The water urbanism fieldwork and interpretative mapping at multiple scales made clear a spectrum of interplays between nature, culture, technique, built fabric and the different water landscapes (the Red River, the network of smaller rivers and canals, and the lakes). Data (statistics, historical maps, contemporary maps, etc.) was combined with on-site observations and photographs, information gained through interviews and guest lectures during an intensive workshop in Hanoi. Participants in the workshop (a mix of international students, young Vietnamese professionals and Vietnamese students) worked on designated themes (water, culture, built, nature) coupled with sites (the Red River, smaller rivers and canals, lakes) for two weeks. The focus on one theme/site – for instance culture/Red River – allowed fieldwork to be screened through a particular lens and new insights to be distilled. Historically, the Red River was a collector and connector of craft village activities – including agricultural as well as religious and community buildings (temples, pagodas, dinhs[5]). There are a number of villages on the Red River north-west of the West Lake that periodically relocate to the opposite bank – responding to the natural processes of erosion and sedimentation of the riverbanks. Ports and areas of sand excavation further animated the riverbanks. As urbanization and modernization surge forward, the role of the river has shifted progressively over time, becoming an urban backside of Hanoi. Today, it is merely part of a system to be tamed and a threshold to be crossed. The 'Red River City' has effectively become a 'City of Seven Bridges' – with seven bridges planned to cross the river in the coming year, connecting Hanoi to an extensive road-based communication network that is strategically dotted with large industrial and export-processing zones.

Other fieldwork and interpretative mapping focused on Hanoi's numerous lakes. A mapping of the historical evolution of the lakes reveals the symbolic importance of water in Vietnam. The ancient, precolonial city of Hanoi was carefully constructed in relation to the lakes. In the French colonial era, land-use planning was

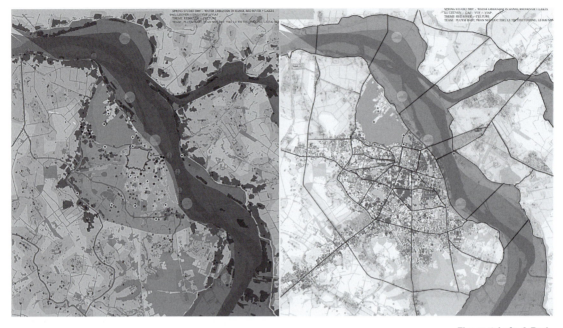

utilized as a mechanism for social and racial control and Hanoi was developed as a bipolar, dual city. The existing, and little-improved, *ville indigène* (for locals) was sepa-rated by a buffer zone from the newly planned *ville moderne* (for foreigners). Mean-while, waterways were developed for both trade and military purposes. A number of the city's lakes – particularly the ones of symbolic importance to the Vietnamese – were filled in by the French as an expression of control over Vietnamese culture. During the socialist era, there was extreme canalization of small rivers and the simul-taneous creation of new lakes, which exploited collective physical labour as part of the socialist regime. Since the initiation of *doi moi*, a relatively ad hoc and frenzied urbanization process has diminished the role of water spaces in the city. Recent development has mostly turned its back to the once-important water bodies, except where the lake is over-exploited as a real estate asset, as in the large West Lake. Over the past decades of urbanization, a great number of the city's lakes have disap-peared with a subsequent decrease in the area of lakes' water surface. As the water bodies shrink, there has been an increase in pollution from both domestic and indus-trial solid and liquid waste discharges. Encroachment and siltation has further dis-rupted the ecological balance of the lakes and a number of them are considered biologically dead. Fortunately, the Hanoi authorities have recognized the importance of the lake system and are busy with a number of ecological restoration pro-grammes.

The short but intensive period of fieldwork and interpretative mapping was succeeded by projective cartographies – in the form of visions (at the territorial scale) and strategic projects (at the urban design scale). Visions were developed to strengthen the existing logics of Hanoi and to steer the spatial development towards a desired future configuration. Visions are a broad frame of reference. They potentially generate a general, open and flexible development strategy and frame social commitments which strive to enlarge the civic realm, to enrich urban culture and to create new, sustainable urban space. Visions are premised upon attractive long-term perspectives and the structuring of the territory as a whole. The abstraction of visions which allow for adaptation to evolving circumstances while protecting non-negotiable, consensually agreed-upon principles, are made concrete through strategic projects.

Strategic projects confront visions with a specific context, with the realities of urban life and development: a real site, a concrete problematic, actual programmes, limited resources, flesh-and-blood actors with tangible interests and legitimate (or other) concerns. Strategic urban projects do not merely make a difference – they make a fundamental difference. Visions alone are meaningless. They must work hand-in-hand with 'strategic projects' which define significant moments in the formation of cities in which clear paradigms emerge, as moments of temporary synthesis in which a concrete economical, political, social and cultural constellation may be mobilized in order to co-act in the production of the city (De Meulder *et al.* 2004).

Three visions were developed at the scale of the Red River Delta and greater Hanoi. The first vision was 'B(l)ending with the Water'. The vision sought to simultaneously address water management, engineering and design and for newly conceived water bodies to influence future urbanization. At the scale of the delta, a new port was proposed significantly south of its present position – with hopes of eventually de-urbanizing Hai Phuong (the country's main port city on the East Sea) and allowing the adjacent Ha Long Bay to recover ecologically. The new location was justified by the predicted sea-level rise and its proximity to newly planned infrastructure. For the delta and greater Hanoi, a number of new water-bodies and flood plains were developed as structural and integrating components of the urban setting, including flood pockets along the Red River, upstream reservoirs, lakes, constructed wetlands and productive/industrial canals. The second vision, 'Cultivating a Structure', built on the delta's fertile soil and Vietnam's existing programme of afforestation. This vision required a more conscious cultivation of particular mosaics of vegetation in order to guide the urban growth of the delta in a determined direction. Among the typologies developed were: ecological corridors connecting forests, mountains and river systems; flood-plain parks; productive timber fields; edge parks between urban and productive land; and productive/recreational park fields. The third vision was 'Raising the City'. The rudimentary tool of topographical manipulation (re-balancing cut and fill) was utilized to create large new areas as raised platforms in the landscape for urbanization while maintaining areas for water to flow through the territory. This vision also included a number of new connections within the Red River Delta intended to support the national and international position of the region and to sustain its vibrant and growing urban economy. Among the infrastructures proposed was a transferium, industrial platforms and various urban plateaus, all counterbalanced by retaining large agricultural fields, water-cleaning and retention basins and large elastic-like water parks responding to monsoon seasons at river confluences.

Strategic project and stakeholders

Strategic projects are considered the principal means for strategically structuring and transforming cities and are a key alternative to the worn-out tradition of master planning. They are a foil to visions. For instance, a strategic urban project for an area immediately south of Hanoi's urban core on the Red River strengthens a number of the visions for the larger territory and city. The site's location is geographically important where essential rail, road, bridge and dyke infrastructures are bundled and where there is the largest collection of lakes for purification and water retention. This is also where urbanization is beginning to encroach on the flood plain of the Red River. A design project suggested a transferium incorporating all Hanoi's urban transport systems, including a new high-speed train. The development of the programme went hand-in-hand with new stakeholder coalitions whereby public investments in infrastructure spur high-end real estate development, resulting in a high-rise city on an urban platform on the Red River. This would in turn generate tax money which can be reinvested in public programmes and social infrastructure. The project is considered 'strategic', fulfils more than merely economic and social objectives, and also contributes to a new social meaning and appropriation of the river which integrates the engineering need for a raised dyke. A new strong metropolitan articulation of the southern gate of Hanoi also works as a flood plain, a soft urban field and edge incorporating floating houses, water transportation, recreation and markets.

Figure 2 **A strategic project for Hanoi's Red River.**

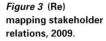

Figure 3 (Re) mapping stakeholder relations, 2009.

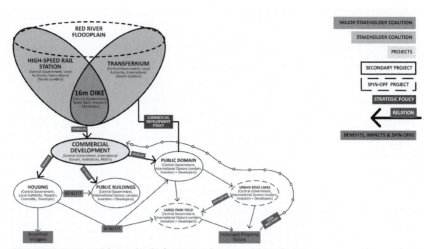

COALITIONS: Focus on High-Speed Rail Infrastructure & Commercial Develoment

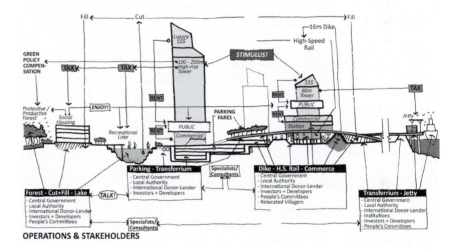

OPERATIONS & STAKEHOLDERS

The projective cartography emerging from the fieldwork developed a new series of stakeholder coalitions which counteract the diminishing political will and the withdrawal of the state, and deals with the gap between the decrease of public budgets and the growth of public needs. These coalitions specifically set out to safeguard the interests of marginalized sectors of the population and to protect the fragile environment. The new coalitions also proposed an array of cooperation between various governmental sectors – a reality that will no doubt take quite some time to realize. It is clear that in an era of economically driven development and in a context of increasing environmental vulnerability, more productive alliances need to be established between the less self-centred forces of civil society – policy-makers who try to articulate new modes of welfare provision and enlightened developers who believe in sustainable economic growth. Strategic urban projects are appropriate vehicles for conceiving, propagating and testing these alliances.

Mapping as communicating

Site-reading strategies and site-design tactics (Meyer 2005) based on extensive field-work are essential for the meaningful design of today's complex regional territories. Complementing the notion of mapping as designing is the fact there is undeniably a communicative quality to cartographic documents which facilitate negotiation between a multitude of stakeholders in urban and regional planning practices. Fieldwork, together with interpretative mapping and projective cartography, has the capacity to build on a particular site's latent spatial possibilities, via a concrete diagnosis and site understanding leading to context-responsive vision and strategic projects and a new interplay between different developmental aspects and actors. As such, fieldwork, mapping and cartography supports a much needed co-productive and project-based urbanistic approach.

Notes

1 The 'water urbanism' studio at KU Leuven is a part of the MaHS (Master of Human Set-tlements)/MaUSP (Master of Urbanism and Strategic Planning)/EMU (European Master of Urbanism). It was taught by K. Shannon and W. Verbakel. Students included: S. Abd El Rahman, D. Assefa, W. Guo, C. Ling, P. Lottens, X. Ma, P. Maro Hayne, B. Mashoodi, C.T. Nguyen, Sp. Nyamato, B. Pluym, A. Siddiqua, E. Sinclair, M. Van De Weijer and C. Yang. The 13-week studio included ten days of fieldwork/workshop in Hanoi where students worked on specific themes/sites and in collaboration with young professionals from the Vietnamese Institute of Architecture and Planning (VIAP) and students from Vietnam's University of Civil Engineering and Forestry University.
2 The present-day obsession with mapping has a number of proponents. In the United States, there are many that are or have been linked to the University of Pennsylvania, Department of Landscape Architecture (including Alan Berger, James Corner, Dilip da Cunha, Anuradha Mathur, Chris Reed, Charles Waldheim). In Europe, there are a number of people engaged in descriptive and projective urbanism via mapping, for instance Raoul Bunschoten, Bruno De Meulder, Xavier De Geyter, Franz Oswald, Bernardo Secchi and Paola Vigano.
3 *Phong thuy* – or *feng shui* (the 'art of geomancy') – determines the propitious siting of habitable areas by identifying sites that are protected from malignant spirits. The specific location of ancient Hanoi (which translates as 'between the rivers') was choreographed amid the To Lich, Kim Nguu and the Red Rivers with the notion that if any evil seeped into the city, it would easily be drained out along the numerous watercourses. At the same time, the waterways could provide clean water, minerals, seafood and prosperity through transportation and communication links. Thanh Long, 'arising dragon', the first name of what is now Hanoi, was situated on the natural higher ground formed by the alluvial deposits by the rivers' dynamics and with protection from behind by the Soc Son Mountains north of the Red River. Gods of the To Lich River and the Long Do hill (Mount Nung) were the tutelary spirits of the ancient capital. To the west, the city was enclosed and protected by the That Dieu – seven low karstic limestone hills arising at the geomorphologic edge of the plains and Truong Son mountain range.
4 The new plan nearly tripled the administrative area of Hanoi to 334,447 km^2 and included an area with a population of over six million (the city previously had a population of just under four million). The spatial consequences extend from servicing the territory with

infrastructure and sociocultural amenities suitable for an ASEAN (Association of South-east Asian Nations) capital to a new formation of urbanization across the territory. All lead to fundamental changes in the environmental dynamics of the region. The decision to expand westward will, on the one hand, relieve the overburdened centre, on the other hand, however, it will reconfigure densities in what is already one of the most densely populated rural areas in the world. The 'rural' component of the Red River Delta averages 1,000 people/sq. km (Shannon 2009).

5   The *dinh* (also called *dinh lang*) is the traditional community house of villages. Historically, *dinh*s were the collective venues of social gatherings, festival celebrations, civil disputes and spiritual pursuits. They served as places where the spiritual and the secular events of life converged.

Open field: Documentary game

Renata Tyszczuk

P.S.

The proposal itself is not as important as the question of why it has been made in the first place.

(Hansen 2005a: 22)

The writing in this chapter emerged out of a combination of research, practice and teaching based in an MArch design studio at the University of Sheffield.[1] It draws on a critical pedagogy that invites attention to entangled cultural, social, economic and ecological processes and a practice that considers the potential of provisional projects.

Open field

Fieldwork in architectural research and practice is an opportunity to confront the assumptions we make in our projects and acknowledge the uncertainties of our encounters with human and material worlds. Disciplinary approaches to fieldwork that draw on an Enlightenment imaginary of discovery and exploration tend to frame our implicit conceptualisations of fieldwork as a process of investigation of a world 'out there' and furthermore, lend substance to a lingering debate which contrasts immersion in the field with distancing oneself in the study or laboratory (Massey 2003; Outram 1996). Latour (1999), however, argues that at each stage of research there is a transformation, an engagement and a process of creation. The field for him is less a space to which one goes and then leaves but is a much more complex and transformative structure that is open, porous and constructed through relations and practices. He offers a shift in the understanding of the locale of the laboratory or field from that of a distanced space, single space or 'single minded space' (Massey 2005: 178) into a multi-faceted site of transformation.

Thinking of fieldwork in architecture or indeed architecture *as* fieldwork and as 'transformative engagement' in an 'open field' where the work is co-constituted blurs the tidily demarcated distance of laboratory and field and the sequential nature of design. This understanding of fieldwork and architecture also asks us to carefully consider our responses and responsibilities to others. It thus calls up the ethical and political implications of 'thinking space relationally' (Massey 2005). In our studio work we have encouraged thinking about fieldwork and the documentation that inevitably accompanies each project as 'games' in order to approach the relational aspects of our practice as architects. The mode of 'serious play' we have adopted in the laboratory/ field space of studio work is in many ways in continuity with the critical, process-based, participatory games and polemics that emerged in Central Europe in the late 1960s and early 1970s. Of particular interest is the diverse practice of the Polish architect Oskar Hansen and his collaborators, which he presented under the rubric '*Forma Otwarta*' – 'Open Form'.[2]

Open Form

The theory of Open Form – *Forma Otwarta* – was developed by Oskar Hansen from the late 1950s. Hansen is credited with developing both a social and decentred conception of space and creativity, and a new way to conceptualise architecture (Crowley 2009). His theory of Open Form had an important influence on Polish concepts of '*dzieła-procesu*' (works of process) and 'performance' in the 1960s and 1970s and is seen as the precursor and proponent of environmental art, the happening, intermedia co-creation and expanded art approaches. Hansen's various ways of intervening in the architectural field were conceived in the laboratory space of Open Form, a way of thinking and doing architecture that extended through cognitive space to a practical engagement with the context. Open Form relied on a blurring of the boundaries of deskwork, studio work and fieldwork, an immersive subjectivity and interchangeable notions of laboratory and environment – an 'open field'.

Not surprisingly, considering his diverse and prolific oeuvre and his interest in pedagogy, Oskar Hansen has exerted significant influence on generations of artists and architects.[3] He is usually remembered for the audacity of his *Linear Continuous System* (Hansen and Hansen 1967), a proposal for a complex open system which could create 'a common home for both town and country people' (Hansen 1970), and the partial implementation of this approach with the 1963 housing estate at Przyczółek Grochowski, Warsaw and the 1966–1968 district plan for Warsaw-Ursynów. Along with the super-scale housing projects and urban plans, and the theories of flexible, evolving and transformable architectures, he is recognised for his ambition to test alternative social and political models in the architecture and his encouragement of participation by many in its process. His idealistic proposals of 'open' relations in these projects are familiar in the discourse of the 1960s and 1970s neo-avant-gardes, and can be dismissed as naive when compared with the bleak reality of the history of these socialist housing estates. Nevertheless, it is important to acknowledge these interventions as 'attempts to negotiate the conditions of designing and dwelling in a socialist everydayness, or at the time when the grandeur mania appeared in Polish architecture' (Świtek, 2009). It is tempting to think of Hansen as the Polish Cedric Price and, just like Price, his importance for pedagogy is based on thinking the unimaginable, and the radicalism of his un-built, rather than built, ideas.[4]

Hansen's theories and pedagogical methods were important in the debates around late Modernist architecture, in particular those of Team 10 and their search for transformed notions of social space (Smithson 1982: 33; van den Heuvel and Risselada 2006: 13). Hansen has said, however, with evident disappointment:

> To understand that period you have to browse through the literature on Team Ten, only not the British. British historians of architecture aren't objective: from that period they only remember Smithson, Smithson and Smithson. There isn't even a mention of *Open Form*.
>
> (Hansen 2003)

The theory of Open Form was publicly expressed by Hansen for the first time at the last CIAM (Congrès international d'architecture moderne) in Otterlo in 1959. He announced: 'Closed Form – decisions made by someone else – I'm uninvolved. You can't find yourself here – your SELF. All these are someone else's memoirs, someone else's emotions, someone else's houses and apartments.' While conversely,

> Open Form will give each of us a sense of a meaningful existence, will help us define ourselves and find our place in the space and time we live in. . . . We'll walk inside it rather than around it. Diverse individuality, with its randomness and activity, will become the wealth of that space – a co-participant.
>
> (Hansen 1959: 5)

His stance was at once an appeal to identity, a call for an engagement with social relations, renewed public involvement in design and an explicit challenge to the particular context of state-directed urbanism and architecture of postwar Poland. As Hansen wrote in 1959, the theory of Open Form was not so much a 'speculative invention of our times', but rather a 'conclusion stemming from the observation of existing systems'. Not one to resist the possibility of a universal application that could reconcile scales, distances and temporalities, Hansen saw Open Form as a way of thinking about the full spectrum of architectural engagements: from large-scale housing estates, exhibitions and public memorials, through to temporary events and participation strategies. This 'scalability' drew on the notion of a space–time continuum, so that the macro scale of the Linear Continuous System (which took as a starting point most of central Europe) was not at odds with the mezzo scale of housing projects, or the micro games and experiments of Hansen's studio and exhibition work (Hansen 2005a: 97).

Hansen's projects were a reaction to the standardisation and typification of architecture which, according to him, whether looking at 'communist times or capitalistic lifestyle', paid scant attention to human issues. As he pointed out, 'Open Form was above all a form of protest against the idea of "optimized" architecture for the "average" user. There isn't such thing as a "typical inhabitant" of a "typical house"!

Every one of us is different' (Hansen 2003). Speaking about the housing projects in particular he warned that 'there is a risk in succumbing to thinking of objects. Like in other matters you have to leave room for change ... the family grows, fads pass. The building has to be a transformable structure' (Hansen 2003). His engagement with architecture in postwar Poland extended to what he called 'humanisation studies', which were intent on integrating the social, environmental and economic aspects of living and work practices, relied on the inhabitants' involvement in the reinvention of existing spaces rather than their demolition, and suggested, for example, the planting of 'roses in place of walls' (Hansen 1979).

Hansen had started from the assumption that the world was inherently unstable and that all art was unpredictable (Hansen 2003). And although he engaged with 'prognostic plans', these avoided the usual predictive tone of visionary architects of this period by instead asking a series of questions: '[h]ow do you think things in Poland are going to develop? What will there be in a couple of years time? What would you like there to be? That kind of thing' (Hansen 2005a: 14, 36). He argued for spatial forms which were open or unfinished, and which therefore required the creativity or participation of viewers or users. In terms of architecture this meant that buildings designed as 'open forms' would be 'incomplete', leaving opportunities for occupants to shape their environment, thus questioning the role of the architect. The ideal open form was ultimately an unauthored and spontaneous one. Space, according to Hansen, needed to be considered in terms of movement, whether in terms of a potential to be reorganised by those who occupied it or in its capacity to change over time (Hansen 1975).

Cognitive space

Open Form allowed for a space within which to rethink the nature of architecture and the critical role of the architect: 'we certainly couldn't squeeze ourselves into social realism', Hansen has said of his particular context of postwar Poland '[a]nd this as I see it today was the first attempt to develop a cognitive space, which is the main element of Open Form.' Hansen's turn to experimental pedagogy is rooted in his search for the nature of this cognitive space. It was an attempt to discover a region where theory and practice were ingeniously inseparable. Open Form suggested a space of potential in which to think, catalyse and enact relations, and invariably oscillated between notions of both laboratory and public space. The openness of this space concerned both the transformative and communicative aspects of space as the basis for architecture.

For Hansen, architecture needed to be adaptive and flexible, taking account of the necessarily unpredictable needs of its users. He therefore saw architecture's contingency as akin to the 'art of events' (Hansen 2005a: 199). Through engaging audiences and users, 'open forms' had the potential to remind individuals of the fact of their own situated understanding and allow them to further test the spaces that they occupied. Hansen theories were developed through his engagement in exhibition design and the freedom to experiment that this offered (2005a: 116). They became for him a testing ground for his architectural propositions. He says,

> exhibitions were the 'laboratory' of Open Form.... the first criterion – transformability: not a rigid closed object but a developing one, openness to change, receptivity to space. A criterion postulating as few details as possible, and a maximum of unsaturated space – the essence of exhibition.
>
> (2005a: 132)

Hansen's rejection of the hierarchical authoritarian model of relations between the artist or architect and the recipient denied the importance of the object and opposed any striving towards notions of an 'ideal form'. The laboratory conditions of Open Form were not concerned with objects but with a relational understanding of the 'creative process', in which the recipient/co-author could actively participate (Ronduda and Wolinski 2006). In Hansen's words (2003),

> [s]pace isn't only the objects that are contained in it – it is the relation between these objects. What I mean is that a focus on objects causes us to perceive space as nothing but a container for objects. It's like watching empty suitcases or bags in a shop window. That's worthless! That's absurd and barbarous! That's precisely Closed Form.

Open Form: 'for-camera activities'

The experimental practices that Oskar Hansen's theories inspired among his students in 1970s Poland were characterised by processual (anti-object, ephemeral, documented) activities – games, visual conversations, interactions – a strong focus on the analysis of the nature of the medium, whether film or architecture, and participative and collective practices that challenged the concept of authorship. What is notable in these works is that there is no clear separation between documentation or art: 'they open a tense field in which the visual space and the space of action stand in relation to one another' (Ronduda *et al.* 2007: 88).

The work, *Open Form*, made in February 1971, was a collaboration between students from the cinematography and acting departments of the Łódź Film School and students and graduates of the Warsaw Academy of Fine Arts' sculpture faculty intent on developing a platform for collective inter-disciplinary work, reforming the teaching process of art schools in Poland and indeed questioning the status quo (Ronduda and Wolinski 2006). *Open Form* consisted of a series of 'for-camera activities' (the artists preferred not to call the work a 'film') divided into seven contrasting 'episodes' made without a script: *Hansen's Studio, Playing on the Actress' Face, Jarnuszkiewicz's Studio, TV Studio, Moses, Library, School, and Location*. During the 'for-camera' work for *Open Form*, the students played the various roles of curators, producers, directors, camera operators, actors and so on. Throughout the improvised process the students continually expanded and developed the set of techniques, strategies, working methods and collaboration models employed. These included 'operations on media', 'interrupted projection' and the 'provocation' of the filmed recipient. 'Provocation' was Hansen's term and involved thinking of the camera as a provocative tool used both to interrupt situations and aid reactions and interactions. The intention was also for the processual work to keep deconstructing itself (it has never been properly edited) and to emphasise the work's materiality (in this case that of photochemical film). The 'unfinished' work of 'for-camera activities' attempted to capture, confront, embody and document the positions and strategies of working collectively in this way, endowing the laboratory space of the studio with the characteristics of a 'conversation' or 'game'.

Playing on the Actress's Face (Gra na Twarzy Aktorki), a scene from Open Form, presents the most conspicuous example of this kind of processual or documented visual game. Every consecutive shot demonstrates the 'move' made by

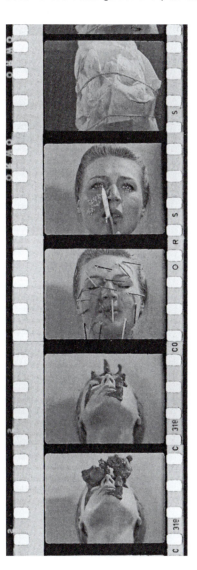

Figure 1 'Game on the Actress's Face', a fragment of the film *Open Form* (1971). Zofia Kulik, Przemysław Kwiek, and: Jan S. Wojciechowski, Paweł Kwiek, Tatiana Dębska, Karol Broniatowski, Andrzej Zalewski, Ewa Lemańska.

each consecutive participant. Each contribution is also a comment on, or response to, the previous one. Like a version of the game of *Consequences*, indeed literally 'exquisite corpse' (*cadavre exquis*), enacted on an actual human body, the 'for-camera actions' remind the viewer of indeterminacy: not only of the myriad choices and possible outcomes of the game but also drawing attention to their own conditions of embodiment. Along with the players, this category of game involves the camera both as a participant and as the potential provocation tool in the game's construction. In turn, the spontaneous character of the game allows different potentially unanticipated conditions of the situation to be revealed. In the practical and theoretical horizon of the sphere of inter-subjective relations, this type of game has been remarked on as 'a school of responsibility in the public sphere' (Ronduda and Wolinski 2006). The various ways of revealing the complex collaborative interactions in the laboratory space of the studio also applied to the moves and counter-moves enacted and documented in the other sequences of *Open Form* 'for-camera activities' that took place outside the studio. These games were located either in the streets of Warsaw or in the landscape (for example, *Game played on Morel's Hill – Gra na wzgorzu Morela*, in Elblag 1971). The 'play' of camera activities is key – not simply in providing adequate documentation of the work, but also in turning viewers into active interlocutors and in acknowledging how all participants, not just those who provoked the activities or game are implied in the work. *Open Form* thus provided a framework, or cognitive space within which to

Figure 2 **Winter Games MArch Studio Six in Nowa Huta, Poland, 2007.**

develop a relational understanding of the work itself as well as possible interventions in the wider context. The unconstructed situations of this work also attempted to dissolve existing hierarchies and notions of expert. If, as according to Joseph Beuys, 'everyone is an artist', and, by extension, 'everyone is an architect', in these works one could also argue that everyone is an amateur and co-creator.

Experimental practice

A consideration of these earlier experimental practices is not concerned with stylistic determinations or in the revival of forms or techniques but in the insights that might be gained for contemporary pedagogy and for architecture. There is a risk, however, of all-too-simple transpositions – the notion of collaboration as good in itself, or of inventing a new kind of formalism whereby discursivity, sociability and co-creativity are pursued for their own sake. We also need to be wary of any analogy between an open work and an inclusive society or any suggestion that a non-hierarchical approach might invoke an egalitarian world. And as for documented work in the field – what if nothing actually takes place? Or what if things don't turn out as expected? If the issue of participation was inextricable from questions of politics or ideology in the 1960s and 1970s Open Form experiments, this is clearly not the case today where participatory techniques have been adopted by the mainstream and collective responsibility is scarce or threatened. At best, attention to the history of Open Form invites a critical pedagogy. A more active politics of participation might depend therefore on stimulating the idea that transformation is possible (Freire, 1996).

Thinking about fieldwork and studio work as documented games is above all about an engagement with the present scope of architectural practice and its potential for transformation. In our MArch research-led design studio, taking part in unscripted and indeterminate games has allowed for a rethinking of the categories and assumptions made about architecture, and also about our interventions and responsibilities as architects. Through a range of activities, working uncomfortably and without a script, in different media, in different locations, we have sought to research and interrogate place, history, change and our imaginary futures.

As part of our collective and discursive approach we have encouraged different attitudes, positions and interventions that in different ways have the potential to test and negotiate agency, social understanding and political action. The process has been non-hierarchical: inviting, welcoming and provoking participation in the research. It has attempted to pose ever more 'inventive questions' in recognition of architecture's role as 'experimental practice' (Grosz 2001: 130). The research and thinking refuses to be academic and detached, it involves learning from unexpected sources and encounters, and engaging with diverse and diverging participants, from passers-by to experts. The processual integrity of this kind of project and its combination of field work, desk work, studio work and laboratory work relies on acknowledging that every experiment is ongoing, that an end result may never transpire, that predictions and determinations don't usually work and that often neither architects nor the public 'participate', or participate as planned. The projects embrace the essential instability, the sometimes bizarre and even threatening connectivity of the world. They are prepared to take a while for ideas to meld, for practices to form, for conflicts to emerge, for things not to work, or to work out in unexpected ways. They encourage thinking about how to produce work without predetermining its outcome and refuse to define space as programmable within the normative logic-dominated techniques of power.

The documentary game is not about the recording and therefore the production of an environment per se, but about understanding architecture as a provisional construction in a paradoxical space of shared interactions – an 'open field'. This kind of experimental practice suggests an alternative and provisional document of architecture's ongoing potential for social and political engagement.

P.S.

The proposal itself is not as important as the question of why it has been made in the first place.

Notes

1   With thanks to MArch Studio Six, School of Architecture, University of Sheffield. Studio Six 'Architecture and Interdependence' (2006–2009) was linked to the Interdependence Day project (www.interdependenceday.co.uk), and explored experimental practice and global environmental change issues. Studio Six fieldwork has involved visits to Berlin, Bergen, Grimsby, Kraków, Nowa Huta and Warsaw.

2   Oskar Hansen (1922–2005) was a Polish architect, urban planner, teacher and theorist of Finnish birth. He graduated from the Technical College in Wilno (Vilnius, Lithuania) in 1942, then studied in the Department of Architecture at the Technical University, Warsaw (1945–1950). In 1948–1950 he visited France, Italy and Britain and studied under Fernand Léger and Pierre Jeanneret; he also became acquainted with Le Corbusier and Henry Moore. From 1950 to 1983 he lectured at the Academy of Fine Arts, Warsaw. He was also a member of the Groupe d'Etude d'Architecture Moderne (GEAM) and a contributor to Team 10. Hansen presented his concepts of Open Form at CIAM 1959, the Team 10 meeting in Bagnols-sur Cèze, 1960 and subsequently the journal *Le carré bleu* dedicated an issue to Open Form in 1961.

3   The Bergen School of Architecture (Bergen Arkitekt Skole, BAS), was founded by Hansen's former student and collaborator Svein Hatloy. BAS still follows the pedagogical methods developed by Hansen and includes instruction on 'Open Form' in its curriculum. The First International Open Form Symposium was organised at BAS in 2001 to celebrate Hansen's eightieth birthday. BAS has continued to host international symposia dedicated to Open Form. With thanks to students and staff at the Bergen School of Architecture, in particular Eva Kun, for her Open Form workshops, and Marianne Skjulhaug, Head of School BAS; and to Sarah Wigglesworth Architects who taught a studio at BAS in 2008–2009.

4   Among Hansen's best-known 'un-built' projects was the submission to the international competition for the monument at Auschwitz-Birkenau (1957; with Zofia Hansen, Jerzy Jarnuszkiewicz, Edmund Kupiecki, Julian Pałka and Lechosław Rosiski), also presented at the CIAM congress in Otterlo, 1959.

The critical *where* of the field

A reflection on fieldwork as a situated process of creative research

Ella Chmielewska and Sebastian Schmidt-Tomczak

This essay is part of a larger project that concerns urban memory in Warsaw and is planned to take the form of a book-object, discursively engaging material, visual and textual evidence. Emphasizing the authors' distinct voices, it expressly dwells on their different articulations of, and positions vis-à-vis, urban objects. In this collaborative research project, the field of fieldwork is seen as mobile, moved by the exchanges and negotiations between the authors. Thus, tracing the critical *where* of the field is here developed as both a strategy for understanding fieldwork and constitutive *of* fieldwork.

Here, a method of close contemplation of materiality developed for Peter Eisenman's field of stelae in Berlin by one of the authors is mobilized by the other author in its deployment in an artist studio in Warsaw. The essay examines the exchanges around this application and argues that the actual fieldwork in collaborative research, while framed by physical displacement, pertains to the movement of the field back and forth between the authors. The field's changing *where*, informed by the authors' critical engagement, theoretical approaches and attitudes, is thus posited as an instrumental device for collaboration. The field's position (procedural, methodological, conceptual, representational, discursive), reframed in each new context, generates productive collisions and translations. It is in transpositions (of thought, language, objects) that collaborative exchanges take place and that fieldwork as creative research practice is articulated.

Sebastian:
Where, within the work, is the field framed and articulated? What is its position in relation to the task or larger project to which it is expected to contribute? How is it inflected by the researcher's familiarity with the site, its texts and surrounding context; by her informed or innocent anticipations?

Figure 1

How and where do we make sense of the field once it is transformed into a set of representations and recordings, now dismembered and re-membered through the ordering of fragmentary images, notations and artefacts? Where do we fold it into the project and what happens with the original field? Is it now exhausted, consumed in the process of data collection, an emptied site left behind?

In this essay we reflect on the position of fieldwork in our collaborative research. In our larger project – a book on urban surfaces, materiality and place memory[1] – collaboration is taken as a process of creative translocation, of 'material thinking', to borrow Paul Carter's concept (2005: 3–5). For us, however, it is not a movement from art to writing as articulated in Carter's work, but from research to research, from looking to looking, *from writing to writing*. It is a process of translation that happens in the transposition of material between the researchers. The focus here is not on movement itself, but on the movement *of*, whereby the object and its *where* are crucial to the procedure.

The process is vectorial, but not unidirectional. It is not dialectic, where the contradictions are sought and negotiated. It is dialogic, though not aimed at resolving implicit disagreements. It is conversational: responsive to the nuance of location, open to changing viewpoints, attentive to the process and to the concrete encounter. The procedure demands alertness to the site and its objects, a close contemplation of the researcher's position. The field here does not enter the process, the fieldwork, as something merely instrumental, *some thing* to be used and discarded but as a productive *place* of work, of gathering thought.

What is central to our project is the specificity of positions, the location of an outsider and an insider within the enquiry, and in relation to the field. The critical *where* from which an outsider is *looking in*, an insider *looking out*; an outsider in a close scrutiny, an insider in making broader connections. In the exchange of looking, in conversation, the specific place of experience is critical: this is *where* possibilities are mobilized.

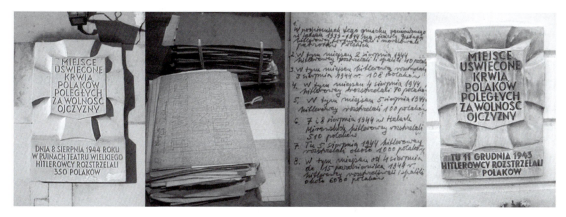

Figure 2

Now, *here*, we are reconstituting, briefly, in consideration of this context, the process of our field/work. We are reflecting on the process through its story, opening it up to *your* scrutiny. De-scribing it, testing our method, as it were, in this *Field/Work* volume.

Ella:

Birkbeck College London, January 2009.

I am speaking at the Symposium *Sites of Memory*. My talk, 'Remembering in Forgetting' – part of my project on surface memory – is a reflection on conflicted place memory in Warsaw. Here in London, it is preceded by two papers on London and followed by one on Paris.[2] I am acutely aware of how my name and accent further locate my paper *in* Warsaw, away from the frame of reference of this London audience. My topic, a 1950s commemorative project by the little-known Warsaw sculptor Karol Tchorek, is familiar to two people in the auditorium, both of whom came especially to hear the paper. Chris is a journalist, a specialist in East European political history; Katy is an artist who inherited Tchorek's works and documents, which are gathered in his studio in Warsaw.[3]

The sculptor's archives contain detailed records of the project that marked the city with stone tablets indicating numerous execution sites from the period of Nazi occupation. With their officially commissioned standard form, they replaced earlier spontaneous acts of local remembrance. Impossible to see in their entirety, unknown as a monument or as the work of a singular artist, indexical and located in discrete places of past trauma, they seem in a dialectical position to Peter Eisenman's Memorial to the Murdered Jews of Europe in Berlin. These stone markers constitute the base of Warsaw's memorial landscape pointing to local politics of memory, to localized voids and absences.

As expected, my talk elicits the kind of questions from the audience that necessitate detailed explanation, translation if you will, of that remote context. At some point, Chris turns to the audience. *I live in Warsaw*, he begins, and with a journalistic facility, proceeds to disentangle historical complexities. His opening makes a palpable impact: *I live in Warsaw* pronounced with his distinct Oxford accent. A few moments later, someone challenges my referring to Tchorek's tablets as artwork. Katy enters, *Let me speak to this. He was my father in law*, she says in her posh Surrey accent,

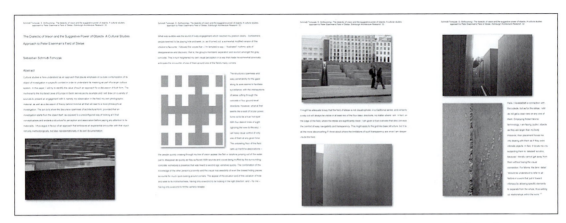

Figure 3

I live in Warsaw ... she follows. The shift becomes apparent: Warsaw's stone tablets have been transposed, dis-located within the room, moved from the obscurity of distance to the proximity of attention. And so has my paper. Now, legitimated by a mere shift of accent ... (the London and Paris papers retreat to the background).

Ella:

Edinburgh, School of Architecture, March 2009.

In his paper for the conference, 'Transilient Boundaries in/of Architecture',[4] Sebastian contemplates Berlin's Stelenfeld memorial, demonstrating through his intense engagement with its form how the 'suggestive power of objects' of architecture (or art) can be revealed in that specific context. In his close attention to materiality, to surfaces, volumes and voids, his position in viewing and the 'experiential encounter' that brings to the site his alert theoretical reflection, he constructs an intricate *critical object*: simultaneously an account of thinking, a methodology for fieldwork, a documentation of an attentiveness to the built form, and a record of what he terms 'a discursive exchange with the object of investigation'. He claims, drawing on Georges Didi-Huberman, that in Peter Eisenman's memorial, 'the remembrance of the unspeakable ... that we cannot look at is what looks back at us from what we see'. It is 'the friction between the evident outside [of the commemorative form] and the uncanny inside [that] reaches embodiment in the observer' (Schmidt-Tomczak 2010: 112). Sebastian insists with the words of German phenomenologist Bernhard Waldenfels.

Sebastian:

'Was unseren Blick beunruhigt, ist nicht etwas, das wir nach Belieben sehen können, sondern etwas das uns *zu sehen* gibt' (Waldenfels 1999: 131).

['What disturbs our gaze is nothing that we can see at will, but something that causes us *to see*.'][5]

Ella:

'What disturbs our gaze is nothing that we can see at will, but something that causes us to *see*.'

'Naszego spojrzenia nie zakłóca to co widzimy, ale to co sprawia, że możemy *zobaczyć*.'

The difficulty of translating the sentence from English to Polish reveals to me an interesting potential of the verb *to see* when mobilized in a different context, in the language that demands specificity of spatial and temporal relation to the object. Employing the verb *zobaczyć*, I am pointing to an acuity and attention as well as to completion: my seeing *having resulted* in completing the act of seeing. *Having seen* that is the realization of the action of the gaze: 'something that causes us to having seen', then. Again, the specificity of language inflects what we see in the event. The place of the event, the field, demands attention to its *Logos*.

What if Sebastian's essay were to be located in the context of Warsaw, in the book on Warsaw's surface memory that I have been working on? What if this essay-object were confronted with texts focused on a different context, on local particularities? Its content set within a different discourse, the object of its reflection placed within Warsaw's fragmented surfaces, ambiguous ruins, its palimpsests of conflicted inscriptions?

What kind of questions would this object pose in the city whose trauma is vaguely indexed by the Berlin memorial? While Eisenman's immense undulating field of concrete blocks references abstract memory of events that happened elsewhere, Tchorek's stone tablets, scattered around the city, speak to the specificity of memories. They address the distinct *here* of trauma, the memory of which also indexes the void there, though the void is differently *concrete* than that inside the Stelenfeld's cement blocks.

Figure 4

What if Sebastian – camera in hand and methodology employed for the Berlin site in mind – were transposed into the field of my work on surface memory, a particular site of my fieldwork in Warsaw? There, at a specific address, all commemorative tablets are held in drawings, blueprints, lists, photographs, notes in the sculptor's personal diary and official correspondence, documents, models and casts.

The place of this archive, the sculptor's studio located in a disfigured fragment of a building hidden in the centre of the city, is simultaneously a place of work for a contemporary artist, Katy Bentall.[6] Through remaking the space, through inhabiting it with her works, collections of art and objects, installations and events, Katy explores the relationship of this place to the city, its memory and personal stories held in its objects and fragments.

Figure 5

Sebastian:

Katy Bentall's studio, Smolna Street, Warsaw, April 2009.

I am leaving the field of smooth surfaces and countless repetitions of a single form, but I am not leaving it behind. I am entering this new space in Warsaw, which also is a field, yet of a different kind. It is easy to imagine the open space in Berlin as a field, the wind sweeping through its channels, rain hitting its surfaces. It is impersonal, indirect, non-specific, and its morphology is ruled by multiplication and multitude. In Warsaw, there, too, is a quantity of objects, but morphological references and similarities are scarce, if they exist at all. The contemporary sofa and period chairs, Christian iconography and abstract paintings, socialist realist sculptures and folk woodcarvings alongside the archive of Tchorek's models and monuments, among Katy's textual works and intricate installations, books and family memorabilia. How did all of these and many other objects get here? Nothing seems out of place, however, so while there is no pattern in the style of an undulating grid of concrete blocks, there must be a connection, a reason why these objects came together. Coming together suggests movement, and, similarly, I am continuing my own mobile enquiry.

Following the gazes of sculpted heads, the reflections of mirrors, the pointing corners of furniture, or the connections established between colours, my attention is directed around the space, falling on new things and surfaces as I move among them. I am part of an unfolding choreography, triggering a close and engaged contemplation. While I am still not sure whether or how I can apply my method from Berlin to this new environment, the exploration of the space feels strangely similar to that *in* Berlin, even though my movement is enacted under entirely different conditions. There is no specific form, but a collection of objects without a clear shape. I am not outside, navigating a concrete form, but inside a fragile space within a fragment of a ruin. I am not looking at an artwork designed in its entirety, delimited by a distinct urban site, but I am *within* an installation, moving around what seems like a deliberate yet contingent arrangement. In fact, I am part of that arrangement in that I am accommodated in Katy's studio.

In Warsaw, as in Berlin, there is an objective of gathering material for research. However, while the visit to Berlin was what shaped the project, its starting point, the visit to Warsaw, is part of an already existing project, my participation in it triggered by the work done in Berlin.

In Berlin, I am perpetually outside, trying to grasp the absence of the Murdered Jews of Europe that is referenced to be elsewhere, alluded to by the possible

Figure 6

void inside the stelae. In this field of concrete, this absence could not be commemorated if it were placed on the personal and specific level on which the field in Warsaw is operating. There, references are direct, the entire space or site is a bundle of objects, held together by someone's past, memory and history.

While in Berlin the clarity of an artistic form could be subjected to an art theoretical reflection based on its materiality resembling minimal art, this is precluded here by an intricate tangle of relationships. They are played out between pluralities of art, history, morphology and language that are bound together in what, too, is an artistic investment, but none that lends itself to analysis through its form. Rather, any theoretical investigation has to start from and scrutinize the mode of apprehension employed to make sense of this very complex and entangled field; not to disentangle it, but to reveal the *intensity of the relationships*, which are enacted through movement.

Ella:

It is not the motion in itself, not filmic mobility of images that matters here, however, but the force of looking that mobilizes thought. For Bill Viola the kind of looking that (time-based) art calls for is not that of an isolated ocular act. It is a close scrutiny of things that, he claims, 'elevates the commonplace to a higher level of awareness' (Viola in Perloff 1998). Viola demands his images to be generative of experiences, to trigger acute events. This kind of looking is not realized by the sense of vision alone but rather by a corporeal presence. For Viola, the closeness of things is based on sensorial complexity that constitutes experience. And it is *experience* that the fieldwork is all about: not separating the senses into text production and ocular scrutiny, but the kind of immersive data *gathering* that necessarily involves the body.

It is not a singular body that Viola specifies for his method of making and demands of his images. 'I want to look so close at things', he writes, 'that their intensity burns through your retina and onto the surface of your mind' (Viola in Perloff 1998). This intensity of looking, then, surpasses the self and the body, and his *completed* looking, his materialized *having seen* – his articulation of the Polish verb *zobaczyć* – has a capacity to burn into my (your) retina, to inscribe itself permanently onto my (your) vision. This materialized insistence goes beyond the experience, exceeds one vision and crosses into another.

For Michel Serres the sense of vision, the act of looking also surpasses the body, goes beyond the self. It is an act of movement, of dislocation, of changing positions. Looking is visiting; it involves displacement and gathers into itself, as he writes, 'the compact capacity of the senses' (Serres 2008: 305). 'In order to see', he follows, 'movements take paths, crossroads, interchanges, so that examination goes into detail or moves on to a global synopsis: changes in dimension, sense and direction' (305). This *looking* both explores and details, it is an action of excursions, 'it always goes beyond its site, by shifting position' (306). Serres insists that while '[t]he subject sees, the body visits, goes beyond its place' (306), goes out from its role and 'plunges into and lives in a perpetual [exchange]' (307).

In order to see, movements must *take paths* in relation to objects of seeing; in approaching, getting closer, moving away, the repositioning of the body informs the relationship to the field and to the considered object. In the shifting position of the self (of the I), in movement, in *trans*action, the *where* of the inside of the place and that of the outside are negotiated.

Figure 7

Sebastian:

Our collaborative fieldwork takes place in the moments of encounter, in productive collisions; when positions and arguments are necessarily vulnerable to change, when exchange, translation and co-thinking in conversation happens.

Like the two concrete surfaces in the last figure, our perspectives collide and create friction that has creative potential. Meeting in a right angle exposes the surfaces to outside forces that can be destructive, chipping the corner, but that thereby create a more varied material landscape. The collaboration forces one to constantly revisit assumptions, implications and aims of the work, luring one out of the comfort zone of the two-dimensional plane and into the dangers of three-dimensional thinking. In certain areas, the two perspectives meet in a perfect edge, making their creative conflicts barely noticeable. In other places, the tectonics of the meeting take off that edge, increasing the distance between the two surfaces. However, any increase simultaneously reduces the angle of their relationship, steadily working towards the spherical geometry of a well-rounded argument, not towards a shared two-dimensionality. The coherence and integrity of the sphere is the ultimate aim of collaboration. It is, however, an ideal concept more than a real possibility. In the discursive mobility that is paramount in the fieldwork project, new sites, texts or histories enter the work, triggering self-reflection that will, chisel in hand, result in the revision of the argument, inflection of voice, forming new edges that will have to be smoothed again in further creative thinking and exchanges.

Notes

1   In this essay, we are focusing on the method as related to the fieldwork, the sites and our specific exchanges. The larger project considers questions of historical context and politics of commemoration. The project is focused on the *iconosphere* of Warsaw, and is based on research of photographic and media archives in Warsaw (National Digital Archive, the Institute of Art, Muzeum Historyczne miasta Warszawy, Tchorek-Bentall Foundation), Marburg (Herder-Institut) and Maryland (The National Archives at College Park).
2   'Sites of Memory: Objects, Traces, Places', 27 February 2009, Department of History of Art and Screen Media, Birkbeck College. For the Polish version of the paper see Chmielewska (2008).
3   Chris (Krzysztof) Bobiński is a journalist, the former *Financial Times* correspondent in Warsaw, publisher of *European Voice* and president of the Unia Polska Foundation. Katy Bentall is an artist, the founder and president of the Tchorek-Bentall Foundation.
4   'Transilient Boundaries in/of Architecture', 30–31 March 2009, University of Edinburgh. See Schmidt-Tomczak (2010).
5   Translation S. Schmidt-Tomczak.
6   See Chmielewska *et al.* (2010).

Field note 2

A voyage into oral field/work

Alan Dein

> Everything audible in the whole world becomes material.
>
> (Walter Ruttmann)

Audio documentary feature-makers like myself are indebted, whether they know it or not, to a remarkable pioneering sound feature called *Weekend*. It was the work of Walter Ruttmann, perhaps best known as a film-maker for his beautiful abstract study *Berlin: Symphony of a Big City* in 1927. Three years later, Ruttmann had returned to the same subject, but crucially this time, captured the noises and snatched conversations of the metropolis in sound only. Recorded directly onto the soundtrack of optical film, Ruttmann championed *Weekend* as 'a completely new acoustic art – new in its means and in its effect'.

Fast forward some 80 years, it appears that the potential of this 'effect' is only now being recognised and channelled into a whole range of possibilities that would surely amaze Ruttmann. The original 11-minute, 10-second audio collage was only played once on German radio and then, unbelievably, it was considered lost until its rediscovery in 1978.

A few years after a copy of *Weekend* turned up in an archive in New York, I was an undergraduate holed up in a polytechnic, surrounded by what was then the miserable and derelict environment of London's East End and uninspired by dour texts on politics and constitution. One book, cannily recommended by a despairing lecturer, would prove to be an enduring inspiration. *Hard Times* (Terkel 1970) by the broadcaster and oral historian Studs Terkel, told what it was like to live through the American Depression of the interwar years in the words of both ordinary and well-known people. As a soundman (Terkel had turned to radio after his popular 1950s TV show was cancelled, a blacklisted victim of Senator McCarthy and his goons), he understood that the authentic voice made history come alive. These voices, even if you couldn't actually hear them, created an emotional and very contemporary impact on the reader. In those days, for a student in the United Kingdom, Terkel's radio shows, broadcast out of Chicago, were way out of reach. It was his books alone that did the talking.

In fact, it was the methodology of oral history, a term also invented in the United States after the Second World War (with Studs Terkel, who died in 2008, still being its most famous practitioner), that first attracted me to interviewing and sound recording. During the 1980s a kind of underground culture of grass-roots local history projects began to mushroom throughout the nation. Their preoccupations were based around an urgent need to fill the gap in the way ordinary people and their environments had been documented, not just by the historians, but by almost everyone else too. This desire to recover *stories-before-it's-too-late* appealed to me, and I joined a growing community of oral historians wielding cassette recorders for local museums, community centres and universities. In 1991 I became the Project Officer for the *Lives in Steel* project initiated by the British Library's National Sound Archive. As a born and bred Londoner it was at first a daunting but, eventually, an inspirational experience to be recording the stories of steelworkers in places that I'd never been, or had ever expected to visit. Places like Port Talbot, Scunthorpe, Redcar, Workington or Motherwell. For the interviewees, 'it was good to talk', just like the old BT advert said. There was the satisfaction, also, that the rituals and rigour of their working lives, which often covered many hours of tape, would be secured forever in an important and accessible archive. It was their voices that would, hopefully, serve the historians of the future.

We were using the technology of audio recording, and this defined the working practice of the oral historian (as opposed to just writing down what people tell us), but how could we best utilise the 'effect' of these sounds? The process of disseminating the recorded interviews still begins with transcribing or logging the audio, and then editing extracts for use in publications or for captions in museum displays. On the whole, harnessing the sound of the voice itself was traditionally less commonplace within the culture of oral history.

For me, radio was the answer. Since 1922 when the BBC first began to broadcast across the ether, there has always been a firm demarcation between speech and music radio. The voice was presented, and broadcast, from a very formal studio setting and the speaker usually read from a pre-written script. Apart from the late 1930s when the BBC's experimental *Radio Symphonies* (not unlike Ruttmann's *Weekend*) hinted at something more adventurous, it wasn't until the invention of portable tape recorders, like EMI's not so very small 'The Midget', that new possibilities opened up. In 1958, the first of the *Radio Ballads* produced by Charles Parker was broadcast on the BBC Home Service. Finely crafted sound portraits of the workplace, a community or in a boxing ring were told in the voices of ordinary people accompanied by the clatter of actuality sounds and all woven around folk music (considered more authentic and radical than mainstream pop or jazz). In all there were just eight *Radio Ballads* broadcast over six years, but for many practitioners, these are reverentially referred to as 'Year Zero' of the sound feature.

In the subsequent years, the Radio Feature concept has become an established art form throughout the world, and I'd argue that many have infinitely surpassed the remit and aesthetic of Parker's *Ballads*. Today, cheap and sophisticated equipment is accessible to all, not just the elite. You don't have to be commissioned by a major broadcaster or a recording company to produce your work. Sound trails, podcasts, documentaries and audio clips of all sonic shapes and sizes proliferate on the Web and it is likely that these will have a dramatic impact on the way we navigate, understand and disseminate our environments.

There's no doubt how seductive a business it is to use a microphone to explore a place or a building or a story. I remember well my first ever BBC radio programme. I presented a portrait of the elderly Jewish community of London's East End. The two key interviews took place in a day centre in Stepney and in someone's living room. The key point of the piece was to explore their relationship with both old memories and current experiences of the same environment. The interviews were very powerful, but it was those snippets of sound, the elderly woman blowing the dust off an old photograph of her as a youngster and the noises off-stage at the day centre, that magnified the stories. Another recording, which I used in a later programme, simply captured in sound the journey a blind man had to make to navigate his way from the street to his fourth-floor flat. The acoustic of the corridor, the noise of a moving lift and the change in ambience of entering through the front door draws the listener into his world.

Figure 1 **Units on Fazeley Street, Birmingham, October 2008.**

Since 2008 I have been presenting BBC Radio 4's *Lives in a Landscape*. It's a series of probing and penetrating observations, each under 30 minutes, of how people interact with others in a landscape, whatever it may be: a building, an island, a city or a club. Its narrative is more unconventional than traditional radio documentaries, though it's certainly less avant-garde in its approach than Ruttmann's *Weekend*. In the episode *Five Units on Fazeley Street*, the producer Laurence Grissell and I portrayed a day in the life of businesses housed in an industrial estate in Digbeth, central Birmingham. The everyday, ordinary setting of such places could actually be anywhere. But unlike modern units on the outskirts of town, regeneration is creeping in. It's unlikely that old-fashioned artisans, car cleaners and steel stockists will be required in such quarters for too much longer. The idea was to create a snapshot of the lives that occupy this spot, even the churchgoers who have a unit for prayer and the unit where a rock band practise their chords into the night. The people may disappear and the ramshackle buildings too but, in between the sounds of the steel shutters rising at dawn and closing at dusk, this pro- gramme was a tale of how ordinary people relate to their spaces.

I suspect that the audio trail, a kind of fusion of oral history, a radio feature and a walking tour, has the wonderful potential of fulfilling Ruttmann's quest for that 'new acoustic art … in its effect'. Here, the audio is still the key resource but it's backed up by a combination of maps, illustrations and text. The *Cally Road Sound Map*, co-produced with the *Guardian* in 2010, offers a pdf of a simple map with numbered points marked along the route of North London's Caledonian Road. The audio is a com- pilation of pre-recorded interviews and sounds that trace the life and times of the street through the voices of local people. The listener/viewer can experience the *Sound Map* in several ways. They can download an mp3, visit the location and follow the walk as it appears on the map or, perhaps, listen to it on the computer, skipping back and forth in any direction and thus creating a different narrative. Or, they can stick with the route and our intended sequence of audio and accompanying photographs. Another downloadable project, the *Argyle Square Sound Trail*, designed as a contributing element to the London Architectural Biennale 2006, is also a walking tour, but this time our guides are solely the voices of the interviewees. There's no narration though, like the Cally Road piece, the titles of the tracks are based on snippets of memories: 'we lost a wonderful playground when they built the Town Hall', 'we were all knitting, then I think I must have lost consciousness' or, 'I wouldn't live anywhere else'.

Noises, chatter and canny editing are all components that Walter Ruttmann used in *Weekend*. I think by introducing another element, a close-up and intimate inter- viewing style, drawing the stories out of people, we sound practitioners have finally helped to turn Ruttmann's audio manifesto into a valuable and very contemporary tool for interpreting our times and indeed, our spaces.

> Not only rhythm and dynamics will be exploited by this new audio art's will to reshape, but also the space created by the whole scale of the sound differences arising.
>
> (Walter Ruttmann)

Sound sources

Dein, A. (1991–1993) *Lives in Steel*, London: The British Library.

Dein, A. and Grissell, L. (2008) *Five Units on Fazeley Street, Lives in a Landscape*, BBC.

Dein, A. and Panetta, F. (2010) *The Cally Sound Map*, London: Guardian News and Media. Online, available: www.guardian.co.uk/caledonian-road.

Parker, C. with MacColl, E. and Seeger, P. (1958–1964) *The Radio Ballads*, BBC (reissued by Topic Records).

Ruttmann, W. (1930) *Weekend*, Berlin Radio.

King's Cross Voices (2006) *The Argyle Square Sound Trail*, London: Camden Council. Online, available: www.camden.gov.uk/kingscrossvoices.

Field/work techniques

Introduction

Victoria Clare Bernie

The chapters which constitute 'Field/work techniques' are concerned with the perceived gap between architectural representation and construction, between the office and the building site, the conventions of notation and the seemingly infinite blur of the late modern city. Throughout this section there is a prevailing sense of loss in the face of this disjunction. In that loss, there is a requirement to remember, borrow and invent, to identify techniques and strategies in order to regain ground and restore significance to the embodied experience of the architect in the site. And the site in question has expanded far beyond its more recent classification, as the footprint or the building plot, to comprise the myriad concerns of lived experience: spatial, temporal, historical, cultural and environmental. It is a field of material and immaterial influences and the role of the architect is increasingly acknowledged as that of navigation over construction.

Navigation of the field, fieldwork, is not a recognised discipline within the formal structures of an architectural education. The site itself is deemed to be contingent and, as Mhairi McVicar observes in her chapter 'Contested Fields: perfection and compromise at Caruso St John's Museum of Childhood', the architect is conventionally required to limit any designation of design intention to the documents and notations of formal contracts, finished drawings and design specifications. Being in the site, acting on the ground and in time, the domain of the earliest architectural practitioners, is lost to the late modern architect. Fieldwork as navigation is primarily the preserve of other disciplines, of science and social science. It is here that the discourses of the researcher and the field are fully developed and the disciplinary paradigms of notation, transcription and translation, observation and participation, documentation and invention may serve to provide a critical resource for the more recent convert to field working.

For architecture, the notion of disciplinary borrowing, the practice of gleaning, is an established methodology. To undertake a second harvest from the practices of others is deemed resourceful, wily in the Greek sense of *metis*, and culturally self-conscious. In recent years this practice has lost much of its critical edge, favouring

instead a careless formal borrowing of images and ideas with little recourse to their cultural significance and disciplinary origins. 'Field/Work Techniques' is a sampling from recent fieldwork investigations as a critical response to the hermeneutic, anthropological, ethnographic, archaeological, geographic and artistic impulses that now inform much of the most interesting work undertaken in architectural design and theory. 'Field/Work Techniques' is an attempt to describe an alternative terrain where the nascent tools of architectural field/working are considered in the context of their intellectual and practical origins and celebrated for their generative power.

Arguing for representation as an act of participation, Paul Emmons deploys a hermeneutic leap to a point of potential fracture in the architectural discipline; the advent of paper and the genealogy of the drawing board in fifteenth-century Europe. For Emmons, the maintenance of an analogical relationship is vital. The connection between the action of the architect on the ground and at the drawing board being maintained in the familial link between the levelling of the site and the preparation of a fine cotton paper laid out upon the responsive surface of a soft wood drawing board. Here, the actions of the field – orientation and marking up, inhabitation and invention – are mirrored on the ground and in the image, serving as exemplars for the reconnection of architect and site through the critical act of drawing.

Borrowing from strategies of ethnography, the participant observer and the fieldnote, Carolyn Butterworth and Prue Chiles reconfigure the professional document, the site diary and the finished drawing in the context of an active engagement with the building process. Recognising the disciplinary identification of drawings and notes as the resource for finite decisions and contractual agreements, Butterworth and Chiles describe an alternative model of documentation and engagement. 'Site notes, scratch notes and head notes' recount the immediate, contingent and generative qualities of the site as re-drawings, adaptations, conversions and conversations on the building site with the craftsmen-builders. Here, the autonomous project of constructing a home, of designing in the expanded field of memory, neighbourhood and family, creates a field for participation and observation in the process of design.

The architect's specification, the primary communication between the designed intention and the site is, of necessity, a point of departure for construction. Writing in relation to a lost detail in Caruso St John's addition to the Museum of Childhood in Bethnal Green, London, Mhairi McVicar describes a professional trajectory away from the evolution of the design in the site, to the prevailing logic of design in the studio and construction on the site. It is here that the ambiguity of the site, the thousand unnamed actions of a negotiated building site, are recognised as contributory factors in the evolution of a design beyond the office. The aspiration of perfection and resolution written into the contractual document and the finite drawing is acknowledged as a beginning, an invocation. The site of the design is refigured as the intention of the office and the experience of the site, the precision of the document and the engagement of the craftsman.

Where the opening chapters of this part borrow extensively from the intellectual ground of history and ethnography to reconfigure the discipline and the site, the

later chapters refer specifically to a technical harvest of materials and strategies. Ways of working initially derived from the logics of optical technology and archaeology and subsequently reformed by the practices of film-making and visual art.

Recognising the implications for architectural convention faced with the global city of speed and blur, Krystallia Kamvasinou offers an alternative mode of engagement, of registration, representation and invention, in the form of video technology. Writing in the context of two experimental video works, Kamvasinou describes a finite and an infinite project: a prescribed account of the Stansted Airport train journey as a linear record and a non-linear edit, and an anecdotal sequence of wildshots and outtakes from a documentary study undertaken in Mumbai. Here, a self-conscious borrowing from visual anthropology, documentary film, ethnographic film and video art aspires to a hybrid methodology where video footage might be directed to operate as record, participant, catalyst and generator. In this way, video is deployed as a form of drawing, an embodied experience and a mediated account. It becomes a critical device, able to operate creatively in the field, identifying and acknowledging objects and events lost to the naked eye, and in the studio, as a resource for the spatial and narrative reconfiguration of a recently designated urban condition.

In 'Blighted', an account of a singular project in an apparently empty lot in North St Louis, Igor Marjanović and Lindsey Stouffer describe an archaeology of the present as a critical unpacking of the seemingly degraded ground of a post-industrial city. Documenting, digging, collecting and collating, borrowing from the formal logics of archaeology, forensic science and conceptual art, the site is reconfigured as a field of objects, of finds, initially deemed to be unrelated but over time, through examination, re-housing, casting and recovery, recognised as vitally connected. Divorced from the site of origin, isolated, cast and drawn, the objects of the site are locked into the familiar logic of the nineteenth-century taxonomy, only to fall victim to the early-twentieth-century fate of collage. The artistic practice of cut and paste creating the ground for invention, for the realisation of architectural forms able to recognise the memory of the site beyond its formal limits; to acknowledge the often silent histories of the urban development project.

Drawing sites : : Site drawings

Paul Emmons

The beginning of modern architectural practice is often traced to the fifteenth century when, following the introduction of paper to the west, architects left the construction site to work at drawing boards remote from building activity (Frascari 2007). In this book's title, the virgule slashing between 'field' and 'work' exemplifies the bifurcated condition between field construction and design work (Parkes 1993). This cleaving, which both joins and separates, is the chiasmus that occurs between the constructions of an architect at a drawing board and those at the building site. Current practice assumes that architectural drawings are created with marks conveying information by arbitrary conventions. However, examining the origins of site drawings shows them to be an index of construction, which allows architects to use drawing to imaginatively project themselves into building. This study reveals three levels of the relationship between field/work and site/drawing: the literal drawing on the site, the analogical site on the drawing and the anagogical drawing beyond the site (Gadamer 1989).

Drawing on site

Plots and plans

Since early in the ancient world, plans of buildings were meaningfully inscribed on the earth through stretching cords and driving pegs into the ground (Rossi 2004). The construction of sacred altars following these practices in India has been identified as the 'ritual origin of Greek geometry' (Seidenberg 1963). The architect worked on site so that drawings of design, full-scale details, layouts on site and the marking of stones for carving were all closely interconnected activities (Wu 2002).

Vitruvius's first-century BCE use of the word *ichnographia* for plans – literally 'foot-marks' – emphasizes that this earlier notion of plan is not the current Cartesian idea of a horizontal section, rather a weighty footprint that is impressed into the earth (Vitruvius 1999: I.II.1). While uncertain, many believe Vitruvius was describing the full-scale marking of the earth on the construction site with the word *ichnographia*. Cesare Cesariano, Milanese architect and the first to prepare a translation and commentary of Vitruvius published in 1521, equates *ichnographia* with the Latin word *vestigium* or 'vestige' – a word Vitruvius uses to describe the footprints of philosopher Aristippus and the geometrical tracings he found on the sandy beach of Rhodes after a shipwreck (Cesariano 1521: I.XIIIv). In this way, the footprint is joined with the geometrical drawing, both of which provide a sign of human presence. Cesariano clearly included site marking as part of his understanding of *ichnographia*, describing the practice of laying out the site by using stakes and ropes, drawing on site in dirt and plaster and walking a snowy site to mark out the future building's plan (Krinsky 1965: 100).

Heaven-sent plans

Cesariano's description of plans as footprints in the snow directly recalls the foundation legend of Santa Maria Maggiore, known as the 'Miracle of the Snow'. Reportedly, during the August heat in Rome in the fourth century, one night the Virgin Mary visited the Pope in a dream asking him to build a church for her where the snow falls. The next morning, upon finding the miraculous snow, Pope Liberious used a hoe to inscribe the plan of the future church into the ground (Strehlke 1987). Masolino's painting of the event (*c.*1428–1432) shows Mary with Christ reaching down, out of the circular clipeus of heaven, to explain divine action in casting snow down to earth. Otherwise painted in tempera, the snow is in oil, used perhaps for the first time south of the Alps, with bold strokes thickly applying the pigment to render a soft, luminous layer of snow with an otherworldly presence (Bellucci 2002: 60).

Numerous medieval religious structures have foundation legends of miraculously outlined plans in snow or frost, often by the footprints of a large beast such as a deer, bear or bull, as proof of the divine origin of the plan (Remensnyder 1995). This circumambulation to describe a plan parallels the ritual consecration of shrines, and defines it as an area set off from the mundane world (Durand 2007: 62). One divinely directed plan was said to be created by an angel drawing a reed through the dew on the ground. An eleventh-century miniature shows the angel's staff extending down from heaven to draw out the ground plan with the future building pictured beyond (Carty 1999: 50). Like architectural drawings, miraculous plans begin to make present an immaterial image, as a meeting place between the visible and the invisible.

Drawing in dirt

Stories of divinely drawn plans probably reflect the actual practices of inscribing full-scale plans on construction sites. For example, the founding legends of the Zurich Fraumünster tell of a stag with flaming antlers leading the founders to the site and later a rope stretched by angels was sent from Heaven to mark the bounds of the building. The rope was preserved in a chest near the high altar until the Reformation (Abegg 2005: 7). The pulling of ropes was commonly used to outline a plan onto the ground

Figure 1 **Conversion of St. Eustace. Athanasius Kircher,** *Latium* **(1671: 186).**

prior to building. As Cesariano compared drawing a plan on paper to outlining the building on site in dust or plaster, so Alberti notes that among the ancients 'it was customary to mark out the line of the intended wall with a trail of powdered white earth' (Alberti 1988: 101). In the Middle East, plans were first drawn on a gridded board in scale and subsequently measured out onto the ground and drawn with plaster or whitewash (Necipoglu-Kafadar 1986: 231). In 401, the architect of Antioch used gypsum to mark out the 'holy church according to the form of the plan' (Creswell 1969: 110). These sort of practices joined practical with ritual significance. When Alexander founded the city of Faro, he directed that flour be used to lay out the plan on the ground, allowing diviners to interpret the future of the city based upon if birds were attracted by the edible plan, which, they concluded, 'foreshadowed that the city would abound in provisions' (Alberti 1988: 381). Perhaps the most vivid example of drawing a plan on the earth at full size was in 762 for the new cosmological circular city of Baghdad. The plan was traced upon the ground with lines of ashes and cotton seeds soaked in naphtha. Then the caliph Al-Mansur entered the city plan through each of its four gates at the cardinal points in turn and, as he reached the location of his future palace at the very center, ordered that the lines be set on fire in order to enable him to see the three-dimensional form of the city (Al-Tabari 1995: 246). The plan on site, elevated into volume by flames, was literally inhabited by the patron. These sorts of ritual layouts of plans in the field inspired later drawing practices.

Site as drawing

Drawing board as site

Direct marking on the site was complemented by scaled drawn architectural plans. The Roman architect Frontinus described plans (*formas*) of aqueducts that could 'have the works before one's eyes, so to speak, at a moment's notice, to consider them as though standing by their side' (Frontinus 1961: 359). This intimacy between the architect's body and the drawn image reinforces the close imaginative relation between earthen plot and drawn plan. In addition to understanding Vitruvius's description of *ichnographia* as full-size site marking, others posit it as scale drawing. Perhaps the ambiguity itself is its clearest meaning – that *ichnographia* cleaves both plot and plan. Cesariano clearly wrote that *ichnographia* includes both markings on site and drawings on paper by comparing the architect walking the compass legs on paper to the architect physically walking the plan on site.

When design drawing first moved off-site, a deep analogical relationship to field construction was maintained. The Florentine architect Antonio Averlino, known as Filarete, wrote in his fifteenth-century treatise: 'As it is necessary to have a site in order to build and to dig the foundations, so too we will first make the site in which we wish to make our drawing' (Averlino 1965: 177r). Leveling the site to prepare for construction is reflected in the preparation of the surface for drawing (Leatherbarrow 2004). Renaissance cotton-fiber paper had an uneven surface that first required flattening by rubbing it with bone or pumice and, like laying gravel for a foundation, benefited from a preliminary dusting 'with a hare's foot' of 'powdered' bone, just as Cesariano wrote of sites (Cennini 1954: 6). This sort of practice continued into the first half of the twentieth century, when drafters prepared tracing linen with powdered chalk (Spiers 1888: 13).

The geometrical drawing of lines on paper is directly analogous to drawing ropes on site. Stretched ropes with knotted measures on stakes at the building perimeter became 'strings' of dimension lines on drawings. Foundation rites related to cutting the earth for building walls are paralleled by drafting practices where stylus-made 'dead lines' incise the paper prior to laying down ink onto the grooves. Drawn vertical lines are equated with construction plumb lines and horizontal lines with levels (Bion 1972: 1). These sorts of similarities are so close and the language between the two almost identical, making distinguishing them sometimes problematic. Geometrical drawing instruments originate in construction tools. The T-square and drawing triangle derive from worksite squares (Shelby 1965). Showing the interrelation of drawing and site tools, Cesariano recommended 'a compass, ruler (*regula*), plumbline, level and measures or squares (*normae*)' for making plans (Cesariano 1521: I.XIIIv).

The drawing table

A key element to flesh out the link between field and work is the architectural drawing table as a building site. From the Latin *tabula* for a flat board, 'table' meant only the top separate from supporting legs (Gloag 1966). In addition to drawing on tracing house

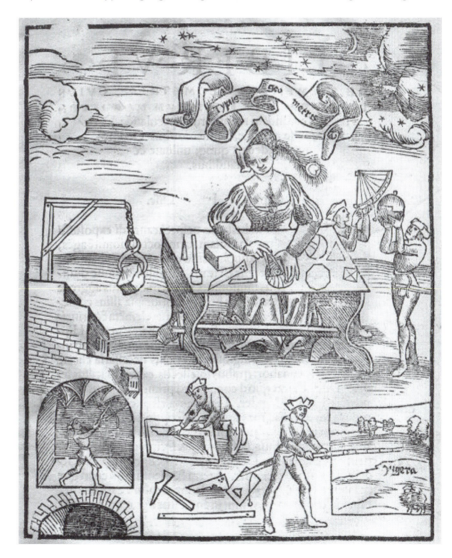

Figure 2 **Typus Geometrie. Gregor Reisch, Margarita philosophica (Basel, 1517 [1504]). Frontispiece Bk. VI, Geometry.**

floors, medieval master masons used a trestle table in their lodges for making drawings and templates (Coldstream 1991: 31). The modern beginnings of the architectural drawing board is the Renaissance library table where the orthography of writing and drawing took place in the study, demonstrating in practice the claim made in Renaissance treatises that architecture is a liberal art. The scholar's table provides the broad, flat surface most amenable to the instrumented geometrical drawing of designers and diviners. The desk, appearing in the fifteenth and sixteenth centuries, began as a portable wooden box to hold writing materials and, when set on a flat table, its slightly angled top was used as a writing surface. Later, like the table, the desk box began to be attached to a frame as a standing desk. Modern drafting tables developed from eighteenth-century mechanical writing desks with adjustable tops (Morley 1999: 277).

Union of horizontal surfaces

The table's planar origins are reflected in the almost interchangeable use of the phrase 'drawing board' with 'drawing table'. Through the drawing board, the table unites with drawing surface to become the site of the drawing. That twentieth-century handbooks advise soft wood for drawing boards because of the way it allows paper to receive pencil and ink shows that the architect's drawing surface is not merely a neutral 'support' awaiting the appearance of meaningful marks (French 1947: 7). The drawing sheet is an active participant that already presents itself as propitious, or, as Li Yang-ping, a mid-eighth-century Chinese calligrapher wrote, it is 'generative paper' in that even when unmarked, it is not empty because fine paper is 'endowed with life like fertile soil' (Hay 1985: 98). Beneath the final drawing surface a multiplicity of planes participate together. In the twentieth century, an underlayment of linoleum or sheet vinyl on the board made a floor for the drawing. This multiplication of horizontal surfaces imparts sacredness to the altar-like drawing board. The presence of many horizontal levels also reinforces the drawing's connection to the world by merging the levels of paper, board, floor, site and ultimately the horizon of the world.

Modern handbooks emphasize the importance of aligning the drawing sheet with the drawing board. In various ways, architects have been admonished for hundreds of years to carefully fix the paper to the table. In 1660, Sir Roger Pratt described 'the manner of designing' as beginning with paper 'laid upon some most smooth table, firmly stretched out, and so fastened to it at each corner, as it can no ways be apt to be moved' (Gunther 1972: 21). The ritual of anchoring drawing paper was achieved over time variously by weights, wax, tacks, glue, staples and tape. The unity of paper and drawing board is so complete that at least since the sixteenth century, the drawing board provided the horizon of the paper by using a T-square against its edge to draft lines (Dickenson 1949–1951). The frontispiece of Andrea Pozzo's 1693 treatise states in part: 'on the Table [*tavola*] exactly squared fix the Paper and having a cross-stock serves as a square by the application of which Stock to the Sides of the Table, you draw' (Pozzo 1989: 13). The T-square and, more recently, the parallel rule entirely unify table, board and paper into a singular construction system. The paper is square with the table, the table square with the window wall to light the working surface, the building square with the cardinal directions and thereby orienting the entire endeavor with the world's horizon. In this way, the paper is fixed to the earth and projectively cleaves together drawing and building site.

It is not an accident that architectural drawing boards are almost exclusively horizontal with only a slight pitch to acknowledge the presence of the drafter's body (Neufert 1936: 168). The plan's priority in architecture and its horizontality ensures the orientation of the architect to the board like that of the site and makes both locations a process of building up an edifice. The horizontal site of the drawing as an analog to the earth invites designers to project their imaginal bodies onto the drawing *as if* actually on site.

Figure 3
Frontispiece. Andrea Pozzo, *Perspective in Architecture and Painting* (1707 [1693]).

Rituals of drawing lines

Drawing the invisible

Cesariano concludes his discussion of Vitruvian *ichnographia* by comparing tracing a building plan to the mythical founder of Rome, Romulus, using a magical staff (*lituus*) to trace the templum of its foundation. Derived from Etruscan rites, a templum or cross of the sky was projected onto the earth to inaugurate a human abode and, by reading the signs disclosed within it such as the flight of birds, ensured that it is amenable to the gods. The spatiality of the human body known through front/back and left/right was oriented with the four cardinal directions of world space: north/south and east/west (Rykwert 1976: 45). Ancient Roman augurs marked out the quadripartite division of the heavens onto the ground, the templum, with the *lituus*. As Marco Frascari (Frascari 2007: 9) has written, for Cesariano, architect/diviners took mental journeys across the image on the paper with the compass legs as the *lituus* staff.

Renaissance site layout practices began with pulling two ropes that bisect the site at right angles to each other to form a cross, not unlike the ancient Roman augurs. Alberti explained:

> Our usual method of defining the foundations is to trace out ... baselines in the following manner. From a midpoint at the front, we extend a straight line to the back of the work; halfway along it we fix a stake into the ground, and through this, following the rules of geometry, we extend the perpendicular. Then we relate all measurements to these two lines.
>
> (Alberti 1988: 62)

This same method of beginning with quadrature occurred in Renaissance drawing. The uneven deckled edges of handmade paper sheets precluded starting from the edge. As Vincenzo Scamozzi wrote in his 1615 treatise: 'we first square up (*quadrato*) the sheet of paper tracing right angle lines lengthwise and widthwise' (Scamozzi 1615: 46). This was a precise analogous relation between physical ropes in the field and drawn lines at the table.

This procedure operates anagogically as the third level of relation between field and work by leading the architect to manifest the invisible within the visible. The drawing of lines, whether ink on paper or rope on site, are not only practical, they also form part of the ritual of architectural creation. Drawing rites consecrate place on paper by inviting the architect to imaginatively inhabit the drawing. In this way, the plan is not an object viewed at a distance or an abstract horizontal section, but a place that the architect's body imaginatively moves within. This is why, when birthing a design, the building's main entrance is almost always at the bottom of the sheet, closest to the belly of the architect. By orienting one's physical body with the drawing, the architect imaginatively steps into the site of the plan and establishes greater meaning in the work itself.

Levels of meaning

The sixteenth-century French architect Philibert de l'Orme not only followed these practices but also theorized them in his 1567 *Premier Tome de l'Architecture.* De l'Orme, emphasizing the importance of drawings and models, described the architect as a specialist in precognition (*précogiter*) or forecasting (Schneider 2008). After describing how the architect creates drawings and models, he discusses a diagram showing three crosses. Regarding the first cross, de l'Orme writes that the work on the drawing as well as on the construction site should begin with the same quadrature described earlier:

Figure 4
Squaring the site:
Diagram of three
crosses, Philibert de
l'Orme, ***Premier tome***
de l'architecture
(1567).

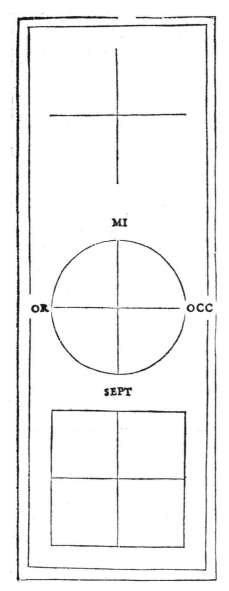

> We say that Architects and Master Masons are not to start a good work, or
> to make a plan as they wish, or models, or to begin tracing and marking the
> foundations, if they do not first draw a straight line, and another perpendicular,
> to 'trace the square' (as the workmen call it).
>
> (de l'Orme 1567: 31v)

This lowest cross in the diagram is shown in a square emphasizing the literal presence of the building site and in a larger sense the fixity of the earth as a square. In addition to describing quadrature as the practical beginning of drawing and building, he next connects this act to the spiritual order of the world in the squaring of the heavens in the second cross of the diagram. They relate, like Romulus's ancient divination, to the cardinal directions and he extends it to the heavenly order of planetary alignments with the earth. De l'Orme cites Marsilio Ficino's neoplatonic philosophy where the astrological influences on the mundane world are focused by the powerful alignment of planets with the lines of the cross, concluding: 'When the stars are at the extremes of the cross of the world, ... they have miraculous and incredible effects [below on the earth]' (de l'Orme 1567: 32v). This statement implies both that a well designed building can bestow celestial powers onto its occupants and that the astrological timing of foundation rituals is crucial. Centered in the diagram, this cross is in a circle to represent the heavenly order and the four winds identifying the four cardinal directions to locate it in the cosmos. Third and finally, he compares the crosses of the building and the world with the heavenly cross of Christ as 'the figure of life and salvation'. Unusual for this time, de l'Orme extends this transcendental relation comparatively across religions asserting the crosses' use also among 'Arabs' and the 'ancient Egyptians' (de l'Orme 1567: 32v). This uppermost cross in the diagram has no other markings and does not take on the form of a Christian cross but instead continues the Greek cross of the two figures below it. The diagram, although composed of minimal lines, organizes a hierarchy of three levels of existence: physical (earth), spiritual (heavens) and transcendent (divine) and suggests through their close similarity the possibility of movement between them. In this way, the ordinary activity of construction through the design drawings of the architect is raised up to a presencing of the spiritual and ultimately the invisible. According to de l'Orme, the right angle of the architect's drawing derives its ultimate authority from the cross of the divine architect (de l'Orme 1567: 2r). Restating this in more modern language, the architect's drawing rituals at the board invite the thinking through of relationships to building on site, relating to the horizons of the greater world, and even to infusing profound meaningfulness.

Through the cleaving of field and work described above, the practices of design in the construction of a plan appear at all three levels: literal, analogous and anagogical. By these acts, subtle speculation is incarnated and theory and practice are connected by the substantial uses which arise from bare contemplation. Architectural drawings are not merely conventional signifiers, they are meaningful manifestations meeting at the intersection of the real and the possible.

Field diaries

Prue Chiles and Carolyn Butterworth

In the squeaky-clean world of the architectural journals the new house is described by a particular sort of building study giving a critical view of formal, technical and material approaches and setting these within the context of other buildings. This information is then summarised in terms of the key roles, cost and contract. The user rarely features either in the text or in the photographs. The house is presented finished, immaculate and empty.

For an architect, to design and build their own house holds a particular attraction, and a particular anxiety. Freed from an external client we relish the chance to pursue our own design ambitions without interference. But, of course, that degree of freedom can leave you feeling exposed, open to the scrutiny of your peers and with no client to hide behind and blame for any mistakes or compromises. For an architect to build their own house is seen as both an indulgence and a risk.

We are both architects and we have both recently designed and built our own houses and it is fair to say that it was the professional context of building that was uppermost in our minds when we embarked upon the process. We were fully aware of the weight that the architect's own house carries in historical and contemporary architectural discourse. When an architect's body of work is assessed it is their own house that is often supposed to be the purest embodiment of their design principles, the material manifestation of the author's will. It's a daunting journey to embark on ... but embark on it we did and very quickly the *actual* site experience of building our own homes became the most memorable part of the process for us and so the subject of this chapter. We began our projects at different times, with different-sized sites and scopes of work and we have used dialogue in this chapter to accentuate the differences and similarities in our attitudes to the processes of building.

In the day-to-day process of design and construction any thoughts of purity very quickly became subsumed by much more mundane concerns. We may not have had external clients but we had partners and children who came with their own expectations and demands and our relationships with builders and neighbours was complicated. Mistakes and compromises occurred as is invariably the case in all projects, but it was our personal involvement with these particular projects that made the contingencies of site far more acute for us and placed us at the heart of a set of relationships and processes that became an *expanded field* for us beyond the conventional notion of *site*.

Site/field

For us, building our own homes changed the notion of site into an expanded field of exploration. The normative definition of site in the architectural design and construction process is the physical location for the building. But, as architecture becomes increasingly affected by recent discourses in contemporary art practice it becomes possible 'to conceive the site as something more than a place' (Kwon 2002: 30) and to recognise 'the multiple expansions of the site in locational and conceptual terms' (Kwon 2002: 30). James Meyer describes this expanded site as 'a process, an operation occurring between sites, a mapping of institutional and discursive filiations and the bodies that move them' (Kwon 2002: 29). Here Meyer was recognising a shift in the nature of the site of contemporary site-specific art practice but we see parallels between this and contemporary architectural discourse. Specifically we see this shift as relevant to the building of our own homes where the expanded site of multiple and layered accumulations of physical locations, relationships, bodies and texts compound into what we define as our architectural *field* of operation. It is this field that then becomes a focus of reflection for our practice, our teaching and our research.

Site diaries/field diaries

As *field* expands out from the normative notion of *site* so its recording should move beyond the conventional way in which site is recorded.

The site is recorded by the site diary; an account of the day-to-day discussions, arguments and decisions taken on site. The site diary is concerned with contractual and professional issues and is the raw material from which the Architect's Instruction and the formal letter springs. It is seen to have no intrinsic value in itself and disappears into the archive once construction is completed to re-emerge only in the event of a dispute or claim. We too have numerous site diaries mouldering on our shelves from previous jobs but we both feel a resistance to consigning the site diaries of the process of building our own homes to the same fate. We see our site diaries as part of a larger accumulation of recordings that were collected to form a description of our expanded sites and we consider the sum total of this material to be our *field diaries*.

This chapter is our first attempt to explain and validate this accumulated material. What light can a ragbag of notes, to-do lists, sketches and photographs shed on the building process? How can our field diaries illuminate new ways of working?

Sitework/fieldwork

All architects work differently and this chapter has made us look at our colliding processes, our similarities and our differences. To narrow the scope of reflection we have confined our comparison of notes to work that took place on site rather than including notes relating to the earlier design process. In part, this decision derives from a concern with the undervalued nature of site work in comparison with the well-researched processes of design, but primarily, it stems from our shared fascination with the parallels between the *field* of making and the anthropological context of *fieldwork*.

In *The Return of the Real*, Hal Foster talks about the contemporary role of 'artist as ethnographer' (1996: 172) where 'artists and critics aspire to fieldwork in which theory and practice seem to be reconciled' (1996: 181). For Foster, ethnography offers 'fieldwork in the everyday' (1996: 182). As architects, trying to explore beyond the normative site, we find the framework of ethnography intriguing as a model to collect and reflect on the everyday processes of making.

We consider our field diaries as artefacts that take advantage of the self-critique and reflexivity that Hal Foster describes as inherent to anthropology. Working as participant observers, scratching beneath the surface of professional protocols and the RIBA stages of work we wish to investigate how being *on site* with your own home differs from any other project and how those differences can impact upon future work.

Site notes/field notes

In *Fieldnotes*, Roger Sanjek describes different ways of recording information and their meaning. Within our projects, field notes include site notes, scratch notes and head notes. Field notes tell us about the anthropological enterprise, how it attempts to work against the divide between science and the humanities, how it distinguishes itself from its sister disciplines, how it creates its own justification and reward for good work. Field notes are 'of the field'. They 'symbolise what journeying to and returning from the field mean to us: the attachment, the identification, the mystique and perhaps above all the ambivalence' (Sanjek 1990: 95). Sanjek argues that, for anthropologists, field notes represent an individualistic, pioneering approach to acquiring knowledge, at times maverick and rebellious. Field notes simultaneously reflect and create the field, forging a connection between the field and the participant observer. In this we can see parallels between the field note and the architect's sketch where both map the development of a relationship between the practitioner and the field.

Traditionally *site notes* are the more formal architect's recording of physical matters, problems, timings and contractual issues. When there is a contract in place they tend to be seen as legal documents and can be vital in any claim from either the client or the contractor. Without a contract site notes record the process of the project. They are anecdotal and essentially more relaxed.

We interpreted *scratch notes* as words or phrases recorded to fix an observation or to recall what someone has just said. They can be surreptitious or they can be public. They can interfere with the process of observation and dialogue but, for the architect, they can also solve problems. 'Scratch notes are sometimes produced in the view of informants, while observing or talking with them and sometimes out of sight' (Sanjek 1990: 93). The production of marks on walls or on paper, often in discussion with the builder or just after, appear quickly and informally. Scratch notes for anthropologists are a reminder, pointers to future investigation and clues to a way forward. Equally, an architect's scratch notes can be instrumental in working through solutions and making practical decisions on site.

In anthropology the phrase 'I am a field note' captures the close identification between participant observer and field. This is illustrated most clearly in the notion of *head notes*, i.e. field notes that are not yet fixed, that remain fluid. 'Head notes' is:

> a felicitous term [that] identifies something immediately understandable to ethnographers. We come back from the field with field notes and head notes. The field notes stay the same, written down [or drawn] but the head notes continue to evolve and change during the time in the field.
>
> (Sanjek 1990: 144)

Site drawings/field drawings

This multiple notion of *field notes* becomes useful as a way to analyse how our drawings changed as we moved from *site* and into the *field*. The first drawings on site are the formal construction drawings that have developed out of the design process. These drawings fulfil a specific contractual function but Lefebvre recognises that they also serve to represent a conceived space that the architect wants to believe is *true*. There is an optimistic determinism at work in the production of these drawings. The architect is seemingly oblivious to the problems, mistakes and contingencies that are bound to lead to changes to the design along the way.

CAROLYN: Lefebvre says that 'the architect ensconces himself' (Lefebvre 1991: 361) as if the drawing becomes a place to nestle, to settle securely in the comfort of a design that is true. There is an emotional attachment suggested here that I recognise in my own attitude towards my design drawings. The gestation of my house had taken so long, four years in fact, to get to the point where we were able to start construction that the drawings I had produced had become like talismans to me and I was well-ensconced in them.

PRUE: My house had also been in my head before any drawings had been done because I lived there; each part evolving and changing. But I too was enormously reassured when the drawings were complete. The design was finally done; the project was in the world, a tangible reality.

CAROLYN: Maybe architects place greater significance on drawings than perhaps is appropriate or useful on site. My builder Ryley Wing, not being personally involved in the project, had a very different attitude to the drawings and saw them purely as tools to build by. To him the drawings were unfinished and incomplete. During the tender negotiations with the builder the drawings took central stage and they were scrutinised for information to finalise costs, programme and contract details. Once on site, however, the role of the drawings seemed much more marginal – many drawings were hardly glanced at and stayed in the site hut accumulating tea rings and biscuit crumbs. The more useful drawings were taken out on site and used, but they were also torn, trodden on and left out in the rain. One drawing got so wet that it glued itself to a roof beam and is still there now, in the depths of the construction. At the time this upset me – how could my house be built as my drawings intended if they were falling apart in front of me?

PRUE: I had a different view of drawings: the design was more in my head; maybe I felt the formal drawings were less personal, less mine. To me dirty drawings were well-used and hence beautiful drawings. Talking to our builder Reg about his attitude to our drawings was surprising – maybe he too was looking with rose-tinted glasses but it struck me as true. First, on dirty drawings he reminded me that some of the drawings remain clean while others are filthy in the same set. If we haven't got to them yet, they remain pristine. 'We try our best to keep them all clean but it is inevitable they will get dirty. Sometimes we hide clean drawings – you will know we haven't looked at them!'

I told him I loved it when they got dirty and scribbled on – 'it looks like you have used them, pored over them, valued them.'

He thinks our drawings have improved over the years and assured me they could not do without any of them. 'You can see the finished article, see what you are aiming for the finished product – this isn't always the case with architects' drawings.'

CAROLYN: However, as my drawings fell apart I was learning to trust Ryley and beginning to understand that despite his lack of care for my drawings he cared very much for the idea of the house that he was making.

We began to work things out on site together, to develop details on the basis of what was happening right in front of us. Initially I would sketch a drawing in my note book and once happy with it give him a copy but then I noticed how often he would communicate with the others on site by sketching on anything to hand; a block, a timber stud, a scaffolding board (Figure 1). We shifted our discussion from my drawing on site to both of us drawing on the site. With these visual scratch notes, we identified a problem, explored options and agreed on a resolution within minutes using marker pen and the building itself (Figure 2).

PRUE: Making drawings together became my favoured way to work too, quick and precise and I felt like I was immediately involved in the making (Figure 3). Then Reg or Scot wrote on the sketches, changing them, and did their own rival drawings. Looking at these drawings again, as inelegant as they are, they mean

Figure 1 One of builder Ryley's messages to the bricklayer, a scratch note.

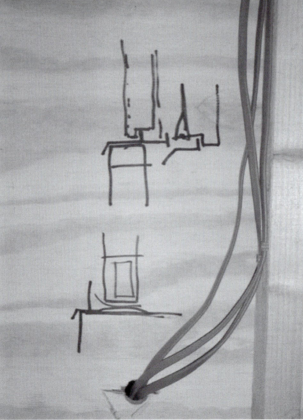

Figure 2 A scratch note on the wall of the house, done in conversation between Ryley and Carolyn.

Figure 3
Additional information for the front door drawn by Prue, dimensioned by the builder, trodden on by everyone.

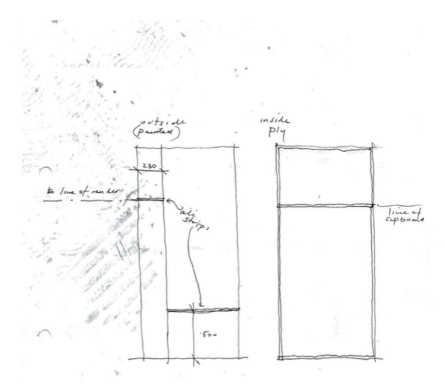

more to me and have memories of difficult decision-making. Once, the builders threatened: 'if you do not put the colour references on the drawings in the next half an hour we will choose the colours.' And another time 'well, we can build that dimension but I don't recommend it...' as they scratched out a dimension for a more sensible mutually agreed one.

CAROLYN: Very often Ryley and I would look at a CAD detail I had drawn previously and then redraw it on a wall while talking it through. Transferring it onto the building itself was a collaborative act that recognised a joint authorship and mutual trust. This placed these scratch notes firmly in the field rather than merely on site, affected by the weather, time pressures, our shifting relationship and the building site's physicality.

My sketchbooks are now shelved and mostly forgotten. My construction drawings now seem so removed from the actual process of building the house that I rarely look at them. It is the scratch notes, the marks on the building itself, that I find myself returning to frequently to remember the process of making that I enjoyed so much. These scratch notes are now embedded in the fabric of the house and can only now be seen as photographs but those images convey the actual experience of making the house in all its messiness, collaboration and craft...

The result of this process for both of us is a desire to encourage a closer more negotiated relationship with builders in future projects.

Construction and craft

The builders, as craftsmen, helped us conduct 'a dialogue between concrete practices and thinking; this dialogue evolves into sustaining habits, and these habits establish a rhythm between problem solving and problem finding' (Sennett 2008: 9). Richard Sennett describes good craftsmanship as 'the higher stages of skill where there is a constant interplay between tacit knowledge and self-conscious awareness, the tacit knowledge serving as an anchor, the explicit awareness serving as a critique and a corrective' (Sennett 2008: 50).

PRUE: The most collaborative parts of the project were those not drawn formally by Howard in my office; the bits round the edges – the kitchen, the balustrade, the external works. I recorded a conversation with Reg Wainwright, our builder who I have known for over 15 years, which confirms to me his attitude to craft:

> REG: When we look at your drawings we can see some parts are crucial and others can be sacrificed.
> PRUE: What does sacrificed mean?
> REG: Well, we might have to think of another way to do it to get the effect you want. We find the bits in the drawings that are most important to us so it is apparent where we are going. I am so experienced now Prue I know where I can make a slight modification and make it better without you noticing, i.e. the timber section.
> PRUE: But that is the bit I always notice – if a builder chamfers an edge or puts a chunkier element in.
> REG: Yes I know that, but I'm talking at a much more subtle level than that, – I'm really good at hiding it. Sometimes we take the impractical suggestions you make and work out how to do it and I find that very rewarding. That is craftsmanship.
> PRUE: Absolutely.
> REG: However, I remember your optimism – I remember the 'just do that, I'm sure it will work out'. We prefer to think before we do something so we only have to do it once. You just charge in with an idea.

CAROLYN: Unlike Prue, I hadn't worked with my builder before and although I knew he had years of experience in construction I hadn't anticipated the level of craftsmanship he would bring to the making of my house. We worked well as a team, our previous experience grounding our discussions in tacit knowledge while both offering critiques that came from a clear appreciation of that site, my family and what I wanted for our home.

Craft and memory

PRUE: Unlike Carolyn, I was dealing with joining on to an old building we had already lived in for years. This was the most difficult part of the building for both the architect and the builder. This involved nostalgic memories of previous conservatories and the memory of my son's first bedroom – now non-existent. The builders did this with a restrained confidence of giving something back to the building – not just taking away. They just made good or left the marks of what had been there before. They were recovering and maintaining history. They were adhering to the 'slow home' (Kannicke 2010) philosophy. Worried initially that this would look a mess, I just accepted it, I needed the builder's reassurance on this and they were right. History was being appropriated through careful crafted manual work.

So craft is, then, distinguished through careful, planned, intelligent thought processes. An anthropologist may say the craft process in this instance is the transformation of an idea into a drawing and then the performance of that drawing into something else. So the process is something of a translation, first of ideas onto paper and then off the paper into action leading to the production of a building. This has parallels with other processes too, such as the playwright developing an idea into a script and the actors and director translating it into a performance. Understanding the building process as a series of translations from one medium to another via collaboration and dialogue with the builder has helped us to unpick our experiences of building our own homes. The notion of field notes has given us a framework by which to pull apart the stages of recording and creation that interweave to form not only the architecture but also the relationships that surround it.

Endnotes

We have both found the experience of building houses for ourselves vastly different from building anything else. Not, as we first thought, because of the heightened expectations and pressure of being scrutinised by our peers but because of the sheer intensity of the process. Through building our own houses we have made the very idea of home tangible, simultaneously mapping existing narratives of family, self and home while creating new ones.

Years later, lying in bed looking at the bedroom door, you also remember the original jamb detail, the conversations about it on site and the sketch buried behind the plasterboard where you and the builder agreed to change it.

And this layering of memories continues because we are constantly in the process of making field notes about our houses; this chapter is one more layer. What started as an image in our heads and became, through a series of translations, first drawings, then a construction site, then a home, continues to shift and change. We are now living inside our fieldwork, still making field notes.

Acknowledgement

We would like to thank Dr Simone Abram (Leeds Metropolitan University) who focused us and added to our interpretation with a keen anthropologist's eye.

Contested fields

Perfection and compromise at Caruso St John's Museum of Childhood

Mhairi McVicar

The constructed work of Caruso St John Architects is shaped by precise control; in a recent interview, partner Peter St John defined a good architect as one who makes fewer compromises (St John 2009). In contemporary architectural practice, architects are professionally advised to avoid compromise by quantitatively defining all aspects of a project prior to construction. Yet as any architectural project progresses from the precise predictions of the office to the inherent ambiguity of the field, it is inevitably subject to compromise. Following the progress of one detail from concept to construction, this chapter examines what even the most seemingly inconsequential of details – in this case, a 25-mm offset in a brick façade above Caruso St John's 2006 Museum of Childhood entrance addition – reveals about contestations between perfection and compromise in the field.

Caruso St John and the Museum of Childhood

Caruso St John Architects' 2006 entrance addition to the Victoria and Albert Museum of Childhood in Bethnal Green, London is predicated upon concepts of precision. A 'simple

Figure 1 **West elevation drawing of Caruso St John Architects' 2006 entrance addition to the V&A Museum of Childhood, Bethnal Green, London.**

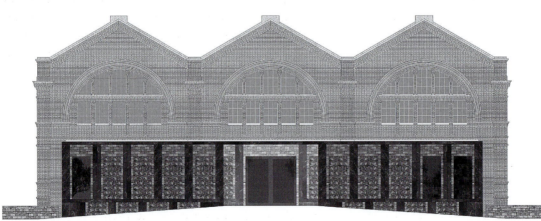

yet intense' box (St John 2009), wrapped in a meticulously detailed patterned stone skin, sits cleanly in front of an ornate brick façade designed by the architect J.W. Wild in 1868–1872. Wild's original proposals for the museum façade included an expansive entrance colonnade which, due to cost constraints, was never built. A much reduced utilitarian entrance was instead constructed, but was criticized as failing to appropriately convey the significance of the museum to its Bethnal Green context and beyond (Caruso St John 2004a: 6; Baxter 2004: 14; Physick 1982: 145). In 2002, Caruso St John began a master plan to renovate the museum, of which phase two proposed a new entrance addition. This entrance addition was charged with the task of creating an appropriately impressive façade, one which would connote the significance of the museum.

Early conceptual sketches from Caruso St John culminated in a simple box form, evoking the patterning and tones of Wild's façade and inlaid decorative mosaics, but reinterpreting Wild's nineteenth-century hand-laid brickwork by specifying CNC (computer numerical controlled) cutting processes to achieve a taut, richly patterned two-dimensional skin of precisely cut stone panels. 'In the nineteenth century', a Caruso St John design report outlined,

> such decoration was carried out by hand. With the rise of industrialized processes in the building crafts, so decoration became prohibitively expensive. However, with recent advances in computer controlled stone cutting it is again possible to achieve complex decorations at an affordable price.
>
> (Caruso St John 2004b: 12)

Caruso St John's early proposals envisaged an assembly of prefabricated non-loadbearing honeycomb panels; an off-site system which promised extremely precise, consistent and predictable tolerances throughout the project, allowing for very fine joints, 'like marquetry' (Caruso St John 2004b: 12). Setting the façade up in a representational rhythm of piers and infill, Caruso St John specified joints as fine as 4 mm between the stone panels to achieve the appearance of a taut, flat skin, proposing an unforgiving surface which would demand minimal dimensional tolerances and permit few compromises in construction. This complex and demanding skin, carrying the weight of conveying the significance of a national civic institution, turned initially to off-site machined processes to deliver a particularly precise kind of quality: one which could only partially be defined numerically. High-cultural, conceptual and civic expectations of care and skill were integrated within this façade; expectations which can be challenging for any architectural office to describe and convey to the builders in the field, in a contemporary professional context which often perpetuates separations between the office and the field.

Negotiations between the office and the field

The professional architect has always been, by definition, largely removed from the field. Franklin Toker, describing the building world of the fourteenth century in 'Gothic

Figure 2 'As built' stone façade of Caruso St John Architects' 2006 entrance addition to the V&A Museum of Childhood, Bethnal Green, London.

Architecture by Remote Control', asserts that the Gothic 'Master' could not be described in the contemporary sense as an architect,

> because their [the Gothic Masters] professionalism consisted in being able to both design and construct, while the professionalism of contemporary architects consists in their ability to draw up buildings with such specificity that they need *not* personally direct their construction.
>
> (Toker 1985: 67)

Toker describes a culture of the 'Master Builder' initially working at a distance by employing a second-in-command on site, noting the presumption that 'it was through drawings that the architect began to manage his building operations by remote control, and that it was this liberation from daily involvement at the construction site which fed his new and higher status' (Toker 1985: 70). Liberation from the field served as a crucial distinction which would define the architect as a profession. In the United Kingdom, the definition of an architect was influenced by Inigo Jones' interpretation of theory as a means of mastery over craftsmen (Crinson and Lubbock 1994: 17), while Sir John

Soane's nineteenth-century definition of the architect as 'a poetic-designer, an intellectual and a manager imbued with high ethics' who could 'lead by virtue of his very distance from mechanical work' (Crinson and Lubbock 1994: 26) cemented the role of the professional architect as one distanced from the field by self-definition. From the nineteenth century to the present day, the architect has become further distanced from the field by the incremental accumulation of multiple specializations within the architectural and building professions. On any contemporary architectural project, an architect, client, project manager, building contractor, structural engineer, façade engineer, environmental engineer, quantity surveyor and numerous specialist consultants and subcontractors may be engaged with the project; many will not previously have worked together. In this specialized and often disjointed context, precise and quantitative communications are posited within the profession as the only means by which the ideals of the architectural office may be correctly translated for accurate construction in the field.

David Leatherbarrow has observed that architects do not build buildings: they make drawings and models (2000: 25). Increasingly, they also write, producing design statements, technical specifications, letters, faxes and emails. The various professional organizations, manuals and journals which advise contemporary architectural practice repeatedly insist that these written and drawn communications, passed between office and field must be, above all else, rational, quantitative and unambiguous. This is, they warn, the only way to maintain control and quality in the field. *The Architects Journal* is representative of this stance in an article by Francis Hall, who states:

> The one certain opportunity available to an architect to set down a definitive and enforceable expression of standard and quality is by way of a properly drafted specification. If this is done, there is understanding and certainty all round. If it is not, there is often disagreement and disappointment.
>
> (1994: 38)

Hall is unequivocal on this matter: 'the objective must be certainty' (1994: 38). Yet, as any practising architect knows, to convey the ambiguity of poetic intentions of any architectural design, and to describe tacit expectations of quality and craftsmanship in a manner which is precise and quantitative is, at best, a formidable task (McVicar 2010). Add to this an organizational structure in which architect, builder and subcontracted specialists may not know – or trust – each other at the onset of a project, and the task becomes near impossible. In such a scenario, professional organizations promote extending the scope of the communications, recommending ever more precise, quantitative and comprehensive instructions which set out, without exception, every detail in a project, and which anticipate uncompromising correlation between the instructions from the office, and the constructed result in the field. Consequently, the sheer quantity of communications between the office and the field has exponentially grown over the last century, from the single-page illustrated contract of 1340 described by Toker, to the hundreds of drawings, specifications, contracts, letters, faxes and emails which now accompany any architectural project. In *Architectural Record*, Robert Spencer Barnett (1995: 32) suggests that the impetus behind this growth is fear, stating that 'Ever-fatter project manuals are often driven by architects' fear that the slightest defect or omission may expose the specifier to liability.' The threat outlined here highlights an underlying condition of contemporary practice: the erosion of trust between the office and the distanced field, in which 'ever-fatter project manuals' act as a substitute for trust. Increased communications cannot in themselves provide the reassurance of absolute certainty, as Walter Rosenfeld inadvertently demonstrates in *Progressive Architecture*: 'No artchitect [sic] or specifier can realistically claim to produce perfect work and contract documents are rarely without some omission, discrepancy, or some other flaw (alas), though perfection is certainly the goal' (Rosenfeld 1991: 47). The specifier is, after all, only human; omissions, discrepancies and errors are, as Rosenfeld highlights, inevitable. Rosenfeld advises the architect to prepare for battle in the event of discrepancy or uncertainty. 'There are times', he concludes, 'when special weapons and tactics are required to carry out the coordination, documentation and execution of the project', referencing the 'game-playing' specifiers must indulge in when 'contractors, architects and owners occasionally behave somewhat deviously in common project-related situations' (Rosenfeld 1984: 46).

In a context in which the architect is distanced from the field, and in which numerous specializations have accumulated to infill the distance between the architect and the field, advice from professional organizations and journals is collectively unequivocal: quantitative definitions are to substitute trust. In a context of distance from the field, communications increasingly bear the burden of precisely defining and upholding, without compromise, all expectations of quality. At the Museum of Childhood entrance addition, a demand for quality began with intensely precise communications as advised; yet even these most precise of communications could not foresee, nor prevent, a 25-mm discrepancy. The constructed project narrates a process by which the poetic intent of a precise project is described through documentation, but in which it is achieved through a reduction of the distance from the field.

Caruso St John and a 25-mm discrepancy at the Museum of Childhood

'It is a battle', Peter St John (2009) concurs of contemporary architectural practice in the United Kingdom, 'we want good working relationships with the builder, but we also want things to be perfect.' Caruso St John's documents exemplify the recommendations of contemporary practice, in that projects are meticulously described in succinctly drawn and written form. 'It is far more likely to work well', St John emphasizes, 'if you put an enormous effort into defining what you want' (St John 2009). At the Museum of Childhood, a project in which the builders had no previous relationship with Caruso St John, drawings and specifications outlined extremely high expectations. These expectations were reinforced by letters, faxes and emails narrating a tightly controlled process, in which every dimension on the drawing and every word in a specification was formally presented as a non-negotiable fact, to be adhered to precisely, without compromise, in the field. 'The dimensional precision and finish', project architect David Kohn faxed to the builder during construction, 'is of critical importance to the building's appearance and we will expect a very high level of workmanship' (Kohn 2006). Despite a succinct and precise set of comprehensive instructions exemplifying all recommendations of contemporary practice, a discrepancy emerged as a compromise; a discrepancy which incurs a sense of disappointment for Caruso St John, yet which attests to the realities of the field and the ambiguous and undocumented negotiations which underpin the quality of any constructed project.

This simple, yet intense, entrance addition was conceived conceptually as sitting cleanly in front of the nineteenth-century façade. As a sequential addition to an existing structure, setting nineteenth-century handcraft against twenty-first-century computer-controlled precision, the proposal could be read as an arrangement of original and addition, brick and stone, hand-laid and machined processes, separated decisively by a 10-mm caulk control joint between Caruso St John's stone addition and Wild's brick façade. The constructed result is, however, more ambiguous and complex, containing unanticipated discrepancies and compromises imposed by the field.

The nineteenth-century entrance structure originally extended across the entirety of the west façade of the museum, concealing rough interior brickwork between the entrance and the museum itself. Following the removal of the original entrance, the end sections of this rough interior brickwork were externally exposed by the narrower Caruso St John addition, and so were demolished, for replacement with new finish brickwork which was to be perfectly matched and aligned with the existing finish brickwork above in order to give the appearance of a complete brick façade. While this condition was carefully predicted and specified, 'in actuality, the new brickwork didn't work as planned', St John recalls (2009).

As a result of the final construction sequence, the façade of the Caruso St John entrance was erected before the replacement brick had been installed. This construction sequence resulted in a discovery, shortly before completion of the project, that the south side of the addition sat too close to the existing façade. The new south elevation of the addition, in fact, encroached 25 mm into the existing brick façade. Consequently, the replacement brickwork could not align perfectly with the existing façade, but was instead forced to push inwards, resulting in a 25-mm offset between the original façade and the reconstructed brickwork. The concept of an addition sitting cleanly in front of an existing structure was constructed in the field as an out-of-sequence structure encroaching 25 mm into a replacement façade. A 25-mm discrepancy may seem insignificant in the overall scope of the project, yet St John recalls the office considering the implications of requesting a reconstruction of the new stone façade two weeks before the formal opening, a demand which could have cost the builder tens of thousands of pounds, and pushed the completion of the project back by several weeks. Concluding the office could never have justified such a correction, the result, St John suggests, remains as a compromise. 'It is imperfect',

Figure 3 Detail of the 25-mm offset between the original brick façade and the reconstructed brick below, V&A Museum of Childhood. The 25-mm offset is located directly above the top of the Caruso St John 2006 entrance addition.

he concludes (St John 2009). Although it is unlikely that anyone will notice the 25-mm discrepancy, which is difficult to locate even when alerted to it, whether anyone will notice it is not the point at stake. It is quite simply the fact that this compromise physically exists. It is not the conceptual clarity which disappoints, nor the specific dimension of the compromise itself, but rather the physical fact of a discrepancy; one which speaks to the underlying disappointment which any architect may face in contemporary practice.

The ambiguity of the field

Compromises between the precise instructions of the office and constructed reality in the field appear to be inevitable within contemporary architectural practice. No matter how detailed a set of instructions, they will, somehow, never be detailed enough to guarantee a perfect alignment between the office and the field. 'Architects involved in Quality Work find that there are never enough drawings, nor enough details drawn', warn Osama A. Wakita and Richard M. Linde, the authors of the US practice manual *The Professional Practice of Architectural Detailing* (1999: vi). *Quality* work – as opposed, this implies, to average work – seems to require *something more* in addition to precise instructions, something which the most precise drawings and specifications cannot in themselves provide or control when they meet the ambiguity of the field.

Architectural communications aim for, yet cannot attain, a comprehensively quantitative definition of architectural intentions, and the field itself remains similarly resistant to quantitative definition. Idealizations of the field have envisaged predictable and consistent conditions for construction. In 'Purity and Tolerance', Katherine Shonfield (1994: 36) referenced Brian Finnimore's recollection of a RIBA Architectural Advisor's idealization of a future building site, 'devoid of mud and of such clinical precision' that it would consist of 'a group of (almost) white-coated, well paid workers, slotting and clipping standard components into place in rhythmic sequence on an orderly, networked and mechanized site, to a faultless programme, without mud, mess, sweat or swearing' (Finnimore 1989: 103). Despite such projections of Fordist control, recent studies of the construction site suggest that the field remains stubbornly messy, muddy, unpredictable and pre-modern: sociologist Darren Thiel's (2007) studies of construction sites observe that the field, changing daily, sometimes hourly, in form, is in actuality organized not by precise predictions, but through an adaptive and responsive process of orchestrated chaos. While activities on the field may be quantitatively predicted before construction, and recorded after construction, daily actions on the site cannot be definitively predicted. The architect's precise instructions are often notably absent from the decision-making processes in the field. 'A thousand times a day', Thiel quotes from Reckman, the worker must decide 'where to place himself and his work amongst the almost infinite possibilities of perfection or compromise' (Thiel 2007: 231). The worker in the field must make hundreds, perhaps thousands, of individual, largely intuitive decisions which will improve, adapt or compromise the ideals of the architectural project, but, as recent research by Kate Ness concluded, the workers who undertake the physical work – the 'bodies', as they are referred to in the construction industry – remain almost invisible in the complex organization of construction. Ness suggests that as construction organizational structures move from the management of employees to the management of subcontractors, the organizational system in construction reaches a point where almost no one knows who constructs a project, nor how they construct it. As Ness suggests, according to the 'traditionalists': 'the degree-qualified construction managers who supervise subcontract packages have no idea what is involved in the practicalities of the work. It is the workers themselves, and the subcontractors' own foremen, who actually organise the work' (Ness 2009). The possibility of achieving perfect alignment between concept and construction remains in the hands of individual builders, yet there is a sense that who they are, and what they actually do, is not precisely known. The builders and their decisions are seldom acknowledged in construction documentations which emphasize predefined processes of control. Regardless of the growing use of prefabricated assemblies, there remains always an unavoidable moment where precisely prefabricated components meet each other, or existing elements, in the ambiguous conditions of the field. Drawings and specifications may precisely specify strict dimensional tolerances, but the field will inevitably exert its own influence. A moment of inattention, a misreading of one dimension, a rainy or windy day may intervene: the builder, too, is only human, and works in unpredictable conditions.

Paradoxically, Shonfield observed, the more construction processes become component-based, the more each joint becomes a primary matter of concern, as an unavoidable moment which must depend on the care and skill of an individual builder. With attention focused on the joint and ever more precise tolerances specified, the joint becomes the least certain moment in construction. As Eric Vastert warned in *Architectural Science Review*:

> The weak spots in the performance of buildings are not so much the building materials, but rather the connections between them. Dimensional variations of products become particularly clear in the joints, where they can disrupt the regularity of façades or tiling.

> (Vastert 1998: 99)

If perfection is the goal, then every joint is of paramount importance, and, as the specification of each joint becomes more precise, the likelihood increases that at least one joint will fail to meet expectations. 'In matters of tolerance', Shonfield writes of the joint, 'statistics are irrelevant' (Shonfield 1994: 37). Only one joint, one moment in construction, must fail in order to engender disappointment if uncompromising perfection is anticipated. While practice journals suggest that only precise communications can avoid disagreement and disappointment, is acute disappointment actually inevitable when precise communications meet the ambiguity of the field?

The philosopher Isaiah Berlin predicted that an acute sense of disappointment is inevitable whenever rational methods are applied to what he terms the 'vague, rich texture of the real world' (1993: 74). Berlin's essay, *The Hedgehog and the Fox*, highlights crucial differences between the measurable and the impalpable, suggesting that it is in the frontier between these fields where the most violent clashes occur. Analysing Leo Tolstoy's descriptions of battlefields in *War and Peace*, Berlin observes that time and time again in Tolstoy's writing, the orderly and rationalized account of what is expected to occur in the battlefield bears little resemblance to the actual events as they play out in the field. The realities of the battlefield as a 'succession of "accidents" whose origins and consequences are, by and large, untraceable and unpredictable' (1993: 20) resonates with the orchestrated chaos of Thiel's construction sites, where precise instructions meet the frontier of the indeterminate field.

'Better, surely, not to pretend to calculate the incalculable', advises Berlin (1993: 77), advice at odds with almost all advice for communications within architectural production. Uncompromisingly quantitative communications are, in this sense, at odds with the nature of architecture itself. Architectural design is an intuitive process. Work in the field, despite all attempts to quantitatively define and control it, similarly appears to remain responsive, adaptive and individual. Any practising architect will acknowledge that, despite the most precise of instructions, ambiguities will occur in the field. Yet such ambiguities continue to be treated as anomalies: unexpected, unwanted imperfections. While contemporary practice advises the architect to plan against and reject any imperfection, we are in reality surrounded by moments where imperfections are present as an inherent condition in a work of high quality.

David Kohn and Cosmatesque imperfections

In 2004, David Kohn, the project architect of the Museum of Childhood, taught an architectural studio at London Metropolitan University in which students measured the twelfth-century Cosmati mosaic pavement in Santa Maria in Cosmedin, Rome, creating a drawing titled *Perfect, Imperfect* by overlaying a drawing of the geometric ideal of the pavement upon a drawing of the 'as built' constructed reality. The differences revealed between the geometric ideal and the constructed reality signified, for Kohn, not a demonstration of error or lack of care, but, rather, an inherent condition of human craft: a demonstration that geometric perfection is unattainable despite the best of intentions, care and skill. The imperfect qualities – the geometrical discrepancies – of Cosmatesque pavements are understood as a quality in themselves, achieved not through precise adherence to comprehensive written and drawn instructions but, rather, through skilful and careful adaptations to conditions in the field. In the case of the Cosmati pavements, 'reality is nothing like the intellectual construct', Kohn suggests, concluding that, 'that difference is being human' (Kohn 2009). Within the Cosmati pavements, the geometric ideal can be understood as a conceptual framework from which work begins; the quality of the construction, however, is determined by the care and skill of the craftsmen in adapting to the field. While the Cosmati pavements are acknowledged as representing good workmanship, they do not achieve geometric precision. 'It is usual', David Pye reflected in *The Nature and Art of Workmanship*, 'to equate "good" with "precise" and "bad" with "rough". To do so is false. Rough workmanship may be excellent while precise may be bad' (1968: 13).

Specifications which demand quantitative precision could perhaps be understood as the beginning of a conversation which seeks to define a shared expectation of quality, in a context where shared expectations of quality cannot initially be assumed. Quality and care are not, in this understanding, guaranteed by an insistence upon precise alignment between the office and the field: rather, they are to be negoti-

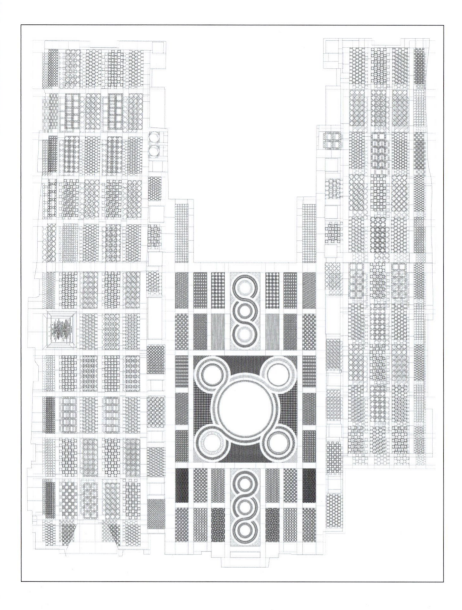

Figure 4 'Perfect, Imperfect' overlay drawing of the differences between the geometric ideal and the 'as built' conditions of the twelfth-century Cosmati pavement in Santa Maria in Cosmedin, Rome, surveyed by Louise Hoffman, James Paul and Sabine Rosenkrantz in 2004 for David Kohn's Undergraduate Studio 5 at London Metropolitan University.

ated by developing shared understandings of what quality and care means in the context of any given project. 'Good workmanship', Pye proposed, 'is that which carries out or improves upon the intended design. Bad workmanship is what fails to do so and thwarts the design' (1968: 13). To achieve good workmanship, all involved with the project – architect, contractor, bricklayer – must reach a common understanding of the overall intent and aims of the project: aims which speak of cultural values that are difficult to quantify. In contemporary architectural practice, architect and builder typically cannot anticipate that they will share common definitions of quality at the beginning of any project. In the absence of familiarity and trust amidst a large and multi-layered team of specialists working together for the first time, precisely describing an inflexible geometric ideal may indeed be the only route to initially define high expectations of the work to be carried out in the field. Yet in *quality* work – work which seems to require *something more* – precise instructions may do no more than serve as a starting point: the introductory remarks in an ongoing conversation. While Francis Hall asserts in *The Architects Journal* that the objective must be certainty, this is, in fact, only a means to an end: the final objective, rather, must be quality.

Kohn describes a process at the Museum of Childhood in which the architectural team began conversations with each layer of management in the construction process, locating those participants who were the most interested, energetic and engaged with the aim of the project; who could be 'cajoled into doing what you want – or into suggesting alternatives which are better' (Kohn 2009), thus building up, through dialogue, a common understanding of what quality might mean in the context of the project. The dialogue of a conversation – in contrast with the monologue of a written instruction – opened up the ability to respond to the unforeseen, yet inevitable, compromises which occurred during construction. At the Museum of Childhood, the acceptance of a compromise was, ultimately, based on an acceptance of trust. 'The collaborative effort of the construction team …', St John wrote to the client, 'will make it difficult for us to be strict with the contractor on all matters' (St John 2006). Collaboration and trust, developed over the course of a project, finally, here, superseded dimensional precision. At the end of any project, we hope to sense, with our soul, that the work is completed to the highest standard possible, despite what any measurement may insist.

Quality in the field

At the Museum of Childhood, even the most precise and comprehensive of communications, meeting all recommendations of contemporary practice, could not deflect a 25-mm discrepancy in the field. The origin of this discrepancy is undocumented, lost within the hundreds of thousands of individual moments buried within the constructed result. That this discrepancy was unpredictable and undocumented, a lacuna in documentation existing only in a final constructed form, attests to the inevitable ambiguity of the field. That this discrepancy, seemingly minor, retains significance as a source of disappointment for the architect attests to the disappointment we all face in contemporary practice, when, despite the best of our efforts, we are compelled to employ quantitative predictions to describe the quality of architectural work.

As with the Cosmatesque pavements, to evaluate quality at the Museum of Childhood by measuring dimensional alignment with the geometric ideal would be to overlook the qualities achieved within the project. At the Museum of Childhood, a rigorous insistence upon perfection throughout the project was vital in first setting standards for high expectations of quality. It served to alert the builders of the value of this civic project: to 'elevate the importance' of this façade, as Kohn emphasizes (2009). The compromise to accept a 25-mm discrepancy, was, however, negotiated by undocumented, direct conversation. The Museum of Childhood façade reads, as intended, as a smooth, flat, taut skin, reinterpreting the hand-laid modelling of Wild's façade as a strictly two-dimensional yet richly patterned civic façade. While specified to extremely precise dimensional tolerances determined by CNC predictions, the façade was ultimately achieved in the field by a hand-laid construction. Located between perfection and compromise, this façade determines its quality not through dimensional perfection, but through the sense of obsessive care which was applied at every stage of the project. Quality, here, was negotiated not simply through the comprehensive set of drawings, specifications, letters, faxes and emails provided by the office – which could provide no more than an initial outline of high expectations – but rather, through the hundreds of undocumented, adaptive and responsive conversations, negotiations and compromises which occurred in the lacuna between the precise predictions of the office and the conditions of the field.

Editing the field

Video tales from globalised cityscapes

Krystallia Kamvasinou

Introduction

The point of departure for this chapter is a reflective account of the making of a short, analogue video (*Stansted*, December 2000, six mins) and a longer series of digital shorts (*Mumbai Tales*, December 2008, in progress, 30 mins). Both videos are about global cities (Sassen 1991), or 'mega-cities',[1] and the novel user experiences these suggest. While both started as parts of research projects that investigated particular conditions of the global city (in the first case, mobility, in the second, water scarcity), their making generated footage that acted as a field for further investigations, revealing aspects of the city that were not part of the researcher's initial thinking. In this way, the videos began to act as the originators of ideas rather than as simple tools for conducting research. This chapter will focus on this dual aspect of video used for fieldwork.

The changing nature of 'field/work'

Physical field

In urban studies, notions of physical field are currently being redefined. New types of urban spaces emerge from new ways of living, urban politics and processes of globalisation: Marc Augé's 'non-places' (Augé 1992); De Certeau's everyday journeys and enactments and their resulting 'space narratives' (De Certeau 1984); J.B. Jackson's 'autovernacular landscapes' (Jackson 1997: 152); and de Morales' 'terrain vague' (de Morales 1995).

We are witnessing a critical move from the contemplation of the architectural object towards the study of the wider field of the city and the body within it. In phenomenological vocabulary this often comes under the definition of 'field perception' instead of 'object perception' (Viola 1995); 'ambiance', an environment composed of several overlapping layers of attention including uncontrollable events;[2] or 'synaesthesia', the crossover between the senses, which is 'the natural inclination of contemporary media' including video (Viola 1995: 164–165). A broader umbrella term might be environmental perception as a condition in which all senses are experienced at once and space literally becomes the medium within which we act (Berleant 1991).

This paradigm shift has led to the proliferation of -scapes, such as 'soundscapes' or 'smellscapes', in addition to or rather in support of the existing 'landscapes' and 'cityscapes'. This shift is fundamental in defining a methodological movement towards research practices such as video-making that are capable not only of registering the qualities of the field, but also of reproducing them.

Virtual field

At the same time, focus has shifted from the crafted, hands-on, material experience of the field to the immense amounts of information received through sources such as television and the World Wide Web. Particularly suited to the increasingly fleeting experience of the world, the moving image or the webpage promise to expand not only the boundaries of knowledge but also of experience. Interfacing with a remote elsewhere, one can be sure to explore the 'virtual' field with a significantly reduced risk of physical danger or effort.

As the notion of field becomes contested in the postmodern context, traditional methodologies of fieldwork appear to follow suit. This change has been led by visual research in the social sciences and in the arts, particularly visual anthropology, documentary film, ethnographic film, and video art (Banks 1998, 2001). Closer to home, disciplines such as product design embrace the use of video studies as a method of collecting information, involving the user, developing design scenarios and finally a product (Ylirisku and Buur 2007). In all cases, video-making is informed by current debates on the status of the camera in film-making, the choice of the physical and cultural viewpoint, the actors' participation, the delineation of the scene, the researcher's role and the relationship of film, exhibition space and the viewing audience.

Video remains closely related to film and by extension to photography. Although technologically video, and in particular digital video, is very different from film,[3] culturally the two can be interchangeable. For the viewer, video represents the latest form of film, 'an edited sequence of photographically created moving images (whether originated on actual film or not), usually with a synchronized soundtrack and usually conforming to a set of narrative and cultural conventions that determine what a "film" should be' (Enticknap 2009: 418). Photographic questions of authenticity and truth are not, however, inherent to video. The sheer capacity of the medium to record, store and infinitely reproduce and manipulate images presents a fundamental shift in moving-image practices, a movement far away from the issues of uniqueness and vulnerability traditionally associated with the reel of film.

Shooting the city: on-site fieldwork

Stansted

The making of the *Stansted* movie was part of PhD research based on motion perception in relation to the development of a design method for working with transitional landscapes. To represent motion in design, one needs to go beyond the traditional tools of architecture and planning. The static conventions are not adequate to the task. Video is 'the medium that conveys most of the detailed richness of a real setting, as compared with text, photos and audio recordings' (Ylirisku and Buur 2007: 27), including, as it does, sensory information such as movement, sound and change of light conditions. In the *Stansted* project, video was used not as a final production, an illustrative tool, but rather as a working tool: first, to document and communicate motion and ambiance beyond maps and drawings (Figure 1), and second, as a sketch tool for development of conceptual ideas. In making a video about a city the architect can represent an urban model, a particular – existing or proposed – urban condition or a less concrete urban experience.

Traditionally, the process of doing fieldwork gradually transforms the architect/researcher from an outsider into an insider, an active participant looking to understand, measure and grasp. In the video-making process, when the collected footage is reviewed back home, the architect/researcher finds herself in an outsider's position once more. This time, the condition is intentional. It is through deliberate detachment and the coincident abandonment of the personal experience of field that we can search for clues in the recorded material as if seen for the first time.

Ten 45-minute videos were recorded on the train trip to *Stansted* over a period of one week. For simplicity, the viewpoint of the camera was always located on the east/south-east facing side of the train, the direction of travel varying between the outward and inward journeys and the camera perspective shifting between different degrees of oblique view and frontal view, following the direction of travel or its opposite. During the ten journeys the camera was set on a tripod and left to record everything that would pass outside the train window. This generated a wealth of recordings, with interesting and sometimes unexpected results. The recorded material became a first-time surveyed meta-field for fieldwork. Detailed information on apparent motion was classified under themes such as 'rotation', 'sweep', 'zoom in and out', resulting in short video studies of each particular condition.

This type of systematic but passive shooting was a deliberate attempt to simulate the experience of someone travelling through space but unable to gain a close, studied understanding of that space. The anticipated outcome was new information, images as raw material caught on video. Although I was there, my presence is rarely felt while watching the footage. One notable exception is a moment when frost and humidity was rapidly building up on the train window. At this point, we get a view of my bare hands wiping the glass. This scene was included in the final six-minute movie as a glimpse of tactile interaction with the transitional landscape, a condition that most of us have experienced (Figure 1).

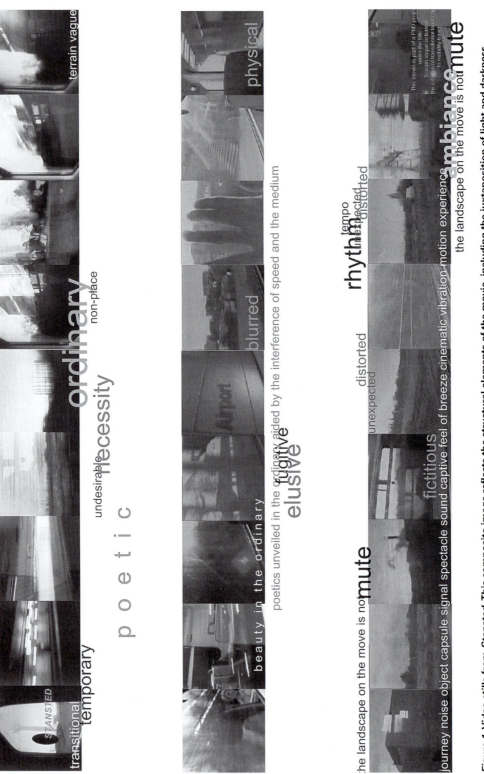

Figure 1 Video stills from *Stansted*. This composite image reflects the structural elements of the movie, including the juxtaposition of light and darkness, alternate travel direction and the superimposition of words/sound.

Mumbai Tales

The making of the *Mumbai Tales* series of shorts was the result of a radically different process. In December 2006, I found myself, video camera in hand, travelling in a rented car in twenty-first-century Mumbai. I was a member of a team working on an AHRC Landscape and Environment documentary project related to water, landscape and social formation. Shooting in Mumbai generated a wealth of footage, some of which was planned and sought (for instance cityscapes recorded from tall buildings and views from and within train), and some that occurred spontaneously in the field. In all cases the camera was active and searching and people behind or in front of the camera were in effect collaborators contributing to the role-play. This is perhaps something that is easier to achieve in a city like Mumbai, familiar with the film-making process and home to Bollywood. While the resulting footage was then classified according to themes and quality, editing *Mumbai Tales* was in effect the result of a conscious decision to work with leftover material, the interlinking rushes discharged in the process of preparing the official 30-minute documentary. Liberated from the need to produce a professional final output with a very tightly determined focus, *Mumbai Tales* was seen as an exercise in defining the methodology itself. The footage was the field, and fieldwork was about discovering the subject of the investigation, experimenting with the limits and possibilities of video for producing edited tales of the city (Figure 2).

If the shooting takes place in Mumbai and the editing in London, where is the real field and where is the fieldwork done? Even before going to Mumbai a range of situations were explored and a range of ideas for filming locations drafted. This was made possible through a literature review and a focused screening of other documentaries, either filmed in India or with similar topics. As a result I would argue that a big part of the 'fieldwork' was conducted before even flying to Mumbai.

Once on location, there were many other issues to master in relation to: the scale of the city and travel, accessibility, orientation, the friendliness or hostility of local residents and consequent negotiations. The physical constraints on the body with regard to the situations and the cityscapes documented were another contributing factor. Physical fitness has to be supplemented by mental fitness; the person behind the camera must have either a trained or a sensitive eye that scans a terrain looking for hidden treasures.

Fieldwork demanded a complex architectural set-up for recording: where will the camera go, what will it point to, where will the interviewee sit, is the light good enough, how will sound be recorded and at what level? These were just a few of the things that had to be addressed before hitting the 'record' button. While recording interlinking rushes, mostly landscape scenes, there was more freedom, and the camera could be handheld, capturing anything that might be remotely interesting to the project.

When filming people, the camera, as well as the presence of the crew filming, actively changed the setting. In retrospect this was seen as an advantage:

Figure 2 Outtakes from *Mumbai Tales*. The six tales are identified by their titles in black. Fluid city; the reflected city; the weeping city; the dream; terrain vague; denCity. The edited tales structure the recorded field into themes intentionally hovering between document and fiction.

people were curious and by providing them with a brief description of the project, we were able to engage with them. In most cases this interaction was achieved through local facilitators who explained the purpose of our visit to the community leaders and thereby allowed the participants some degree of control over the filming event and their presence within it. We were actively interested in their communities and lives and, through the process of designed mediation, they felt empowered to contribute to the making of the movie. In one instance, an unplanned filming sequence created an opportunity, a discovery impossible to predict and delightful to record. Amidst the film-making crowd, a slum dweller opened the door to her house to reveal a small 'ethno-graphic museum' in the form of a collection of brass pottery. For that moment of serendipity video operated as a form of 'designer clay' (Ylirisku and Buur 2007: 25) a medium able to capture the anecdotal and the prescribed with equal accuracy and care.

There are similarities between *Stansted* and *Mumbai Tales*, and the ways in which one built on the knowledge gained from the other. Extensive experience of recording moving landscapes through train windows in *Stansted* was referenced in the Mumbai recordings where similar footage was sought and planned in advance. It was anticipated that such footage would enable the researchers to survey the city according to the formal and spatial logics established in the earlier work. However, although the technique used was the same, the knowledge of the field transmitted through the final images was very different. In Mumbai, issues of the physical, social and cultural content far outweighed the more structural concerns of the *Stansted* work.

Through my work with video I have begun to envision the potential for a hybrid methodology, a working practice able to operate between the positivist approach, the objective camera recording anything that is caught within its frame, and the interpretative–hermeneutical approach where the camera becomes a cata-lyst/analyst of the phenomena it observes (Henley 1998; Banks 1998, 2001). In this mode of practice video-recording can be utilised to produce an edited version of the field, part document part fiction, able to reveal the unnoticed and the hidden, the political and the sensual, the intricate nuances of the field that are lost to direct contact.

Editing the city: video as a meta-site

The *Stansted* movie followed basic rules of editing, repetition, juxtaposition, tempo, pause and superimposition of music. In the one-minute introductory section of the movie there is a sequence of photographic images of the terrain in transit. Here, speed is frozen and we are able to view its traces in the form of lines of lights or trails of a blurred landscape. A structural rule throughout the movie involved the juxtaposition of scenes depending on the direction of travel. One scene, from the train going north, showed the landscape 'moving' southwards, the next scene showed the movement north. A further requirement was the contrast of light; after a bright scene, a darker one followed. A similar rule of contrast was applied to the use of sound. The movie began with no musical background, just the narration of keywords spelt out one after another with slight variations in tone. The sequence continued with a musical piece (by Tomaž Grom) inserted to accompany the flow of movement and underline the trance-like or hypnotic nature of the visual experience. This sequence also involved pauses with no music. Here the presence of others in the carriage could be felt through their talking. Notably, the absence of people in front of the camera suggests, that we, the viewers, are actually the key actors, and the camera's viewpoint represents us, looking through the window (Figure 1).

Mumbai Tales takes the form of several video stories stitched into a video collage, exposing different aspects of city life and cityscape in the context of a twenty-first-century mega-city. 'Fluid city', the 'reflected city', the 'weeping city', 'The Dream', 'terrain vague', 'denCity' are the short tales that constitute the movie. Water is one of the linking elements. Here, people only appear in passing and the footage of interviews has been deliberately omitted. The purpose of the movie was to rework, survey and creatively experiment with an excess of leftover footage, after the making of the main documentary.

Each Mumbai tale is also a collage, a reconfiguration of geographically con-trasting but thematically similar scenes. Original source footage for the work reflected the geography of the city, each videotape capturing a particular location. These clips were then reorganised according to themes. In this way, a systematic method of working with the footage was discerned not in the shooting itself, the *Stansted* model, but in the edit. 'Fluid city' deals with the movement of people, vehicles, water and goods. The 'weeping city', visually underlined by leaking pipes and superfluous water features, looks at the extremes and necessities of human labour in the poorest quar-ters of Mumbai in opposition to the affluence experienced elsewhere in the city. 'The Dream' is a collection of eccentricities, out-of-place incidents occasionally shown in slow or fast motion for emphasis (Figure 2).

The work of the *Mumbai Tales* is ongoing. There is no requirement for it to end. If there is to be an end, it will have to do with factors outside the city and the movie, to do with an end of resources, of time and money, allocated to the project. In a sense, the production of a final movie, no matter how un-polished, somehow defeats the purpose of this process of fieldwork. The final *Mumbai Tales* will have to be an open-ended, abruptly cut, curiously inconclusive, full of wonders, *Edited-Field*.

Acknowledgements

I would like to acknowledge the AHRC Landscape and Environment Programme under which the project 'Liquid City: Water, Landscape and Social Formation in 21st Century Mumbai' was funded, and Prof. Matthew Gandy, Department of Geography, UCL, for useful discussions.

Notes

1 The two cities are London and Mumbai. Both cities have populations well beyond ten million (estimated over 20 million in the case of Mumbai, 60 per cent of which lives in slums). Mumbai is the fifth-fastest-growing mega-city, while London has a much lower growth rate.

2 See the work of Erik Satie and later John Cage in music. See also Brian Eno (1996).

3 According to Enticknap (2009: 418), film describes 'a flexible, transparent solid on to which is coated a photosensitive emulsion, which in turn records an image when exposed to light'.

Blighted

Igor Marjanović and Lindsey Stouffer

> ***Blight*** n. **1.a**. Any of numerous plant diseases resulting in sudden conspicu-
> ous wilting and dying of affected parts, especially young, growing tissues.
> **b.** The condition or causative agent, such as bacterium, fungus, or virus,
> that results in blight. **2.** An extremely adverse environmental condition such
> as air pollution. **3.** Something that impairs growth, withers hopes and ambi-
> tions, or impedes progress and prosperity. **-blight** *v.* **blight-ed**, **blight-ing**,
> **blights**. *-tr.* **1.** To cause (a plant, for example) to undergo blight. **2.** To have a
> deleterious effect on; ruin.
>
> (*The American Heritage Dictionary* 1992: 202)

The term 'blighted' is used to describe the distressed landscape of many postindustrial
American cities. These so-called 'rust-belt cities' thrived on the industrial production of
the nineteenth century, but suffered steep economic decline as the urban population
fled to the suburbs in the second half of the twentieth century. In this reversion of
progress, once-thriving urban neighborhoods became abandoned, trapping poorer
residents who did not have the means to follow the flight to the suburbs. Starting in
the 1950s and 1960s, many urban renewal projects were initiated across North
America, aiming to address this issue. In the process, planners, developers and politi-
cians designated urban areas as 'blighted' in order to radically remedy the problem
through total demolition. The erasure of these traditional neighborhoods paved the way
for the burgeoning trend of new large-scale housing projects, which, despite their
social promise, only traded one form of poverty for another. These extreme measures
deeply affected local communities and exacerbated the suburban flight, leaving city
centers almost virtually vacant.

St Louis followed this trajectory too faithfully. As its historic neighborhoods
were labeled 'blighted', they faced the wrecking ball and a new tragedy ensued. The
city's public housing policies became entangled with social, economic and political pre-
dicaments, undermining humane concerns for habitation and community. For some,
the term 'blighted' signified a state of decay beyond repair; for others, it meant the

loss of home. Today, we reflect upon this term as politically problematic – it was appropriated from plant pathology to suggest a form of physical disease, wilting and decay; yet, we will argue, it also suggested a crisis of development and public policy, whereby architecture became a tool of debasement and political propaganda.

This crisis is most evident in the Pruitt-Igoe Housing Project designed by Minoru Yamasaki, architect of the World Trade Center in New York City. Completed in 1955, it featured a series of 33 rectangular buildings, each 11 stories tall. A concrete icon of modernity, it was built to celebrate governmental policies, economic progress and social idealism. A mere 17 years later in 1972 demolition workers carefully placed explosives at the lower levels of Pruitt-Igoe. Its large concrete slabs were gone in a widely publicized cloud of dust. Seen around the world, the demolition was so iconic that it prompted historians and critics to reflect upon its significance, including Charles Jencks's poignant words:

> Modern Architecture died in St Louis, Missouri on July 15, 1972 at 3:32p.m. (or thereabouts) when the infamous Pruitt-Igoe scheme, or rather several of its slab blocks, were given the final *coup de grace* by dynamite.... Boom, boom, boom.
>
> (Jencks 1986: 9)

Colin Rowe extended this sentiment in his influential essay 'Collage City', where he lamented upon the outcomes of modern planning next to a full-page reproduction of Pruitt-Igoe demolition (Rowe and Koetter 1975: 73). Yet, despite their strong critique of modern planning, Jencks's and Rowe's texts reveal little about local communities. They remain focused on the success and often on the failure of grand plans, with their texts as signifiers that the spectacle of destruction replaced the spectacle of ribbon-cutting and opening of new housing projects. Yet, once the TV crews, critics and general public left these demolition sites, a solemn reality settled – St Louis lost a large portion of its urban fabric, and vacant lots started to dot its troubled map.

One of these lots is the focus of our ongoing study – located only blocks away from the former Pruitt-Igoe site is the Wellston Loop, a small urban community on the fringe of North St Louis. Its scarred landscape is all too familiar – a mix of leftover housing projects and a combination of distressed yet tenacious urban neighborhoods that seem like islands in a sea of empty lots. Most buildings are vacant. Of the few that are occupied some are maintained but most are beyond repair. The dust of Pruitt-Igoe's demolition certainly reached this part of town – both literally and figuratively. This urban image – frustrated, withered and complex – is located at the heart of our pedagogy.

Surveying

A small group of first-year architecture students arrives at an empty lot in Wellston Loop. Only last summer they were waking up in their parents' homes just finished with

high school. Most have never lived independently, never had an architecture course
and have never intentionally been in this type of neighborhood. As they disperse in
groups, they are given blue rubber gloves, ropes, labels and archival bags. These are
the physical tools with which they survey the empty lot – they measure it, draw it and
slowly uncover its 'depth', looking for traces just below the surface. Acting as urban
archeologists, the students dig, sniff and probe. They deny the lot's emptiness, revealing clues to its past and present through a plethora of found objects. Beneath the
muddy grass is a set of old letter blocks; against the brick wall an armchair; hidden in
the bushes a pair of headphones. A surprising richness is discovered. This site that initially seemed *blighted* is revealed as a record of memories and objects.

Many thinkers have noted the significance of objects found in the field. In
his book *Space and Place* Yi-Fu Tuan argues that places are akin to objects:

> Place is a type of object. Places and objects define space, giving it a geometric
> personality.... Objects and places are centers of value. They attract or
> repel in finely shaded degrees. To attend to them even momentarily is to
> acknowledge their reality and value.
>
> (Tuan 1977: 17–18)

Paul Adams, Steven Hoelscher and Karen Till further elaborate on the value of found
objects, speaking about surface and texture as carriers of meaning. 'Although we may

Figure 2
Collecting:
Fragments of
collected objects are
re-classified into a
site taxonomy.

think of texture as a superficial layer, only "skin deep", its distinctive qualities may be profound', they wrote. 'A surface is, after all, where subject and object merge; the shape, feel, and texture of a place each provides a glimpse into the processes, structures, spaces, and histories that went into its making' (Adams *et al.* 2001: xiii). The metaphorical depth of found objects surpasses the site's 'skin-deep' physical depth, enabling a field narrative to be woven with creative interpretation. It is precisely this enigma of excavation, reconstruction and reconfiguration that drives our studio pedagogy and challenges the students to approach the site not as an abstract map but as a layered narrative made of fragmented objects and experiences.

Collecting

Initially discarded in this empty lot, the objects are further displaced into the world of architectural design studio to be studied. Catalogued fragments in bags are arranged on a wall and labeled. Suddenly, a rich history of this place is revealed through the collections of things that at once seemed random. As we gaze at the collection, we search for stories inscribed in the objects, exploring their patina and seeking relationships. Our challenge is to create order from chance, the magical from the ordinary. We resort to collecting, measuring and documenting, constantly reflecting on our fieldwork. The resulting site plans document the objects through words and images, starting to imply new narratives. These maps expose the enigma of a piece of furniture, a texture of a wall, the porosity of ground … The site plans reveal a narrative, imbuing a deep sense of proximity between the students and their site through reconfiguration of studied objects.

Once the objects are organized into a taxonomy, they become types, they are relational. Matthias Winzen characterizes the typological relationship between the collected and the collection by saying:

> Collecting introduces meaning, order, boundaries, coherence and reason into what is disparate and confused. The paradox of the similarly dissimilar, [is] the idea that the unique, singular object … express[es] its uniqueness in relation to other, similarly dissimilar unique objects. It is a paradox of compromise that reduces every individual to type.
>
> (1998: 23–24)

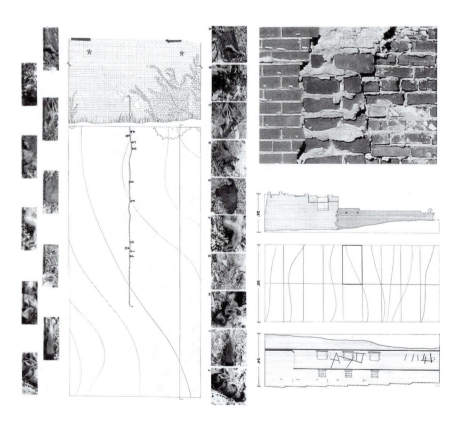

Figure 3 Site plans: Maps of found objects and textures. Collage and drawing by students, Katherine Hered, Alexander Plutzer and Anna White.

Thus, our studied objects suggest a typology of experiences that augment traditional built typologies, suggesting a contextualization of architectural work within more personal and lived experiences. Our site plans suggest a reading of found objects and a history that is embedded in subjectivity – a form of site analysis too often absent from urban renewal plans.

Casting

We look at our site taxonomy not as empirical evidence – its conclusions are rather incidental. Yet, we take it seriously as we believe that it holds clues to past users and their narratives. We also try to be inspired by these objects as designers in search of beauty. We seek ways to understand and transform them. We submerge the objects in small plaster casts and excavate them again. What was recently uncovered is hidden and something new is found. Despite the apparent order of plaster cubes and their labels, their exact contents are mysterious. Our curiosity is triggered – we want to discover their interior. We reflect on diverse action verbs with which we can start to transform these cubes. In order to structure our second process of digging – this time in the studio space – we use these verbs to guide our spatial actions, similarly to Richard Serra's 'verb list', which he used to describe actions to be taken on materials. 'To crumple, to shave, to tear, to chip, to split, to cut…' – these are only a few of Serra's verbs whose exact meaning is only understood in their direct interaction with the material itself (Serra 1994: 3). Our project parallels a similar verbal and spatial path.

Poured, buried and labeled, the objects are ready to be rediscovered through a series of verbs and corresponding tools. Our verbs of transformation and action are: carve, drill or slice. The delicacy with which we acted on site – the attention to fragility and archeological intricacy – is now substituted with the 'roughness' of our new tools: drill, band saw and disk sander. These tools give us courage to alter the cubes and discover new geometries. Gradually, the surprising interiors of the cubes are revealed. What was a recognizable fragment on site becomes an abstraction. Headphones emerge as delicate curves; old letter blocks become thin lines weaving through the plaster mass. The possibilities for sectional interpretation are endless.

Drafting

We draw a series of plans and sections that map each plaster fragment, reconstructing its inner geometry. Our drafting methods are informed by the slicing of the cubes. The cutting on the band saw is replicated through a cut on paper – a series of sectional drawings document the cut pieces in great detail. We draw the objects relying on the precision of drafting, but also on an inherent poetry. How can we interpret what we just did? What kind of context did we create for our work by divesting the objects of their shape, use-value and location? In her book *The Body in Pieces: The Fragment as*

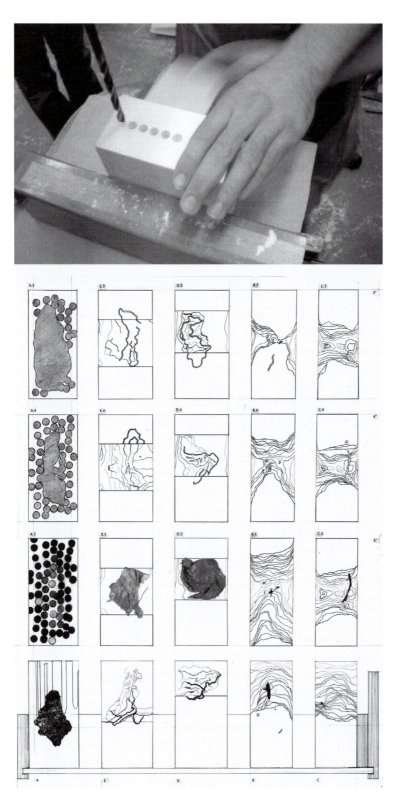

Figure 4 Casting and drawing: Transformation of found objects through submerging, carving, drilling, slicing and drawing. Collage and drawing by student, Jennifer Mills.

a *Metaphor of Modernity* (1994), Linda Nochlin argues that 'the representation of the body in our century can only be at the price of fragmentation, and that collage is the characteristic sign of this' (Nochlin quoted in Bann 2002: 139). Our drawings reconcile fragments produced by the powerful lesions in the living body of American urbanism. Its fragmented interests, structures and narratives are exposed in these sliced plaster cubes and their intricate drawings – a series of two- and three-dimensional collages.

Tracing

Found objects are both traces and traced. Now we trace the plaster sections in search of new form to be built on the site where we started. We explore varying systems of lines and their orientations. The lines are endless; so are their potential interpretations. The layers of tracing papers accumulate on our drafting boards, recreating the layered quality of the site itself. Emerging from these layers is a series of design proposals for small urban structures. A pause, a quiet pavilion, an unknown – this is our elusive program. This small intervention does not 'save' the site, yet it preserves some of its poetic and reveals internal contradictions. Through this discursive process a natural and societal imbalance is exposed, similar to director Godfrey Reggio's depiction of Pruitt-Igoe's demolition in his seminal film *Koyaanisqatsi* (1982). Describing the phenomenon of *Koyaanisqatsi* (Hopi for life out of balance), he used images in absence of dialogues and vocalized narrations to amplify important ethical concerns. Our proposals seek to restore a balance through critical reflection and attention to existing circumstances that result in a series of design proposals that are inherently malleable.

Calibrating

By surveying the blighted streets of St Louis, we inhabit the void spaces of the city. We valorize discarded urban spaces and their marginalized narratives by examining material traces. Our archeology of the present becomes meaningful in opposition to the work of developers and planners. Their 'blight' determines a level of physical decay beyond repair. Where they see blight, we seek beauty – a design pursuit essential to our work. In her book *On Beauty and Being Just*, Elaine Scarry contends 'that beauty, far from contributing to social injustice actually assists us in the work of addressing injustice' (2001: 62). To the introductory architecture student the motive force is to pay attention – to see and appreciate. This project challenges students to cross boundaries between rich and poor, safe and unsafe – both literally and conceptually. Earlier we spoke of Yi-Fu Tuan's comparison of places with objects. He goes on to assert that 'an object or place achieves concrete reality when our experience of it is total, that is, through all of the senses as well as with the active and reflective mind' (Tuan 1977: 18). This idea forms the foundational experience that we believe is important to teaching young architects to make important design decisions. By locating our fieldwork within the discursive realm of design practices, we hope to contribute to the transformation of abstract 'spaces' into specific 'places'. We do not claim to provide students with a total understanding of this place. They have touched its skin and in so doing have reached more deeply inside than would have been possible without their fieldwork.

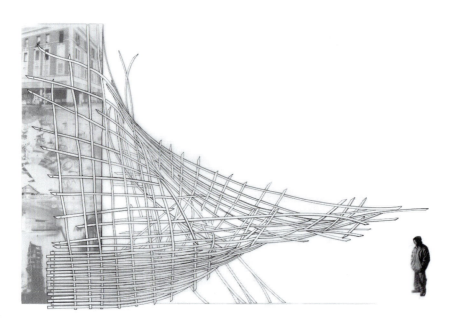

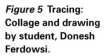

Figure 5 Tracing: Collage and drawing by student, Donesh Ferdowsi.

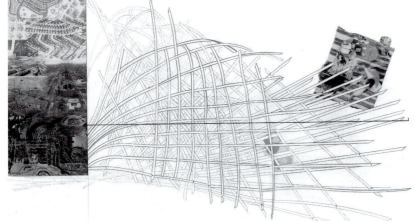

Field note 3

'Refuge' – moving between research and practice

Philipp Misselwitz and Can Altay

I am going to be talking about a project that I have been working on over the last couple of years together with Philipp Misselwitz, also working in Istanbul.[1] This has enabled us to deal to a great extent with certain questions which were intriguing to us: of urban professions, spatial practices and the kinds of limitations of existing modes of practice.

The project is trying to deal with this notion which we call *refuge*, derived into old French from the latin *refugium*. Refuge is commonly understood as a place or state of safety. Those seeking refuge wish to be thrown into a protective space or environment. In colloquial language, the notion of refuge is used quite freely. It can refer even to a holiday retreat, or a place of hiding, some sort of resort or safe haven.

Figure 1 **Still from** *White Butterfly Laundries,* **by Anne Misselwitz and Gunnar Kohne (2009).**

Others instantly associate the word of refuge with refugee-hood or being a refugee. According to the narrow definition developed in the twentieth century, for mainly legal and humanitarian purposes, 'refugee' refers only to forcefully displaced persons who have escaped to safety across a national boundary.

We are proposing that the motive or concept of *refuge* has become one of the key denominators of urban transformation, the urban fragmentation taking place throughout the globe. So in a sense, to try to cast aside the myriad or alternative understandings around refuge, we try to base our concept of refuge relating to three main conditions. The first one being a moment of conflict which results in a choice or forced displacement within a city or within a geography which always includes a repressed trauma and helps create this state of suspension. In both instances it also manifests itself spatially. The collapse of the urban condition or urbanity, in the sense of a civic space, due to conflicts which remain un-negotiated and unresolved, somehow bypassed or postponed through the condition of movement. The second condition is clear spatial manifestation, both in the sense of the very rich seeking refuge from the rest of the city, and literally the space of refugees, but always the creation and manifestation of boundaries between spaces or within spaces. These boundaries always exclusively keep out or contain in. Keep out, in the case of the gated community, means keeping out the masses, keeping out the unwanted side of the city. Whereas at the opposite end, boundaries contain the refugees so that they do not get out. The third condition is a kind of emergence of new behavioural norms and how this feeds the systems of governance, the systems of governance of cities, the systems of these territorial zones, and a state of exception becoming the norm. All of these are a suspension of civic politics, of the politics of the city. What I am referring to can be a very daily life of any city that goes through a certain regeneration or transformation which creates these boundaries, but can also be a much more severe condition of war, of any other un-negotiated condition of conflict.

The main question is what to make of architecture, planning or spatial practices in general in such a context? How can we position ourselves vis-à-vis, in relation to, or within, such conditions of refuge and such states of suspension? How do you really operate when all the norms and rules and regulations of your own practice, your own discipline, your own field, in a sense can no longer operate? How can you operate when traditions or customs of practice are all turned upside-down? How do you work when cities lose the capacity to transform conflict into the civic? Can some civic space still be carved out within this, maybe above or below this state of suspension?

So, then it comes to the relation to practice, the relation to field/work. What really is the professional responsibility to act in such a context? How do you negotiate this struggle to, in a sense, pass the threshold of research, to feed into practice? How, as spatial practitioners, can we leave safe territories of our own fields and disciplines and step into this severe field of polarised society or context where there are no longer clients, no longer commissions, no longer stated budgets, or calculated audiences?

Note

1   The text is an edited extract from the *Field/Work* conference keynote, presented by Can Altay on Saturday, 21 November 2009, which was accompanied by a showing of the documentary film, *White Butterfly Laundries* by Anne Misselwitz and Gunnar Kohne.

Can Altay and Philipp Misselwitz co-curated the exhibition titled 'Refuge: Architectural Proposals for Unbound Spaces' as part of the 4th International Biennale of Rotterdam (Rieniets, Sigler and Christiaanse, 2009). Within 'Open City Istanbul' three exhibitions took place at De po/tütün, Istanbul: *Open City Forum* curated with Tim Rieniets, *Refuge* and *BAS Princen: Fire Cities Portfolio* (2010).

Afterword

Working (through) the field : /

Jane Rendell

What follows are some speculative thoughts on the relation between the terms 'field' and 'work' articulated in response to the fascinating chapters and projects contained within *Architecture and Field/Work*. My purpose is to offer some ideas about how the research encapsulated within this book can be considered with respect to the wider context of inter-disciplinary spatial practice and to reflect upon how future research in architectural design and other practice-led arenas might make productive links between academia and the profession, specifically, as this book suggests to me, by 'working (through) the field'.

When disciplines exchange they come together in dialogue, but there is often also competitive tension and, frequently, disputes over territory. When claims are made for the particular meaning of conceptual terms and the specificity of disciplinary methods what seems to be at stake is the wish to put into play terms that dissolve fixity and valorise ambiguity. This current volume is situated at a point of interchange between architecture and anthropology and as such is concerned particularly with the relevance of 'field work' for architecture, a set of ethnographic techniques, which form the heartland of anthropological methodology. When I asked editor Suzanne Ewing how she understood the distinction between site and field, for example, she pointed out that:

> site is a place to practise in/on/with, and field is a place to learn from/in ... 'To site' implies definitive moves, an author(s) and of course specificity. 'To field' is more contingent, responsive, and depends on flowing, pervasive conditions, clouds, indeterminate edges[1].

Both site and field are spatial terms, which in recent times have provided exciting points of departure and operative mechanisms for new architectural research, but the way in which Ewing draws the distinction between them indicates the emphasis she wishes to place on learning, and also her decision to flag up indeterminacy as a desirable feature of the exchange. So in *Architecture and Field/Work* the emergence of a new term – 'field' – in architecture is given value in relation to a more established term – 'site' – by virtue of its potential as a location of learning and for its indefinite qualities.

This desire to discover new terms, which allow the production of, and the claims for, knowledge to be unfixed, is part of a larger project in spatial theory and practice. Elsewhere I have explored how cultural geography and other allied fields have, over the past 30 years, continually sought to discover unfixed or relational qualities in given spatial terms so demonstrating that space is an active ingredient, not a passive backdrop, in social and cultural life (Rendell 2006: 15–20). In the 1970s, for example, one of the main projects for cultural geographers was the 'reassertion of space in critical social theory' (Soja 1989). While time, as history, through the dialectical processes of historical materialism in Marxist thought, had been taken to be the active entity in shaping social production, space was taken to be merely the site in which social relations took place. To argue for the importance of space in producing change geographers such as David Harvey, Doreen Massey and Edward Soja turned to the work of French philosopher Henri Lefebvre (Harvey 1989, Massey 1994). In *The Production of Space*, Lefebvre suggests that the relation between space and the social is two-way: 'Space and the political organization of space express social relationships but also react back upon them (Lefebvre [1974] 1991: 8).' Soja describes this concept of Lefebvre's as the 'fundamental notion of the socio-spatial dialectic: that social and spatial relations are dialectically inter-reactive, interdependent; that social relations of production are both space forming and space contingent' (Lefebvre [1974]1991: 8)[2]. This meant then that space was not inert but an active ingredient, not only socially produced, but also, and importantly, vital in the production of social relations.

This highlighting of the importance of space rather than time in the postmodern period encouraged a 'turn' to spatial theory in the late 1980s and early 1990s. Academics from all kinds of disciplines, from art history to cultural studies, looked to geography for a rigorous and theoretically informed analysis of the relationship between spatial and social relations. Published in 1993, Michael Keith's and Steve Pile's edited collection of essays, *Place and the Politics of Identity*, marked the moment in the debate when place started to become more central to discussions (Keith and Pile 1993). By interrogating the reciprocity of the relation between the politics of place and the place of politics, the introduction and many of the essays in the collection highlighted an interest in 'unfixing' place (Keith and Pile 1993: 5). Doreen Massey had already been arguing in favour of an understanding of place as 'unfixed, contested and multiple'. For Massey, although a place may constitute one articulation of the spatial or one particular moment in a network of social relations, each point of view is contingent on and subject to change (Massey 1994: 4–5).

As an intellectual tool, the 'unfixing' of place operated as a critique of writings in human geography and architectural theory that had emphasized the special qualities of particular places as if they were somehow pre-given and not open to change or connected to wider conditions. The focus on 'genius loci', in architecture in particular, had essentializing tendencies[3]. While other work, including Yi-Tu Tuan's notion of topophilia and Gaston Bachelard's concept of topoanalysis, had been far more valuable in emphasizing a humane, but also an imaginative and sensual understanding of place[4].

In 2002 cultural geographers came to reflect on the 'seminal' theorists whose 'spatial thinking' had influenced geography's so called 'spatial turn', (Crang and Thrift 2000). In *Thinking Space*, editors Mike Crang and Nigel Thrift identified a number of new themes in spatial thinking such as experience and travel, trace and deferral, mobility, practice and performance (Crang and Thrift 2000: Introduction, 19–24). All the qualities noted indicated that space had become mobilized as experiential and practice-oriented, not only from a social perspective, but also in a way which somehow emphasized temporal qualities – not the 'old' time of history but other temporalities – flow, flux, duration, ephemerality, event – arguably setting up discussions that are now being termed the 'performative turn' (Rendell 2009: 20).

Over a similar timeframe discourses around public, context-based and site-specific art developed an understanding of site beyond its location as the physical coordinates of the work but instead in relation to performance and also to ethnography. Some authors made their arguments with particular reference to the practice of place, Nick Kaye, for example, made a strong argument for site as a performed place (Kaye 2000). Also drawing on Michel de Certeau's 'notion of space as a practiced place' (de Certeau 1988: 117), in my *Art and Architecture: A Place Between* (2006), I identified an inter-disciplinary mode of practice, located between art and architecture, which I termed 'critical spatial practice', to describe works that intervened into specific sites in order to offer both a moment of self-reflection on their own methods as well as social critiques of those sites and their cultural histories and contemporary social uses[5].

Miwon Kwon's *One Place after Another* (2002) also used place as a term from which to begin a critique of site-specificity. Kwon noted that site-specificity had been 'embraced as an automatic signifier of "criticality"' in current art practice and argued instead that there was a lack of criticality in much site-specific work and that while site-specific practice might have a radical potential it is always open to co-option by institutional and market forces (Kwon 2002: 1). The title of her book sounded a warning of 'undifferentiated serialization', one of the dangers associated with taking one site after another without examining the differences between them (Kwon 2002: 166). Kwon looked to Homi Bhabha's concept of 'relational specificity' as a way of emphasizing the importance of thinking about the particularity of the relationships between objects, people and spaces positioned, akin to James Clifford's notion of site as a mobile place, between fixed points (Clifford 2000: 52–73).

Meanwhile Alex Coles's edited collection, *Site Specificity: The Ethnographic Turn*, positioned art's interest in site within an ethnographic perspective that included the research processes of fieldwork as well as the role of the artist as a contemporary ethnographer (Coles 2000). This approach also defined sites not in terms of geometry but in relation to the cultural and spatial practices that produced them, including the actions of their researchers and investigators. Indeed, following Hal Foster's seminal essay, self-critique, along with culture, context, alterity and inter-disciplinarity, were taken to be the key aspects of anthropological research to impact on fine art practice (Foster 1996: 171–204, Foster 2002: 91).

When locating the new collection of essays in *Architecture and Field/Work* within the broader development of spatial terms, it is important to note that the emergence of 'field' in architecture, alongside space, place and site, is explicitly anthropological in its reference. It is not the first time that architects have been interested in anthropology; in the late 1960s and early 1970s research into the use of architectural spaces drew greatly on anthropological approaches[6]. In more recent work, it is an explicit interest in ethnographic processes which characterizes the inter-disciplinary encounter. The fascination with certain methodological qualities certainly seems to overlap with fine art's attraction to ethnography as noted by Foster. Architectural practitioners and cultural critics in *Architecture and Field/Work* are interested in shifting the focus from the architectural product to the whole production process and its various constituents as a field of enquiry. While earlier engagements with anthropology emphasized the 'users' of architecture as producers of cultural space, this current interaction also highlights the role of the building industry in the construction of architecture, and shifts the terminology employed to discuss producers and users towards the ethnographic term 'participants', thus questioning the line drawn between researcher and researched, and bringing ethical issues concerning researching subjects and their objects of study – people as well as buildings – into the frame.

Of particular interest in this book's specific engagement between architecture and anthropology is the decision to focus on 'work'. For this reason the chapters and the projects discussed in this collection produce an original take on the broader cultural project I have described so far and its concern in revitalizing spatial terms. Thus far in order to (re)activate spatial terms critics have shown how they interrelate with social and temporal categories, from the socio-spatial dialectic, to the unfixing of place, to site as a performed place. Rather than space, place or site, *Architecture and Field/Work* explores the potential of the spatial term 'field', and it examines field's relation to the social-temporal category not of unfixing or performance but of work; and it does so not with explicit reference to the dialectic but rather through the operation of /.

Work is an action, it refers to the act of labour, but it is also a term used to describe a process in psychoanalysis – the 'working-through' of resistance. For Sigmund Freud, resistance is a response, it comprises actions that are performed to avoid the process of remembering painful events that have been repressed: 'The greater the resistance', Freud says, 'the more extensively will acting out (repetition) replace remembering.'[7] The therapeutic process of psychoanalysis allows analysands to work through material that has been repressed, to bring unconscious elements of the psychic structure into relation with consciousness. So how might this psychoanalytic process of working-through be relevant to field/work?

I suggest that a consideration of work in terms of 'working-through' brings to mind the need to work-through disciplinary resistances, the ways in which disciplines foreground and value certain patterns of enquiry and knowledge production, and ignore, marginalize and even repress others. Perhaps then the very interest that architecture currently has in ethnographic practice is present precisely because these methodologies contain qualities and activities that have been and are currently cast aside and devalued in architecture, or maybe because adopting such research procedures which engage with a range of participants can shift attitudes towards that which has been repressed in architecture.

Strands of the architectural profession have pragmatic needs that often favour short-term economic gain; when working within a capitalist system procedures need to be simplified in order to make design work profitable. It is also the case that the university, with its managerialist attitudes and bureaucratic structures, is a field of knowledge production deeply embedded within capitalist modes of production and consumption, and more recently with the scandalous bail-out of the banks, it is facing, along with the whole of the public sector, a future raided of finance. Higher education is located within the current crisis of capitalism, but does not face quite the same restrictions or priorities as the architectural profession – as long as the funding alloc-ated to academics still allows original knowledge to be generated that does not have to be entirely focused on economic impact, the possibility remains for the development of new research cultures which might allow for a working-through of resistance to see what has been repressed in architectural practice.

I would like to end with a note on the /, or forward slash, that links field to work. A major feature of *Architecture and Field/Work* is the in-depth discussion, more explicitly made in the editorial introductions but also implicit in the individual contribu-tions, of the different relations that exist between the terms field and work as: field work, fieldwork and field/work. Ewing has highlighted her own interest in how the shift from field work to fieldwork is a change from verb to noun. I have been exploring a par-allel interest in my site-writing project, but rather than a shift from verb to noun, I take a noun and a verb and join them together to produce a hybrid[8]. It was the hyphen which provided me with an exciting opportunity to create a new term noun-verb out of two others, and I find the use of the slash in field/work even more provocative. The forward slash is often employed instead of the hyphen or dash to connect two terms, but it can also indicate alternative terms. So what does this specific use of the forward-facing slash here in *Field/Work* suggest? Does the connection made between the two terms also highlight a distinction, so making their combination one of amalgamation, hybridity and of differences juxtaposed? And where does this forward-facing mark point to, who and how might it join and split, and what is it capable of doing?

Notes

1   Personal email correspondence, 17 May 2010.
2   This quote from Henri Lefebvre emphasized by David Harvey is discussed in Soja (1989: 81).
3   See, for example, Christian Norberg-Schulz, *Genius Loci: Towards a Phenomenology of Architecture* (New York: Rizzoli, 1980).
4   See Gaston Bachelard, *The Poetics of Space*, translated by Maria Jolas (Boston: Beacon Press, 1969) and Yi-Fu Tuan, *Topophilia: A Study of the Environmental Perception, Attitudes and Values* (Englewood Cliffs, NJ: Prentice Hall, 1974). See also

Paul C. Adams, Steven Hoelscher and Karen E.Till (eds) *Textures of Place: Exploring Humanist Geographies* (Minneapolis: University of Minnesota Press, 2001) pp. xix.

5   The term 'critical spatial practice' was first introduced in my article, Jane Rendell 'A Place Between Art, Architecture and Critical Theory', *Proceedings to Place and Location* (Tallinn, Estonia, 2003), pp. 221–33 (published in English and Estonian) and later consolidated and developed in my book *Art and Architecture*.

6   See for example, Amos Rapoport, *House Form and Culture* (New Jersey: Prentice Hall, 1969); Amos Rapoport, *Human Aspects of Urban Form* (Oxford, Pergamom Press, 1977); Anthony D. King (ed.), *Buildings and Society: Essays on the Social Development of the Built Environment* (London: Routledge a Kegan Paul, 1980); and Anthony King, *The Bungalow* (Oxford: Oxford University Press, 1995). See also the work of anthropologist Shirley Ardener, 'Ground Rules and Social Maps for Women', Shirley Ardener (ed.), *Women and Space: Ground Rules and Social Maps* (Oxford: Berg, 1993), pp. 1–30.

7   Sigmund Freud, 'Remembering, Repeating and Working Through' (1914) *The Standard Edition of the Complete Psychological Works of Sigmund Freud, Volume XII (1911–1913): The Case of Schreber, Paper on Technique and Other Works*, translated from the German under the general editorship of James Strachey (London: The Hogarth Press, 1958) pp. 145–156.

8   My aim in my site-writing work is to write sites rather than write about them – to remake the material qualities of the sites in textual form – and in so doing, to shift the relation between subject, verb and object, so that instead of an author, as subject, writing about a site, as object, a different relation is created, where a new site, produced through writing, operates as an object as well as a process, a noun as well as a verb, so setting up a set of relations between sites as subjects and objects. My site-writing project was initiated as a pedagogic tool at the Bartlett School of Architecture, UCL, from 2001, and as a mode of spatializing writing first in Jane Rendell, 'Doing it, (Un)Doing it, (Over)Doing it Yourself: Rhetorics of Architectural Abuse', Jonathan Hill (ed.) *Occupying Architecture* (London: Routledge, 1998) pp. 229–46, and then developed through a whole series of essays and works, brought together in Jane Rendell, *Site-Writing: The Architecture of Art Criticism* (London: IB Tauris, 2010).

Bibliography

Abegg, R. and Wiener, C.B. (2005) *The Fraumünster in Zurich*, Berne: Society for the History of Swiss Art.

Adams, P.C., Hoelscher, S. and Till, K.E. (2001) 'Place in Context: Rethinking Humanist Geographies', in P.C. Adams, S. Hoelscher and K.E. Till (eds) *Textures of Place: Exploring Humanist Geographies*, Minneapolis: University of Minnesota Press: xiii–xxxiii.

Alberti, L.B. (1988) *On the Art of Building in Ten Books*, trans. J. Rykwert, N. Leach and R. Tavernor, Cambridge, MA: MIT Press.

Al-Tabari (1995) *The History of al-Tabari, Abbasid Authority Affirmed*, vol. 28, trans. J. McAuliffe, Albany: State University of New York Press.

Altork, K. (1995) 'Walking the Fire Line: The Erotic Dimension of the Fieldwork Experience', in D. Kulick and M. Wilson (eds) *Taboo: Sex, Identity, and Erotic Subjectivity in Anthropological Fieldwork*, London: Routledge: 107–139.

American Heritage Dictionary of the English Language, The (1992) Boston: Houghton Mifflin Company.

Amit, V. (ed.) (2000) *Constructing the Field: Ethnographic Fieldwork in the Contemporary World*, London: Routledge.

Archives of American Art (Dwan 1967), Smithsonian Institution, Robert Smithson and Nancy Holt Papers, 1905–1987, microfilm 3832, frames 967–973: Letters from Virginia Dwan to county clerks in Pine Barrens region, dated 21 April 1967.

—— (Dwan 1984), Smithsonian Institution, Virginia Dwan interviews, 21 March–7 June 1984.

—— (Flavin 1966), Smithsonian Institution, Robert Smithson and Nancy Holt Papers, 1905–1987, unfilmed material: Postcard from Dan Flavin to Robert Smithson, postmarked 12 February 1966 from Cold Springs, New York.

—— (Graham 1966), Smithsonian Institution, Robert Smithson and Nancy Holt Papers, 1905–1987, microfilm 3832, frame 848: Letter from Dan Graham to Robert Smithson, postmarked 11 March 1966.

—— (McConathy 1966), Smithsonian Institution, Robert Smithson and Nancy Holt Papers, 1905–1987, microfilm 3832, frames 843–844: Letter from Dale McConathy to Robert Smithson, dated 22 January 1966.

—— (McPhee 1967), Smithsonian Institution, Robert Smithson and Nancy Holt Papers, 1905–1987, microfilm 3836, frames 357–377: Part II of John McPhee's 1967 Pine Barrens article in *The New Yorker*.

—— (Robbin n.d.), Smithsonian Institution, Robert Smithson and Nancy Holt Papers, 1905–1987: Undated audiotape interview with Robert Smithson by Tony Robbin.

—— (Smithson 1967), Smithsonian Institution, Robert Smithson and Nancy Holt Papers, 1905–1987, microfilm 3832, frames 501–508: Robert Smithson's 1967 date book, which ends with the month of June.

—— (Smithson 1972), Smithsonian Institution, Oral history interview with Robert Smithson, 14–19 July 1972.

Artforum (1968a) [Gallery advertisement for 'Earth Works'], September 1968.

—— (1968b) [Gallery advertisement for 'Earth Works'], October 1968.

Augé, M. (1992) *Non-places: Introduction to an Anthropology of Supermodernity*, London: Verso.

Averlino, A. (1965) *Filarete's Treatise on Architecture*, trans. J. Spencer, New Haven: Yale University Press.

Bahn, P.G. (2007) *Cave Art: A Guide to the Decorated Ice Age Caves of Europe*, London: Frances Lincoln.

Bahn, P.G. and Vertut, J. (2001) *Journey through the Ice Age*, Berkeley: University of California Press.

Bakhtin, M.K. (1968) *Rabelais and his World* (1965), trans. H. Iswolsky, Cambridge, MA: MIT Press.

—— (1984) *Problems of Dostoyevsky's Poetics* (1929), ed. and trans. C. Emmerson, Minneapolis: University of Minnesota Press.

Ballantyne, A. (2004) 'Misprisions of Stonehenge', in D. Arnold and A. Ballantyne (eds) *Architecture as Experience: Radical Change in Spatial Practice*, London: Routledge: 11–35.

Banks, M. (1998) 'Visual Anthropology: Image, Object and Interpretation', in J. Prosser (ed.) *Image-based Research: A Sourcebook for Qualitative Researchers*, London: Falmer Press: 9–23.

—— (2001) *Visual Methods in Social Research*, Thousand Oaks, CA: Sage.

Bann, S. (2002) 'Mould, Rubble, and the Validation of the Fragment in the Discourse of the Past', in B. Neville and J. Villeneuve (eds) *Waste-Site Stories: The Recycling of Memory*, Albany: State University of New York Press.

Barfield, T. (1997) 'Fieldwork', in T. Barfield (ed.) *The Dictionary of Anthropology*, Oxford: Blackwell: 188–190.

Barnett, R.S. (1995) 'Choosing Our Words Carefully', *Architectural Record*, 183 (6): 32.

Bataille, G. (1980) *Prehistoric Painting: Lascaux or the Birth of Art*, trans. A. Wainhouse, Geneva: Skira; London: Macmillan.

Baxter, A. & Associates (2004) *The Museum of Childhood at Bethnal Green Conservation Plan*, unpublished report prepared for the Museum of Childhood.

Bear, L. and Sharp, W. (1970) 'Discussions with Heizer, Oppenheim, Smithson', *Avalanche*, 1 (1): 48–71.

Beattie, M. (2003) 'Hybrid Identities: Public and Private Life in the Courtyard Houses of Barabazaar, Kolkata, India', in S. Menin (ed.) *Constructing Place: Mind and Matter*, London: Routledge: 154–165.

—— (2005) 'The Marketplace as Hybrid Space: Re-reading Barabazaar and the City', unpublished PhD thesis, University of Newcastle, Newcastle upon Tyne.

—— (2008) 'Hybrid Bazaar Space: Colonialisation, Globalisation and Traditional Space in Barabazaar, Calcutta, India', *Journal of Architectural Education*, 61 (3): 44–55.

Bellucci, R. and Frosinini, C. (2002) 'Working Together: Technique + Innovation in Masolino's and Masaccio's Panel Paintings', in C. Strehlke with C. Frosinini (eds) *The Panel Paintings of Masolino and Masaccio: The Role of Technique*, Milan: Five Continents: 29–68.

Bennett, D. and Bhabha, H.K. (1998) 'Liberalism and Minority Culture Reflections on "Culture's In Between"', in D. Bennett (ed.) *Multicultural States Rethinking Difference and Identity*, London: Routledge: 37–47.

Berger, R. (1993) 'From Text to (Field)work and Back Again: Theorizing a Post(modern) Ethnography', *Anthropological Quarterly*, 66 (4): 174–186.

Berleant, A. (1991) *Art and Engagement*, Philadelphia: Temple University Press.

Berlin, I. (1993) *The Hedgehog and the Fox: An Essay on Tolstoy's View of History*, Chicago: Elephant Paperbacks, Ivan R. Dee.

Bhabha, H.K. (1994) *The Location of Culture*, London: Routledge.

Bion, N. (1972 [1758]) *The Construction and Principal Uses of Mathematical Instruments*, trans. E. Stone, London: Holland Press.

Birch, E. (1986) 'The Observation Man: A Study of William H. Whyte', *Planning Magazine*, March: 4–8.

Boettger, S. (2004) 'Behind the Earth Movers', *Art in America*, April: 54–63.

Bradburd, D. (1998) *Being There: The Necessity of Fieldwork*, Washington, DC: Smithsonian Institution Press.

Brianard, G., Mehta, R. and Moran, T. (2008) 'Grand Tour', *Perspecta 41*, The Yale Architecture Journal, Cambridge, MA: MIT Press.

Burns, C.J. and Kahn, A. (2005) 'Why Site Matters', C.J. Burns and A. Kahn (eds) *Site Matters: Design Concepts, Histories, and Strategies*, London and New York: Routledge: vii–xxix.

Careri, F. (2002) *Walkscapes: Walking as an Aesthetic Practice*, Barcelona: Ed. Gustavo Gili.

Carter, P. (2005) *Material Thinking: The Theory and Practice of Creative Research*, Melbourne: Melbourne University Press.

Carty, C. (1999) 'The Role of Medieval Dream Images in Authenticating Ecclesiastical Construction', *Zeitschrift für Kunstgeschichte*, 62 (1): 45–90.

Caruso St John Architects (2004a) *Planning Report, Museum of Childhood at Bethnal Green*, unpublished report.

—— (2004b) *Stage E Detail Design Report, Museum of Childhood at Bethnal Green Revision A*, unpublished report.

Castaneda, C. (1968) *The Teachings of Don Juan: A Yaqui Way of Knowledge*, New York: Washington Square Press.

Cennini, C. (1954) *The Craftsman's Handbook 'Il Libro dell' Arte'*, trans. Daniel Thompson, Jr., New York: Dover.

Cesariano, C. (1521) *Vitruvius, De Architectura*, Como.

Chapman, M. and Ostwald, M.J. (2009) 'Unstable Ground: Scientific Frictions in the Analytical Techniques of *Learning from Las Vegas*', *Architectural Science Review*, 52 (4): 245–253.

Chmielewska, E. (2008) 'Niepamięć w upamiętnianiu: szczególność miejsc traumy a typowość pamięci w ikonosferze Warszawy', in K. Chudzimska-Uhera and B. Gutowski (eds) *Rzeźba w Polsce (1945–2008)*, Orońsko: Centrum Rzeźby Polskiej: 101–106.

Chmielewska, A., Tchorek, M. and Carter, P. (2010) 'A Warsaw Address: A Dossier on 36 Smolna Street', *The Journal of Architecture*, 15 (1): 27–29.

Clifford, J. (1983) 'On Ethnographic Authority', *Representations*, 1 (2): 118–147.

—— (1988) *The Predicament of Culture: Twentieth-Century Ethnography, Literature and Art*, Cambridge, MA: Harvard University Press.

—— (2000) 'An Ethnographer in the Field', interview by Alex Coles in *Site Specificity: The Ethnographic Turn*, London: Black Dog Publishing.

Clifford, J. and Marcus, G.E. (eds) (1986) *Writing Culture: The Poetics and Politics of Ethnography*, Berkeley: University of California Press.

Coffey, A. (1999) *The Ethnographic Self: Fieldwork and the Representation of Identity*, London: Sage Publications.

Cohen, A.P. (1992a) 'Post-Fieldwork Fieldwork', *Journal of Anthropological Research*, 48 (4): 339–354.

—— (1992b) 'Self-Conscious Anthropology', in J. Okely and H. Callaway (eds) *Anthropology and Autobiography*, London: Routledge: 221–241.

Coldstream, N. (1991) *Medieval Craftsmen: Masons and Sculptors*, Toronto: University of Toronto Press.

Coles, A. (ed.) (2000) *Site-Specificity: The Ethnographic Turn*, London: Black Dog Publishing.

Corner, J. (1999) 'The Agency of Mapping: Speculation, Critique and Invention', in Denis Cosgrove (ed.) *Mappings*, London: Reaktion Books: 211–252.

Cosgrove, D. (1984) *Social Formation and Symbolic Landscape*, Madison: University of Wisconsin Press.

—— (2008) *Geography & Vision: Seeing, Imagining and Representing the World*, London: I.B. Tauris.

Crang, M. and Thrift, N. (eds) (2000) *Thinking Space*, London: Routledge.

Creswell, K.A.C. (1969) *Early Muslim Architecture: Umayyads, A.D. 622–750*, vol. 1, part 1, Oxford: Clarendon.

Crinson, M. and Lubbock, J. (1994) *Architecture: Art or Profession? Three Hundred Years of Architectural Education in Britain*, Manchester: Manchester University Press.

Crowley, D. (2009) 'Architecture and the Image of the Future in the People's Republic of Poland', *The Journal of Architecture*, 14 (1): 67–84.

Cupples, J. (2002) 'The Field as a Landscape of Desire: Sex and Sexuality in Geographical Fieldwork', *Area*, 34 (4): 382–390.

Dalby, L. (1983) *Geisha*, Berkeley: University of California Press.

D'Amico-Samuels, D. (1991) 'Undoing Fieldwork: Personal, Political, Theoretical and Methodological Implications', in F.V. Harrison (ed.) *Decolonizing Anthropology: Moving Further Toward an Anthropology for Liberation*, Washington, DC: Association of Black Anthropologists, American Anthropological Association: 68–87.

De Certeau, M. (1984) *The Practice of Everyday Life*, Berkeley: University of California Press.

Delamont, S. (2002) *Fieldwork in Educational Settings: Methods, Pitfalls, and Perspectives*, 2nd edn, London: Routledge.

De l'Orme, P. (1567) *Premier Tome de l'Architecture*, Paris.

De Meulder, B., Loeckx, A. and Shannon, K. (2004) 'A Project of Projects', in A. Loeckx, K. Shannon, R. Tuts and H. Verschure (eds) *Urban Trialogues. Visions, projects, co-productions: Localizing Agenda 21*, Nairobi: UNCHS (United Nations Center for Human Settlements): 187–197.

Derrida, J. (1976) *Of Grammatology*, trans. G.C. Spivak, Baltimore: Johns Hopkins University Press.

De Sola-Morales Rubio, I. (1995) 'Terrain vague', in C.C. Davidson (ed.) *Anyplace*, Cambridge, MA: MIT Press: 118–123.

Dewey, J. (1954) 'Search for the Great Community', in *The Public and Its Problems*, Athens, OH: Swallow Press.

Dickenson, H.W. (1949–51) 'Ancient Drawing Tools', *Transactions of the Newcomen Society*, 27: 73–83.

Didi-Huberman, G. (2005) *Confronting Images: Questioning the Ends of a Certain History of Art*, trans. J. Goodman, University Park: Pennsylvania State University Press.

Doherty, C. (ed.) (2004) *Contemporary Art: From Studio to Situation*, London: Black Dog Books.

Duiker, W. (1995) *Vietnam: Revolution in Transition*, Boulder, CO: Westview Press.

Durand, G. (2007) *The Rational Divinorum Officiorum of William Durand of Mende: A New Translation of the Prologue and Book One*, trans. Timothy Thibodeau, New York: Columbia University Press.

Eno, B. (1996) *A Year with Swollen Appendices: Brian Eno's Diary*, London: Faber & Faber.

Enticknap, L. (2009) 'Electronic Enlightenment or the Digital Dark Age? Anticipating Film in an Age without Film', *Quarterly Review of Film and Video*, 26 (5): 415–424.

Ewing, K.P. (1994) 'Dreams from a Saint: Anthropological Atheism and the Temptation to Believe', *American Anthropologist*, 96 (3): 571–583.

Ewing, S. (2009) 'Choosing (What) to Learn from: Las Vegas, Los Angeles, London, Rome, Lagos...?', in S. Chaplin and A. Stara (eds) *Curating Architecture and the City*, London: Routledge: 23–38.

Finnimore, B. (1989) *Houses from the Factory: System Building and the Welfare State 1942–74*, London: Rivers Oram Press.

Fischli, P., Koolhaas, R. and Obrist, H.U. (2009) 'Flaneurs in Automobiles: A Conversation between Fischli, Koolhaas and Obrist', in H. Stadler and M. Stierli (eds) *Las Vegas Studio: Images from the Archives of Robert Venturi and Denise Scott Brown*, Frankfurt: Deutsches Architekturmuseum.

Forty, A. (2006) 'Primitive: The Word and Concept', in J. Odgers, F. Samuel and A. Sharr (eds) *Primitive: Original Matters in Architecture*, London: Routledge: 3–14.

Foster, H. (1996) 'The Artist as Enthnographer', *The Return of the Real: Avant-Garde at the End of the Century*, Cambridge, MA: MIT Press: 171–204.

Foster, H. (2002) *Design and Crime (and other Diatribes)*, London: Verso.

Frampton, K. (1992) *Modern Architecture: A Critical History*, London: Thames & Hudson.

Frascari, M. (2007) 'A Reflection on Paper and Its Virtues within the Material and Invisible Factures of Architecture', in M. Frascari, J. Hale and B. Starkey (eds) *From Models to Drawings: Imagination and Representation in Architecture*, London: Routledge: 23–33.

Freeman, D. (1983) *Margaret Mead and Samoa: The Making and Unmaking of an Anthropological Myth*, Canberra: Australian National University Press.

—— (1996) *Margaret Mead and the Heretic: The Making and Unmaking of an Anthropological Myth*, Harmondsworth and New York: Penguin Books.

—— (1999) *The Fateful Hoaxing of Margaret Mead: A Historical Analysis of Her Samoan Research*, Boulder, CO: Westview Press.

Freilich, M. (ed.) (1970) *Marginal Natives: Anthropologists at Work*, New York: Harper & Row.

French, T. (1947) *Engineering Drawing*, New York: McGraw-Hill.

Freud, S. (1950) *Totem and Taboo: Some Points of Agreement between the Mental Lives of Savages and Neurotics*, trans. J. Strachey, London: Routledge & Kegan Paul.

Friere, P. (1996) *Pedagogy of the Oppressed*, trans. M. Ramos, London: Penguin Books.

Frontinus, S.J. (1961) *Aqueducts of Rome*, trans. C. Bennett, Cambridge, MA: Harvard University Press, Loeb Classical Library.

Fuller, S. (2000) *Thomas Kuhn: A Philosophical History for our Times*, Chicago: University of Chicago Press.

Gadamer, H. (1989) *Truth and Method*, trans. J. Weinsheimer and D. Marshall, New York: Continuum.

Gewertz, D. and Errington, F. (1991) 'We Think, Therefore They Are? On Occidentalizing the World', *Anthropological Quarterly*, 64 (2): 80–91.

Giedion, S. (1962) *The Eternal Present: The Beginnings of Art, a Contribution on Constancy and Change*, London: Oxford University Press.

—— (1964) *The Eternal Present: The Beginnings of Architecture, a Contribution on Constancy and Change*, London: Oxford University Press.

Gilbert, L. and Moore, G. (1981) *Particular Passions: Talks with Women Who Have Shaped Our Times*, New York: Potter.

Gloag, J. (1966) *The Social History of Furniture Design from 1300 BC to 1960 AD*, London: Cassell.

Goldberger, P. (1999) 'Champion of the City', *Architecture*, 88 (4).

Golec, M.J. (2009) 'Format and Layout in Learning from Las Vegas', in A. Vinegar and M.J. Golec (eds) *Relearning from Las Vegas*, Minneapolis: University of Minnesota Press: 31–48.

Good, K. (1991) *Into the Heart: An Amazonian Love Story*, London: Penguin Books.

Gronewald, S. (1972) 'Did Frank Cushing Go Native?', in S.T. Kimball and J.B. Watson (eds) *Crossing Cultural Boundaries*, New York: Chandler: 33–50.

Grosz, E. (2001) *Architecture from the Outside: Essays on Real and Virtual Space*, Cambridge, MA: MIT Press.

Gunther, R.T. (ed.) (1972 [1660]) *The Architecture of Sir Roger Pratt*, New York: Benjamin Blom.

Hall, F. (1994) 'Specifying for quality', *The Architects Journal*, 199 (8 June 1994): 38.

Hannerz, U. (2006) 'Studying Down, Up, Sideways, Through, Backwards, Forwards, Away and at Home: Reflections on the Field Worries of an Expansive Discipline', in S. Coleman and P. Collins (eds) *Locating the Field: Space, Place and Context in Anthropology*, Oxford: Berg: 23–42.

Hansen, O. (1959) 'Forma Otwarta' ('Open Form'), *Przegląd Kulturalny*, 5, trans. M. Wawrzyniak; reprinted in J. Gola (ed.) (2005) *Towards Open Form / Ku Formie Otwartej*, Warsaw: Foksal Gallery Foundation, Revolver, Warsaw Academy of Fine Arts Museum.

—— (1970) 'LSC. Linearny System Ciągły', *Architektura*, 4–5: 126–137.

—— (1975) 'To Break down the Barriers between the Audience and the Actor', *Poland (Polska)*, 10: 38; reprinted in J. Gola (ed.) (2005) *Towards Open Form / Ku Formie Otwartej*, Warsaw: Foksal Gallery Foundation, Revolver, Warsaw Academy of Fine Arts Museum.

—— (1979) 'To Demolish or Not?', *Poland (Polska)*, 5: 6–7; reprinted in J. Gola (ed.) (2005) *Towards Open Form / Ku Formie Otwartej*, Warsaw: Foksal Gallery Foundation, Revolver, Warsaw Academy of Fine Arts Museum.

—— (2003) excerpts from an interview with Hans Ulrich Olbrist, Phillipe Parreno for *Domus* magazine, December 2003; reprinted in J. Gola (ed.) (2005) *Towards Open Form / Ku Formie Otwartej*, Warsaw: Foksal Gallery Foundation, Revolver, Warsaw Academy of Fine Arts Museum.

—— (2005a) *Towards Open Form / Ku Formie Otwartej*, J. Gola (ed.), Warsaw: Foksal Gallery Foundation, Revolver, Warsaw Academy of Fine Arts Museum.

—— (2005b) *Zobaczyć Świat*, ed. J. Gola, Warsaw: Zacheta Narodowa Galeria Sztuki.

Hansen, O. and Hansen, Z. (1967) *Linearny System Ciągły* [*Linear Continuous System*], Warszawa: ZPAP.

Hardgrove, A. (1999) 'Community as Public Culture in Modern India: The Marwaris in Calcutta, c. 1897–1997', unpublished PhD thesis, University of Michigan.

Harley, J.B. (2001) *The New Nature of Maps: Essays in the History of Cartography*, Baltimore and London: Johns Hopkins University Press.

Harvey, D. (1989) *The Condition of Postmodernity*, Oxford: Blackwell.

Harrison, F.V. (ed.) (1991) *Decolonizing Anthropology: Moving Further Toward an Anthropology for Liberation*, Washington, DC: Association of Black Anthropologists, American Anthropological Association.

Hay, J. (1985) 'Surface and the Chinese Painter: The Discovery of Surface', *Archives of Asian Art*, 38: 95–123.

Henley, P. (1998) 'Film-making and ethnographic research', in J. Prosser (ed.) *Image-based Research: A Sourcebook for Qualitative Researchers*, London: Falmer Press: 42–59.

Hensel, M., Hight, C. and Menges, A. (eds) (2009) *Space Reader: Heterogenous Space in Architecture*, Chichester: John Wiley/AD.

Herzfeld, M. (1987) *Anthropology through the Looking Glass: Critical Ethnography in the Margins of Europe*, Cambridge: Cambridge University Press.

Hight, C. (2008) *Architectural Principles in the Age of Cybernetics*, London: Routledge.

Hinson, G. (2000) *Fire in my Bones: Transcendence and the Holy Spirit in African American Gospel*, Philadelphia: University of Pennsylvania Press.

Hobbs, R. (1981) *Robert Smithson: Sculpture*, Ithaca, NY: Cornell University Press.

Holt, N. (2004) Public lecture (title unknown) by Nancy Holt at the Museum of Contemporary Art, Los Angeles, December 2004.

—— (2009) Personal correspondence Nancy Holt to Emily Scott (email, 20 April).

—— (2010) Personal correspondence Nancy Holt to Emily Scott (email, 21 January).

Holt, N. and Scott, E. (2009a) [Author interview] Nancy Holt interview with Emily Scott, 11 March.

—— (2009b) [Author interview] Nancy Holt interview with Emily Scott, 28 November.

Jackson, J.B. (1997) *Discovering the Vernacular Landscape*, New Haven, CT, and London: Yale University Press.

Jackson, V. and Sinclair, A. (2007) *Archaeology Graduates of the Millennium: A Survey of the Career Histories of Graduates 2000–2007*, London: The Higher Education Academy.

Jaschke, K. (2005) 'Mythopoetic Modernism: Aldo van Eyck: Architecture as/and Art', in E. Laaksonen and M. Vainio (eds) *Architecture and Art: New Visions, New Strategies*, Helsinki: Alvar Aalto Foundation/Alvar Aalto Academy: 56–62.

—— (2009) 'City Is House and House Is City: Aldo van Eyck, Piet Blom and the Architecture of Homecoming', in V. Di Palma, D. Periton and M. Lathouri (eds) *Intimate Metropolis: Urban Subjects in the Modern City*, London: Routledge: 175–194.

Jencks, C. (1986) 'The Death of Modern Architecture', in *The Language of Post-Modern Architecture*, New York: Rizzoli.

Johnson, N.B. (1984) 'Sex, Color, and Rites of Passage in Ethnographic Research', *Human Organization*, 43 (2): 108–120.

Jones, E.M. (1993) *Degenerate Moderns: Modernity as Rationalized Sexual Misbehaviour*, San Francisco: Ignatius Press.

Kannicke, A. (2010) 'Nostalgia in Private Space: Domesticating Time', paper presented at *Home Cultures*, Sheffield, January 2010.

Kayden, J.S. (2000) *Privately Owned Public Space: The New York City Experience*, New York: John Wiley & Sons.

Kaye, N. (2000) *Site Specific Art: Performance, Place and Documentation*, London: Routledge.

Keesing, R.M. and Strathern, A.J. (1998) 'Fieldwork', in *Cultural Anthropology: A Contemporary Perspective*, Fort Worth: Harcourt Brace: 7–10.

Keith, M. and Pile, S. (eds) (1993) *Place and the Politics of Identity*, London: Routledge.

Killick, A.P. (1995) 'The Penetrating Intellect: On Being White, Straight and Male in Korea', in D. Kulick and M. Wilson (eds) *Taboo: Sex, Identity and Erotic Subjectivity in Anthropological Fieldwork*, London: Routledge: 76–105.

Kipfer, B.A. (2007) *The Archaeologist's Fieldwork Companion*, Malden, MA: Blackwell.

Kohn, D. (2006) '176 Museum of Childhood: Concrete Works', Fax (9 May 2006).

—— (2009) [Author Interview] David Kohn interview with Mhairi McVicar (1 May).

Krinsky, C. (1965) *Cesare Cesariano and the Como Vitruvius Edition of 1521*, PhD dissertation, New York University.

Kuhn, T. (1962) *The Structure of Scientific Revolutions*, Chicago: University of Chicago Press.

Kulick, D. (1995) 'The Sexual Life of Anthropologists: Erotic Subjectivity and Ethnographic Work', in D. Kulick and M. Wilson (eds) *Taboo: Sex, Identity and Erotic Subjectivity in Anthropological Fieldwork*, London: Routledge: 1–27.

Kulick, D. and Wilson, M. (eds) (1995) *Taboo: Sex, Identity and Erotic Subjectivity in Anthropological Fieldwork*, London: Routledge.

Kuper, A. (1988) *The Invention of Primitive Society: Transformations of an Illusion*, London and New York: Routledge.

Kwon, M. (2002) *One Place after Another: Site Specific Art and Locational Identity*, Cambridge, MA: MIT Press.

LaFarge, A. (ed.) (2000) *The Essential William Whyte*, New York: Fordham University Press.

Lassiter, L.E. (2005) *The Chicago Guide to Collaborative Ethnography*, Chicago: University of Chicago Press.

Latour, B. (1987) *Science in Action: How to Follow Scientists and Engineers through Society*, Cambridge, MA: Harvard University Press.

—— (1999) *Pandora's Hope: Essays on the Reality of Science Studies*, Cambridge, MA: Harvard University Press.

—— (2005) *Reassembling the Social: An Introduction to Actor-Network-Theory*, Oxford: Oxford University Press.

Leach, N. (1999) *The Anaesthetics of Architecture*, Cambridge, MA: MIT Press.

Leatherbarrow, D. (2000) *Uncommon Ground: Architecture, Technology, and Topography*, Cambridge, MA: MIT Press.

—— (2004) 'Leveling the Land', in *Topographical Stories: Studies in Landscape and Architecture*, Philadelphia: University of Pennsylvania Press: 114–130.

Lefebvre, H. (1991) *The Production of Space*, Oxford: Blackwell Publishing.

Leroi-Gourhan, A. (1968) *The Art of Prehistoric Man in Western Europe*, trans. N. Guterman, London: Thames & Hudson.

—— (1993) *Gesture and Speech*, trans. A.B. Berger, Cambridge, MA: MIT Press.

Lévi-Strauss, C. (1955) *Tristes Tropiques*, London: Jonathon Cape.

—— (1963) *Structural Anthropology*, New York: Basic Books.

Lewis-Williams, D. (2004) *The Mind in the Cave: Consciousness and the Origins of Art*, London: Thames & Hudson.

Logan, W. (2000) *Hanoi: Biography of a City*, Sydney: Select Publishing, University of New South Wales Press.

McGowan, J.M. (2008) 'Ralph Erskine, (Skiing) Architect', *Nordlit*, 23 (vår 2008): 241–252.

—— (2010) 'Ralph Erskine, Colonist? Notes towards an Alternative History of Arctic Architecture', in A. Müller (ed.) *Arctic Perspective Cahier No. 1: Architecture*, Ostfildern: Hatje Cantz Verlag.

McPhee, J. (1967a) 'Profiles: The Pine Barrens – I', *The New Yorker*, 43, 25 November: 67–68ff.

—— (1967b) 'Profiles: The Pine Barrens – II', *The New Yorker*, 43, 2 December: 66–68ff.

—— (1968) *The Pine Barrens*, New York: Farrar, Straus and Giroux.

McVicar, M. (2010) 'Passion and Control: Lewerentz and a Mortar Joint', in A. Dutoit, J. Odgers and A. Sharr (eds) *Quality out of Control: Standards for Measuring Architecture*, London, New York: Routledge.

Massey, D. (1994) *Space, Place and Gender*, Cambridge: Polity Press.

—— (2003) 'Imagining the Field', in M. Pryke, G. Rose and S. Whatmore (eds) *Using Social Theory: Thinking Through Research*, London: Sage and the Open University: 71– 88.

—— (2005) *For Space*, London: Sage.

Mayerfeld Bell, M. (1997) 'The Ghosts of Place', *Theory and Society*, 26: 813–836.

Mead, M. (1928) *Coming of Age in Samoa: A Study of Adolescence and Sex in Primitive Societies*, New York: HarperCollins.

Meyer, E. (2005) 'Site Citations: The Grounds of Modern Landscape Architecture', in C. Burns and A. Kahn (eds) *Site Matters: Design Concepts, Histories and Strategies*, New York and London: Routledge: 29–129.

Meyer, J. (2001) 'The Mirror of Fashion', *Artforum*, May: 134–138.

Minh-Ha, T.T. (1989) *Woman, Native, Other: Writing, Postcoloniality and Feminism*, Bloomington: Indiana University Press.

—— (1991) *When the Moon Waxes Red: Representation, Gender and Cultural Politics*, New York: Routledge.

—— (1992) *Framer Framed*, New York: Routledge.

Morley, J. (1999) *The History of Furniture: Twenty-five Centuries of Style and Design in the Western Tradition*, Boston: Bulfinch.

Morton, H. (1995) 'My Chastity Belt: Avoiding Seduction in Tonga', in D. Kulick and M. Wilson (eds) *Taboo: Sex, Identity and Erotic Subjectivity in Anthropological Fieldwork*, London: Routledge: 168–184.

Myers, J. (2006) 'No-Places: Earthworks and Urbanism Circa 1970', unpublished PhD thesis, University of California, Berkeley.

Nancy, J.-L. (1996) 'Painting in the Grotto', in *The Muses*, trans. P. Kamuf, Stanford, CA: Stanford University Press.

Narayan, K. (1999) 'Ethnography and Fiction: Where is the Border?', *Anthropology and Humanism*, 24 (2): 132–147.

National Recording Project Database [NRPD] (undated) London: Public Monuments and Sculpture Association.

Necipoglu-Kafadar, G. (September, 1986) 'Plans and Models in 15th- and 16th- Century Ottoman Architectural Practice', *Journal of the Society of Architectural Historians*, 45 (3): 224–243.

Ness, K. (2009) 'Not Just about Bricks: The Invisible Building Worker', in Dainty, A.R.G. (ed.), 25th Annual ARCOM Conference, 7–9 September 2009, Albert Hall, Nottingham, Association of Researchers in Construction Management, 1: 645–654.

Neufert, E. (1936) *Bau-Entwurfslehre*, Berlin: Bauwelt.

Newton, E. (1993) 'My Best Informant's Dress: The Erotic Equation in Fieldwork', *Cultural Anthropology*, 8 (1): 3–23.

—— (2000) *Margaret Mead Made Me Gay: Personal Essays, Public Ideas*, Durham, NC: Duke University Press.

Nochlin, L. (1994) *The Body in Pieces: The Fragment as a Metaphor of Modernity*, London: Thames & Hudson.

Norvell, P.A. (1969) 'Robert Smithson: Fragments of an Interview with P.A. Norvell, April, 1969', in L. Lippard, *Six Years: The Dematerialization of Art*, New York: Praeger: 87–90.

Oakes, T. and Price, P. (eds) (2008) *The Cultural Geography Reader*, London: Routledge.

Outram, D. (1996) 'New Spaces in Natural History', in N. Jardine, J. Secord and E. Spary (eds) *Cultures of Natural History*, Cambridge: Cambridge University Press: 249–265.

Paglen, T. (2008) 'Experimental Geography: From Cultural Production to the Production of Space', in N. Thompson (ed.) (2008) *Experimental Geography: Radical Approaches to Landscape, Cartography, and Urbanism*, New York: Independent Curators' International: 26–33.

Parkes, M.B. (1993) *Pause and Effect: An Introduction to the History of Punctuation in the West*, Berkeley: University of California Press.

Perec, G. (2008) *Species of Spaces and Other Pieces*, trans. J. Sturrock, London: Penguin Books.

Perloff, M. (1998) 'The Morphology of the Amorphous: Bill Viola's Videoscapes', Online: http://epc.buffalo.edu/authors/perloff/viola.html (accessed 21 November 2009).

Petrescu, D. (2007) 'The Indeterminate Mapping of the Common', *Field*, 1 (1).

Physick, J.F. (1982) *The Victoria and Albert Museum: The History of Its Building*, Oxford: Phaidon.

Pickles, J. (1995) *Ground Truth: The Social Implications of Geographic Information Systems*, New York: Guilford Press.

Pozzo, A. (1989) *Perspective in Architecture and Painting*, an unabridged reprint of the English and Latin edition of *Perspectiva Pictorum et Architectorum* (1693), New York: Dover.

Prasad, S. (1998) 'The Havelis of North India: The Urban Courtyard House', unpublished PhD thesis, Royal College of Art, London.

Pye, D. (1968) *The Nature and Art of Workmanship*, Cambridge: Cambridge University Press.

Rabinow, P. (1977) *Reflections on Fieldwork in Morocco*, Berkeley: University of California Press.

Raphaël, M. (1946) *Prehistoric Cave Paintings*, New York: Pantheon Books.

Rattenbury, K. (2008) *Robert Venturi and Denise Scott Brown: Learning from Las Vegas*, London: Routledge.

Reggio, G. (dir.) (1982) *Koyaanisqatsi*.

Remensnyder, A. (1995) *Remembering Kings Past: Monastic Foundation Legends in Medieval Southern France*, Ithaca, NY: Cornell University Press.

Rendell, J. (2006) *Art and Architecture: A Place Between*, London and New York: I.B.Tauris.

—— (2009) 'Constellations: or the Reassertion of Time into Critical Spatial Practice', David Cross and Claire Doherty (eds) *One Day Sculpture*, Bielefeld: Kerber Verlag, pp. 19–22.

Reznikoff, I. and Dauvois, M. (1988) 'Dimension sonore des grottes orneées', *Bulletin, Societé Préhistorique Française*, 85 (8): 238–246.

Rieniets, T., Sigler, J. and Christiaanse, K. (2009) *Open City: Designing Coexistence*, Amsterdam: SUN.

Rinella, H.K. (2006) *The Stardust of Yesterday: Reflections on a Las Vegas Legend*, Las Vegas: Stephens Press.

Robben, A.C.G.M. and Sluka, J.A. (eds) (2007) *Ethnographic Fieldwork: An Anthropological Reader*, Malden, MA, and Oxford: Blackwell Publishing.

Roberts, J.L. (2004) *Mirror Travels: Robert Smithson and History*, New Haven, CT, and London: Yale University Press.

Ronduda, L. and Wolinski, M. (2006) 'Gry i Rozmowe Plastyczne, Działania Współdziałania' ['Games, Visual Conversations, Activities and Interactions'], *Piktogram*, 5 (6): 14–125.

Ronduda, L., Wolinski, M. and Wieder, A.J. (2007) 'Games, Actions and Interactions: Film and the Tradition of Oskar Hansen's Open Form', in L. Ronduda and F. Zeyfang (eds) *1,2,3…Avant-Gardes: Film/Art between Experiment and Archive*, Berlin and Warsaw: CCA Ujazdowski Castle/Sternberg Press: 88–103.

Rosaldo, R. (1989) *Culture and Truth: The Remaking of Social Analysis*, Boston: Beacon.

Rose, G. (1995) 'The Interstitial Perspective: A Review Essay on Homi Bhabha's *The Location of Culture*', *Environment and Planning D: Society and Space*, 13: 365–373.

Rosenfeld, W. (1984) 'Games Specifiers Play', *Progressive Architecture*, 65 (12): 46–47.

—— (1994) 'Specifications: Killer Clauses', *Progressive Architecture*, 72 (2): 47.

Rosengren, M. (forthcoming) *Cave Openings*, Göteborg: Art Monitor.

Rossi, C. (2004) *Architecture and Mathematics in Ancient Egypt*, Cambridge: Cambridge University Press.

Rowe, C. and Koetter, F. (1975, August) 'Collage City', *The Architectural Review*.

Rykwert, J. (1976) *The Idea of a Town: The Anthropology of Urban Form in Rome, Italy and the Ancient World*, Princeton, NJ: Princeton University Press.

—— (1981) *On Adam's House in Paradise*, Cambridge, MA: MIT Press.

Said, E. (1997) *Beginnings: Intention and Method*, London: Granta.

Sanjek, R. (ed.) (1990) *Fieldnotes: The Makings of Anthropology*, Ithaca, NY, and London: Cornell University Press.

Sassen, S. (1991) *The Global City: New York, London, Tokyo*, Princeton, NJ: Princeton University Press.

Scamozzi, V. (1615) *L'Idea della Architettura Universale*, Venezia.

Scarry, E. (2001) *On Beauty and Being Just*, Princeton, NJ: Princeton University Press.

Scheper-Hughes, N. (1995) 'The Primacy of the Ethical: Propositions for a Militant Anthropology', *Current Anthropology*, 36 (3): 409–420.

Scheyvens, R. and Storey, D. (eds) (2003) *Development Fieldwork: A Practical Guide*, Thousand Oaks, CA: Sage.

Schmidt-Tomczak, S. (2010) 'The Dialectic of Vision and the Suggestive Power of Objects: A Cultural Studies Approach to Peter Eisenman's Field of Stelae', *Edinburgh Architecture Research*, 32: 107–114.

Schneider, M. (24 June, 2008) 'Self-invention and Deviance: Philibert de l'Orme's Role in the Creation of the Savant Professional Architect', *Discoveries*, 25, (1): 1–10.

Schofield, J., Klausmeier, A. and Purbrick, L. (eds) (2006) *Re-mapping the Field: New Approaches in Conflict Archaeology*, Berlin: Westkreuz Verlag.

Schön, D. (1983) *The Reflective Practitioner: How Professionals Think in Action*, London: Temple Smith.

—— (1985) *The Design Studio: An Exploration of its Traditions and Potentials*, London: RIBA Publications.

Scott Brown, D. (1976) 'On Architectural Formalism and Social Concern: A Discourse for Social Planners and Radical Chic Architects', *Oppositions*, 5: 99–112.

Seidenberg, A. (1963) 'The Ritual Origin of Geometry', *History of the Exact Sciences*, 1: 487–527.

Sennett, R. (2008) *The Craftsman*, Harmondsworth: Penguin Books.

Serra, R. (1994) 'Verb List, 1967–68', in *Writings, Interviews*, Chicago: University of Chicago Press.

Serres, M. (2008) *The Five Senses: A Philosophy of Mingled Bodies*, trans. M. Sankey and P. Cowley, London: Continuum.

Shannon, K. (2009) 'Greater Hanoi: Mega-city in the Making', *Topos*, 66 (March): 98–103.

Shelby, L.R. (Spring, 1965) 'Medieval Masons' Tools II: Compass and Square', *Technology and Culture*, 6 (2): 236–248.

Shonfield, K. (1994) 'Purity and Tolerance: How Building Construction Enacts Pollution Taboos', *AA Files*, 28 (Autumn): 34–40.

Smithson, A. (ed.) (1982) *The Emergence of Team 10 out of C.I.A.M*, London: Architectural Association.

Smithson, R. (1966a) 'The Crystal Land', *Harper's Bazaar*, May: 72–73.

—— (1966b) 'Entropy and the New Monuments', *Artforum*, June: 26–31.

—— (1967a) 'Atlantic City (H-13)', unpublished writing from 1967, in J. Flam (ed.) (1996) *Robert Smithson: The Collected Writings*, Berkeley: University of California Press: 332.

—— (1967b) 'The Monument: Outline for a Film', unpublished writing from 1967, in J. Flam (ed.) (1996) *Robert Smithson: The Collected Writings*, Berkeley: University of California Press: 356–357.

—— (1967c) 'A Tour of the Monuments of Passaic, New Jersey', *Artforum*, December: 48–51.

—— (1968) 'A Sedimentation of the Mind: Earth Projects', *Artforum*, September: 44–50.

Soja, E. (1989) *Postmodern Geographies: The Reassertion of Space in Social Theory*, London: Verso.

Spiers, R.P. (1888) *Architectural Drawing*, London: Cassell.

Stierli, M. (2009) 'Las Vegas Studio', in H. Stadler and M. Stierli (eds) *Las Vegas Studio: Images from the Archives of Robert Venturi and Denise Scott Brown*, Frankfurt: Deutsches Architekturmuseum.

St John, P. (2006) '176 Museum of Childhood', letter (11 December 2006).

—— (2009) [Author Interview] Peter St John interview with Mhairi McVicar (11 May 2009).

Strathern, M. (ed.) (1995) *Shifting Contexts: Transformations in Anthropological Knowledge*, London: Routledge.

—— (2004) *Partial Connections*, Walnut Creek, CA: AltaMira Press.

Strehlke, C.B. and Tucker, M. (1987) 'The Santa Maria Maggiore Altarpiece; New Observations', *Arte Cristiana*, 75: 105–124.

Sunderland, P.L. (1999) 'Fieldwork and the Phone', *Anthropological Quarterly*, 72 (3): 105–117.

Świtek, G. (2009) 'When Architecture Fails: Representations of Homeworld', published conference proceedings 'A+P2' *Architecture and Phenomenology 2*, international conference, Kyoto Seika University, June 2009.

Swyngedouw, E. (2004) *Social Power and the Urbanization of Water: Flows of Power*, London: Oxford University Press.

Tedlock, B. (1991) 'From Participant Observation to the Observation of Participation: The Emergence of Narrative Ethnography', *Journal of Anthropological Research*, 47 (1): 69–94.

Terkel, S. (1970) *Hard Times*, New York: Pantheon.

Thiel, D. (2007) 'Class in Construction: London Building Workers, Dirty Work and Physical Cultures', *The British Journal of Sociology*, 58 (2): 227–251.

Toker, F. (1985) 'Gothic Architecture by Remote Control: An Illustrated Building Contract of 1340', *The Art Bulletin*, 67 (Part 1): 67–95.

Tsai, E. (1991) 'Interview with Dan Graham by Eugenie Tsai, New York City, October 27, 1988', in E. Tsai (ed.) *Robert Smithson Unearthed: Drawings, Collages, Writings*, New York: Columbia University Press: 8–22.

Tuan, Y.F. (1977) *Space and Place: The Perspective of Experience*, Minneapolis: University of Minnesota Press.

Turner, E. (1999) 'Relating Consciousness, Culture and the Social', *Anthropology Newsletter*, January: 46.

van den Heuvel, D. and Risselada, M. (eds) (2006) *Team 10: In Search of a Utopia of the Present 1953–1981*, Rotterdam: NAi Publishers.

van der Haak, B. (dir.) (2005) *Lagos Wide and Close: Interactive Journey into an Exploding City*, Amsterdam: Submarine.

Vastert, E. (1998) 'Specification of Visual Requirements for Regularity of Joints', *Architectural Science Review*, 41 (3): 99–104.

Venturi, R. Scott Brown, D. and Izenour, S. (1977) *Learning from Las Vegas: The Forgotten Symbolism of Architectural Form*, rev. edn, Cambridge, MA: MIT Press.

Vidler, A. (2008) *Histories of the Immediate Present: Inventing Architectural Modernism*, Cambridge, MA: MIT Press.

Vinegar, A. (2008) *I Am a Monument: On Learning from Las Vegas*, Cambridge, MA: MIT Press.

Viola, B. (1995) *Reasons for Knocking at an Empty House, Writings 1973–1994*, London: Anthony d'Offay Gallery.

Vitruvius (1999) *Ten Books on Architecture*, trans. Ingrid Rowland, Cambridge: Cambridge University Press.

Wakita, O.A. and Linde, R.M. (1999) *The Professional Practice of Architectural Detailing*, 3rd edn, New York: Wiley.

Waldenfels, B. (1999) *Sinnesschwellen. Studien zur Phänomenologie des Fremden 3*, Frankfurt am Main: Suhrkamp.

Walker, J. (1979 [1917]) *The Sun Dance and Other Ceremonies of the Oglala Division of the Teton Sioux*, New York: AMS Press.

—— (1982a) *Lakota Belief and Ritual*, ed. Raymond J. DeMallie, Lincoln: University of Nebraska Press.

—— (1982b) *Lakota Society*, ed. Raymond J. DeMallie, Lincoln: University of Nebraska Press.

—— (1983) *Lakota Myth*, ed. Elaine A. Jahner, Lincoln: University of Nebraska Press.

Watson, C.W. (ed.) (1999) *Being There: Field-work in Anthropology*, London: Pluto Press.

Whitehead, T.L. and Conaway, M.E. (eds) (1986) *Self, Sex, Gender in Cross Cultural Fieldwork*, Chicago: University of Illinois Press.

Whyte, W.H. (1980) *The Social Life of Small Urban Spaces*, Washington, DC: The Conservation Foundation.

—— (dir.) (1988) *The Social Life of Small Urban Spaces*, produced by the Municipal Art Society of New York, Santa Monica: Direct Cinema Ltd.

—— (2000) *A Time of War: Remembering Guadalcanal, a Battle without Maps*, New York: Fordham University Press.

—— (2002) *The Organization Man*, Philadelphia: University of Pennsylvania Press (foreword by Joseph Nocera).

—— (2009) *City, Rediscovering the Center*, Philadelphia: University of Pennsylvania Press (foreword by Paco Underhill).

Whyte, W.H. and the Editors of *Fortune* (1958) *The Exploding Metropolis: A Book for People Who Like Cities and a Critique of the Plans of People Who Don't*, New York: Doubleday & Co. Inc.

Whyte, W.H. and the New York City Planning Commission (1969) (Ghostwriter of) *Plan for the City of New York*, New York: New York City Planning Commission and co-creator of its promotional film *What is the City but the People*.

Winzen, M. (1998) 'Collecting, So Normal So Paradoxical', in I. Schaffner and M. Winzen (eds) *Deep Storage*, Munich and New York: Prestel-Verlag.

Wolcott, H.F. (2005) *The Art of Fieldwork*, 2nd rev. edn, Walnut Creek, CA: AltaMira Press.

Wu, N. (2002) *Ad Quadratum: The Practical Application of Geometry in Medieval Architecture*, Aldershot: Ashgate.

Ylirisku, S. and Buur, J. (2007) *Designing with Video: Focusing the User-centred Design Process*, London: Springer-Verlag.

Yoshinori, Y. and Shinda, V. (eds) (2004) *Monsoon and Civilization*, New Delhi: Roli Books.

Index

Figures are indicated by **bold** page numbers.

DATE DUE